the complete

MEDIA &
COMMUNICATION

h a n d b o o k

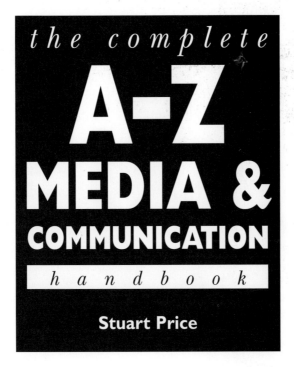

the complete

A-Z
MEDIA &
COMMUNICATION
handbook

Stuart Price

Hodder & Stoughton

A MEMBER OF THE HODDER HEADLINE GROUP

To my sons,
Edward and Huw

British Library Cataloguing in Publication Data

A catalogue entry for this title is available from the British Library.

ISBN 0–340–69131X

First published 1997
Impression number   10 9 8 7 6 5 4 3 2 1
Year   2001 2000 1999 1998 1997

Typeset by GreenGate Publishing Services, Tonbridge, Kent.
Printed and bound in Great Britain for Hodder and Stoughton Educational,
a division of Hodder Headline plc, 338 Euston Road, London NW1 3BH,
by Redwood Books, Trowbridge, Wilts

HOW TO USE THIS BOOK

The *A–Z Media and Communication Handbook* is designed for ease of use. The most important concepts in the field, together with factual references, have been set out in alphabetical order. The intention is to provide a source which can be consulted throughout the study of media and communication.

The entries begin with a one-sentence definition, which should help you understand the precise meaning of each term. Longer entries are devoted to the more important concepts, and to issues which require careful explanation. Quotations from established threorists provide a useful insight into the issues and controversies encountered in the subject. Illustrations, photographs and diagrams are provided where they help to support individual ideas.

Your understanding of media and communication can be increased by using the cross-references set out in italics, which appear either in the main body of each entry or in brackets at the end. These cross-references direct study to related concepts.

Although you will require further reading to ensure a good grasp of the subject, the Handbook provides substantial descriptions of many areas of study. You should continue to check your understanding of ideas and issues by consulting the entries as your studies progress.

To assist revision, the book includes an explanation of examiners' terms, revision lists, guides to writing essays and in-depth assignments, and advice on carrying out textual analysis. All the Media A-level syllabuses have been consulted, together with the AEB Communication Studies syllabus, a number of Access courses, and modules from two separate Media Arts undergraduate programmes.

Stuart Price

ACKNOWLEDGEMENTS

My thanks are due first to Lucy Byrne whose presence always makes tasks like this easier. Tim Gregson-Williams and Clare Smith at Hodder & Stoughton were most helpful. I would like to acknowledge the efforts of Alan Nanson who so ably interpreted my suggestions for the cover illustration, and all at GreenGate Publishing Services for their hard work. Thanks also to Tony Nandi at Thames Valley University for the contact sheet and Raoul Wedge-Thomas for use of the storyboard blank. Peter Kennard allowed the reproduction of his excellent photomontage. In addition, I would like to mention the kind interest shown in this project by my sister, Sharon Price.

The author and publishers would like to thank the following for permission to reproduce material in this volume:

The Guardian for the use of their front page and circulation figures; Greg Evans International for the photographs of country houses (one of which was shot by Greg Balfour Evans); Mirror Syndication International for the use of their front page; PA News for their photograph of a demonstration of sacked dockers, Dec 1997, shot by Michael Stephens; Getty Images for their photograph of mounted police clashing with demonstrators, 1990, shot by David Hoffman; The Gernsheim Collection, Harry Ransom Humanities Research Center, The University of Texas at Austin for their photograph of the view from Nièpce's window at Gras, 1826; Paul Trowler and HarperCollins Publishers for the reproduction of their pie-chart, found in Investigating Mass Media, by Paul Trowler, (1996).

While every effort has been made to trace copyright holders, this has not been possible in all cases; any omissions brought to our attention will be remedied in future printings.

A

ABC: American Broadcasting Company, one of only three major commercial networks (until the arrival of cable channels like *CNN*) which fought for domination of post-war US television. ABC was originally part of the *NBC* radio network, which was broken up by the Federal Communications Commission in 1941. ABC was overshadowed by its two rivals (NBC and CBS) until the mid-1970s. There have been several attempts to establish a fourth commercial channel, the most successful of which was probably the Fox network.

ABC: the 1978 'ABC' trial in Britain, in which three journalists (Aubrey, Berry and Campbell) were charged under the Official Secrets Act. Their offence was the publication, in May 1976, of an article in the magazine 'Time Out'. This revealed information about the government's surveillance headquarters in Cheltenham, highlighting the way in which successive administrations had 'eavesdropped' on the electronic communication of individuals and groups regarded as a threat. The case itself was dismissed in September 1978 but its lasting effect was to illustrate the continued existence of a 'secret state' in Britain, engaged in the surveillance of its own population.

ABC: the Audit Bureau of Circulations, a British organisation which authenticates the circulations claimed by *newspapers* and periodicals.

abend: American term for the termination of a computer programme through some form of software or hardware failure (see *abort*). It comes from *ab*normal *end*ing.

aberrant decoding: *decoding* is the process of interpreting coded messages, so a sense of the original or intended meaning is gained (see *code*). For example, the reader of a book will use his/her knowledge of written English to decipher the signs on the page. 'Aberrance', on the other hand, means straying from the correct or usual path. Therefore, 'aberrant decoding' suggests a mistaken or deficient interpretation of a message. However, when Umberto *Eco* first coined the term in 1965 (in 'Towards a semiotic enquiry into the television message'), he used it to describe a variety of misunderstandings, not all of which could be described as mistakes. He began by taking an example from history, referring to 'the artist of the palace of Knossos in Crete', who 'produced a message (in this case a coloured stucco relief called the Prince of the Lilies) for a well-defined community of receivers'. According to Eco, this community would have had 'the same reading code as the artist: it knew for instance that the stick held in the left hand stood for a sceptre ... that the yellow-brown colour of the face meant youth; and so forth'. Here, each part of the painting is interpreted according to an established code, so that the intentions of the artist are clearly understood. Eco then described the reaction to the artist's work by another group outside the community – the Achaen conquerors of Crete who, because they used different codes, could only misinterpret the images. This misunderstanding, in Eco's words, 'was purely accidental to the communication itself ... an *aberrant decoding* which the artist would never have thought of'.

So, in this example, misunderstanding arises because sender and receiver simply do not share the same code. In other words, a message encoded using one code, is decoded using another. At this point aberrant decoding is presented as a 'mis-communication' between different cultures, rather than an error made within one culture's code. In all possible cases, however, Eco maintains that 'the aberrant decoding was the unexpected exception, not the rule'.

In the case of the *mass media*, however, Eco takes a different view – that aberrant decoding is actually the rule. He argues that the transmitter of the message (the media industry) 'works within a communicative code which [it] knows a priori [knows beforehand] is not shared by all the receivers'.

This idea requires updating. If they are to make a successful impact, all television 'messages' have to use codes which an audience can understand. The television audience is no longer, if it ever was, 'undifferentiated' (a mass in which individuals and groups cannot be told apart). The television industry has developed a set of codes which are capable of a more universal appeal.

In the later part of his essay, Eco moves beyond the theory of aberrant decoding, arguing that the transmitting organisation, the 'technical interpreter' and the audience, each possess a 'significance system'. This is made up of the 'system of meanings pre-existent to the message' (*ideology*) and the codes and subcodes used by all parties (which Eco calls *rhetorical devices*).

The idea of 'cultural reference' (also found in Eco's essay) shows how members of a society are able to draw on a range of shared concepts, in order to make successful interpretations of public communication.

ABN: American Broadcasting Network, the original designation of the American Broadcasting Company's (ABC) radio network.

above the line: the promotion of a product through media outlets such as magazines, newspapers, television, radio and so on (contrasted with *below the line*, where products are advertised through sponsorship and trade promotions).

abridgement is the process of 'condensing' a book so that a more concise version can be published.

absence: a concept in *structuralism* which refers to the inferred absence of a particular *sign* in a *syntagm* (a sequence or unit of meaning). The idea that a sign creates meaning because it is present on a page, or on a screen, or because it exists in some other obvious form, seems straightforward. But the concept of 'absence' seems to suggest that meaning can also be produced by elements which are missing.

This idea depends on the process of choice and rejection. The author of a radio drama, for instance, will choose certain units of meaning from a *paradigm* (in this case, language). These will be phrases, sentences, complete exchanges, and so on.

Structuralists argue that choosing some elements means rejecting other options, and maintain that such exclusion is significant. Of course, the theorist will only be able to work out what is missing by studying what has been included; that is why the absence is 'inferred' – no one can be certain which absent alternative out of many options is the most significant.

However, certain signs might be expected to occupy particular positions in a syntagm; when they do not appear, this allows the theorist to guess at some of the options that have been rejected. Thus, the signs which have been chosen (units of meaning in language, or sequences of film, for example) are meaningful because they form a contrast to what Hartley in O'Sullivan (p. 2) calls 'the absent possibilities'. The implication is that the beliefs and values of all those involved in public exchange (speakers, writers, programme makers, advertisers and so on), may be revealed by treating the finished act of communication as a process of exclusion.

Post-structuralism, (and in particular the deconstructionist movement) treats the concept of presence/absence differently. Writers like *Derrida* argue that the concept of presence is itself paradoxical. In Derrida's view, every sign is a 'deferred presence'. A sign is not the thing itself, only a reference to that thing. It is not entirely absent, either, because it remains as marks on the page, sounds in the air, images on the screen. Therefore, absence becomes a quality of all communication acts, and is no longer simply a reference to 'rejected' choices of sign. (See *deconstruction*.)

absence: in film theory, the concept of 'absence/presence' refers to the way in which the *cinema* creates the illusion of spatial and temporal presence; individuals, objects and events, recorded on *film*, seem to have certain 'real' qualities. They look and sound like elements of the world we know, and appear at times to share a similar 'time frame', but in fact no longer belong to the same dimension; they are 'absent'. Absence also refers to the practice of allowing individuals on-screen, to discuss characters who are off-screen, providing a film's audience with information about the strengths/weaknesses of that character. In addition, absence can mean the way in which women are excluded from certain genres of film, and more generally how they become a symbolic 'other' in the cinema, removed from the world of cinematic *discourse*.

Academy: before the introduction of the widescreen format, 'Academy' was the standard screen format used by the Hollywood studios. It was based on 35 mm film stock and had an aspect ratio of 4:3.

Academy of Motion Picture Arts and Sciences: the US organisation that has, since 1928, awarded the Oscars at an annual ceremony.

accent: in reference to public and private speech, this is the national, local, or individual mode of pronunciation. Accent is one component of *dialect*, which also includes grammar and vocabulary. In accent, vowel sounds may differ according to the regional background of the speaker. When studying the act of *speech* in general, accent means the prominence given to a syllable in speech, through the use of stress or pitch. (See also *language*).

access is the idea that opportunities should be provided for individual members of the public, special interest groups and non-commercial organisations, to produce their own programmes or articles for broadcast or print. Such access is supposed to be free of editorial interference. Demands for access became more pronounced in the 1970s, when the BBC began its 'Open Door' series and the Sunday Times devoted half a page of each issue to non-staff commentators. Phone-in programmes such as 'Any Answers' are still a feature of radio broadcasts, while Channel 4's 'Right to Reply' encouraged viewers to respond to controversial issues by setting up a number of 'video boxes' where opinions could be recorded by members of the public.

The concept of access has its limitations, however. O'Sullivan and his co-writers say ('Key Concepts', p. 4) 'demands for access are based on a reflection theory of the media – that is that the media ought to reflect the plurality of different groups, politics or lifestyles that can be identified ... in social life'. It is seen by some as a sop to democracy which leaves the structures, personnel and working-practices of the media untouched. Gill and Adams (p. 5) note that 'such access programmes as there are, are timed to reach smaller audiences. The mass communicators keep a firm grip on the broadcasting schedules ... the role of the producer is still dominant'. Ellmore ('Mass Media Directory', 1990), writing from a US perspective, calls access to media (see p. 4) 'the non-existent right of individuals to obtain air time or print space in the media'.

access in computing terms means the process of retrieving and using information which is electronically stored (as in 'accessing data').

access cablecasting is an American term meaning the channel space which is set aside for individuals and organisations within a 'cable community'. *Federal Communications Commission* rules specify that there must be channels which allow public access.

access code: a group of characters or numbers that identifies the user of a personal computer, to the computer system itself.

access time: the interval between the time that computer data is called up, and the time it appears on screen.

accessed voices: an academic concept referring to the media practice of including statements, interviews and opinions from groups and individuals, in news reports and other documentary material. The 'range' of individuals allowed expression, depends on the nature of the reports themselves, but writers like John Hartley believe that official voices (police, members of parliament, experts, etc.) are more likely to be sought out.

acoustic signal: the *sound* waves produced by any source, natural, animal, human, mechanical or electronic.

acoustics: the technical control of *sound* and sound environments.

acquisition of language: the processes through which infants gradually acquire all the attributes of a fully-formed adult language. Observation of children from different language groups seems to demonstrate that the stages of language acquisition are the same for all individuals.

The first noises made by a new-born infant are 'stimulus controlled'; they are involuntary responses to the child's environment, and are not part of early language formation. The infant does possess, however, the ability to recognise phonetic contrasts in the speech of adults.

The first stage of language development proper, occurs around the sixth month, when the infant begins to 'babble'. Babbling sees the production of phonemes, which take the form of combinations of vowels and consonants, such as 'ma', 'ba', 'ga' and so on.

Petitto and Marantette (McGill University) discovered that the forms of intonation used at this stage by infants, begin to resemble the 'intonation contours' of adults. Petitto's (1991) view that humans are predisposed to discover the units of linguistic meaning, supports Noam *Chomsky's* argument that human beings are predisposed to acquire language.

By nine or ten months, babies go through a period of phonetic 'contraction', during which the phonemes used are restricted to those belonging to its native tongue; the babbling of two babies from different language groups no longer sounds similar.

Just after their first year, children begin to use the same combination of sounds to refer to the same things, demonstrating that they have learned that sounds are related to meaning. This is sometimes known as the 'holophrastic' phase, when one-word 'sentences' are produced (ie. words that indicate a complete response to a situation). Gross (p. 779) indicates that single words can be used in a range of different contexts to mean different things; ' 'milk' might, on one occasion, mean, 'I want some more milk', and on another occasion, 'I don't want to finish my milk'. The 'one word' stage ends around the age of eighteen months, followed by the 'two-word' stage which begins between eighteen months and two years of age. The combination of two words allows a greater range of expression.

One theory which attempts to explain language acquisition is the notion of imitation, in which the child imitates what it hears; a similar idea is reinforcement, during which the child learns correct speech-forms by repetition (guided by an adult). However, rather than imitate exactly what an adult says, a child will continue to follow the grammatical rules and the word-forms it already uses; Fromkin and Rodman (p. 402), give the example of a child who persists in saying 'my teacher holded the baby rabbits and we patted them', despite the adult's repetition of 'held' as an alternative to the 'over-regularised' form used by the child.

Chomsky (1959) argued that, when children (or adults for that matter) hear a sentence, they do not retain the exact grammatical structure of the utterance, but retain an understanding of its meaning. In other words, surface structure is transformed into *deep structure*. According to this theory, linguistic ability pre-exists the exercise of coherent speech.

acronym: a word composed of the initials of several words (sometimes the title of an institution, a series of letters which stand for a particular theory, or shorthand for a social type etc.). A 'nimby' for example (dating from 1986), is the name given to someone who is content to see urban development, nuclear dumping, or the growth of motorways, provided such things do not occur anywhere near their own home; 'nimby' stands for 'Not In My Back Yard'.

act: a thing which is done, an identifiable unit of deliberate behaviour which has meaning to the actor and/or to the witnesses of the act (see *speech act*).

ACT: Action for Children's Television, an American group which lobbies against the airing of commercials during children's television.

action research is a form of social research dedicated to bringing about a practical change in society.

actioner: a film industry term (dating from the late 1960s) which has become fairly commonplace slang, an actioner is a spectacular action film, usually produced in *Hollywood*.

active audience: the idea that audiences are not misled by broadcasters and other powerful forces, but are intelligent and discriminating, capable of interpreting messages and of 'negotiating' meaning. The 'active' audience thesis was a response to approaches which concentrated on the text. In 'Television Culture' (1987), John

Fiske argued against the views of writers like Colin MacCabe. In Fiske's opinion, McCabe saw the audience as (p. 62) 'relatively powerless and inactive' because audiences in general were understood 'as textual subjects', entirely shaped by the film, radio programme, newspaper article etc., being consumed. This approach emphasises the power of the text to 'position' the subject. Shaun Moores, in 'Interpreting Audiences' (1993), attributes this to (p. 6) the 'old mass society thesis' which saw audiences 'as almost entirely subjected to the ideological work performed by the media'.

In contrast to the 'textual subject', Fiske drew attention to the 'social subject', an individual with a place and a history. Fiske went on to say that social subjectivity is more important than textual subjectivity because the latter exists 'only at the moment of reading'.

This approach marks a turn away from what Justin Lewis (see 'Viewing, Reading, Listening', p. 19) calls the more 'speculative and literary' concerns of *textual analysis* and paves the way for a closer engagement with real audiences.

However, if audiences are active, what form does this activity take? One of the more usual answers is that audiences can become 'critical' of media texts. Schlesinger (1992) argues this confuses 'the capacity ... to interpret what we see and hear with the exercise of real political power'. According to Fiske, activity begins not only when an audience (an interpretive community or 'sub-cultural grouping') starts to create its own 'readings', but when these readings make a new input into culture. He believes the balance of power lies in the audience's favour, citing the 'inflexibility' of the powerful and the 'creativity' of the weak. Price, ('Media Studies', 1993), argues that this view underestimates the ability of the dominant class to produce a variety of 'sub-cultural' references in media texts (p. 26); 'cultural artifacts do not reflect the interests or ideas of the dominant class simply because they have been produced within its dominant mode of production'.

The emphasis on audience activity relies ultimately on the view that media texts are indeed being used to present 'ideologically loaded' points of view to audiences. Although 'dominant' viewpoints exist, media industries recognise that they must create texts which appeal to groups of consumers; this means such texts must reflect their audiences' cultural outlook. To complicate things further, the actual preferences audiences express are bound to include 'mainstream' ideas previously encountered through the media. Therefore, a variety of discourses are bound to be circulated in media forms.

active file: a computer file that is in use.

actualisation: properly speaking, 'self-actualisation', a term used by Abraham Maslow in 1954. Maslow believed that behaviour was motivated by unsatisfied needs, and produced a 'hierarchy' of human requirements, from the most basic physical requirements of life, to those *social needs* which include companionship, belonging, and so on. The last level described by Maslow is *self-actualisation*, where an individual attains (or tries to attain) the highest degree of their potential. (See *hierarchy of needs*.)

actuality: a term used by media professionals to refer to material obtained on location; sounds and images drawn from reality, as opposed to studio or archive sources. Actuality is thought to convey the essence of an event effectively, but it is usually used only as a brief extract, and is always placed in the context of a formal news report. This leads some commentators to see its use as entirely manipulative, as a 'key device in producing ideological closure' (Hartley, in O'Sullivan, p. 5). The idea is that the 'preferred reading' intended by the news organisation is 'anchored' by the indisputable reality of the actuality material. In other words, that the material is used to illustrate a 'dominant' point of view only. Hartley sees it as 'a device for naturalising meaning'.

This does not allow for the fact that actuality can speak for itself and, depending on the content shown, can set the agenda for the discourses which surround it; the increasing use of 'non-professional' actuality has encouraged new perspectives on news. The Rodney King tape, where white Los Angeles policemen were shown beating a black motorist, would be a difficult candidate for the kind of 'ideological closure' Hartley has in mind. (For a thorough study of actuality, see 'Media Culture and Society', Vol. 18 No. 1, January 1996).

additive process is an obsolete film process in which each primary colour is printed separately to produce a single colour image.

address: an *address* is the deliberate direction or delivery of a message (eg. an utterance, written passage, public display and so on), from an individual, group or institutional source, to any type of recipient, individual or collective. All speech, writing and mediated communication is directed at (or 'addressed to') various individuals and groups. Even supposedly private forms of communication, like diaries, have a sense of audience. An address can be a single formal act (like a public lecture), but address as a generic term refers to a whole process of communication. This process begins when an addressor (eg. a speaker, writer, or broadcaster), wishes to produce an effect in an audience. The addressor's knowledge or impression of that audience, helps him/her to put the message *content* into a suitable *form*. An address is an intentional act of communication. The media often imitate personal forms of address in order to create a kind of 'intimacy' between performer (actor, game-show host, reporter, etc.) and audience. An address with a *will to power* is called *interpellation*.

Adobe Photoshop is a 24-bit image processing program, designed by Adobe Systems Inc. for the Apple Macintosh computer. Photoshop allows designers to manipulate images/graphics by the use of painting and drawing tools. It also acts as a colour correction and darkroom system.

ADR: Additional Sound Recording is a post-production process in cinema, in which actors re-record their lines whilst watching their original performances on a loop of film, to ensure that their words match the lip movements on the film (*lip-sync* or *lip synchronisation*).

advance copies: in magazine publishing, a limited number of copies of an edition, which are checked before a full print run. In book publishing it refers to copies of a book which are sent out to reviewers, the publisher's 'reps', prominent individuals and the author, before the official publishing date. The gap between advance copies and publication can be anything between two weeks and a month, depending where the book has been printed (print runs from overseas take longer to return to the publisher) and on the urgency of market requirements.

advertisement: a public announcement of goods or services which are for sale; most examples of modern advertising are carried by mass media outlets. The term advertisement is often used to refer to the broadcast, printed or other form taken by an individual commercial message. (See facing page.)

advertising is the practice of making public announcements about the availability of goods and services; closely related forms of public address include the promotion of political and corporate bodies. Advertising can be divided into the following types:

- consumer advertising (the most important is that directed at the mass market)
- trade and specialist advertising, sponsorship (where an advertiser supports an event or activity to keep its name in the public eye)
- state advertising (public information campaigns or more controversial announcements like share issues)
- charitable appeals.

Other promotional forms include corporate advertising (used to enhance the reputation of a company), public relations (a form of promotion or news management) and party political broadcasts.

Advertising Advisory Committee: a body made up of representatives from the advertising industry, consumer groups and medical experts, which oversees and regulates the code of Advertising Standards and Practices. (See *Advertising Standards Authority.*)

advertising agency: an organisation which buys advertising space for clients, prepares and manages their accounts, and produces copy for various types of advertising campaign. The *client* may be an individual but is more usually a company. From the client's requirements, a brief for the campaign will be set out. Within the agency, the point of contact for the client is the 'account handler', whose job is, according to John Josling in 'The Practice of Advertising', (p. 43), to: '... maintain contact with his [sic] client, building up a full understanding of that client's advertising and marketing situation'. An agency will *conceptualise* the audience it has been asked to reach, attempting to define the characteristics of its market. Agencies will usually consist of the following departments:

- client management (including the Board Director, Managing Director, Account Director and so on)
- media
- planning and research
- creative
- traffic
- print production and progress.

In some cases, the agency will not have its own creative group, and will go to specialist companies for such work.

advertising as medium: although advertising is 'carried' by the mass media, it is important in two respects. First, the revenue it produces is essential for the survival of the commercial media. Secondly, it is generally regarded as a central force in the reproduction of culture. Armand Mattelart (in 'Advertising International,' Preface, ix) declares that: 'Advertising is now an essential actor within public space'. According

—and he wonders why she said "NO!"

 Could he have read her thoughts he would not have lost her. A picture of neatness herself, she detested slovenliness. And not once, but many times, she had noticed his ungartered socks crumpling down around his shoe tops. To have to apologize to her friends for a husband's careless habits was too much to ask. So she had to say "NO"—and in spite of his pleading couldn't tell him WHY.

No SOX Appeal Without

PARIS
GARTERS
NO METAL CAN TOUCH YOU
25c to $2
Dress Well and Succeed

SINGLE GRIP

DOUBLE GRIP

© 1928—A. STEIN & COMPANY—MAKERS—CHICAGO, NEW YORK, LOS ANGELES, TORONTO

Advertisement for Paris garters, 1928

to Mattelart, it has become 'a mode of communication' in its own right. Leiss, Kline and Jhally ('Social Communication in Advertising', 1990, p. 1), maintain that 'advertising represents a privileged form of discourse' in society, replacing older forms of privileged discourse like 'church sermons, political oratory, and the words and precepts of family elders'. Andrew Wernick (in 'Promotional Culture' Preface, vii) writes that 'advertising [is] not just a commercial phenomenon ... promotion [his term for advertising in the widest sense] is a rhetorical form diffused throughout our culture'.

In the pre-industrial era, advertising was confined to proclamation and announcement; the 'reach' of modern advertising is much greater, and is inextricably linked to the power of the industrialised world, which can ensure the international dissemination of advertising messages.

Since the 1950s, the critics of advertising (Packard, Galbraith, Leymore, Mattelart and others) have drawn attention to its supposedly negative *effects* on the consumer and on society in general. These have been variously thought to include 'brainwashing', the creation of desires that once did not exist, the promotion of acquisitive values, encouraging timidity among programme-makers and so on. Some advertising companies have become particularly well known: the Saatchi agency in the 1980s was credited with the successful promotion of the Conservative Party.

Modern advertising is closely associated with the practice of *lifestyle* profiling and audience *segmentation*, in which the population is divided into groups according to factors like product choice, mode of consumption, residential location, and various psychological characteristics. The elements which make up audience *subjectivity*, such as class, sex and age, still provide a useful guide for the segmentation of the marketplace.

Advertising Standards Authority: a British organisation, set up in 1962, which oversees standards in advertising, monitors complaints, publishes reports and on occasion removes advertisements from circulation. One of its central aims was 'to make sure that the non-broadcast advertisements that appear in the UK are legal, decent, honest and truthful' (from the ASA guide 'Advertising Under Control'). Only cigarette advertisements have to be cleared before they are published and circulated, but some advertisers contact the ASA for guidance before proceeding with their campaign. The Authority carries out regular surveys in order to search for breaches of the British Codes of Advertising and Sales Promotion. There are six general rules which introduce the Code, and twenty-one other points, from questions of legality to how free offers should be made.

Some adverts which have passed the ASA codes are still withdrawn by their sponsors; this trend can be explained by the nervousness that can infect some corporate environments (in 1997, Nike withdrew a poster showing the feet of Christ nailed to the cross, with the slogan 'Marathon. 26 miles, 285 yards and 2 feet'). Controversy has, however, helped to raise the profile of many companies and products (Benetton and Tango are two brand names which have benefited from high-profile campaigns).

aesthetics: the study or judgment of beauty in art or nature. In its original Greek form, aesthetics was the philosophical study of sense experience in general, but by the late-eighteenth century it had become increasingly concerned with the sensuous appreciation of fine art and landscape. The German philosopher Emmanuel Kant argued that aesthetics, though a social process, was more subjective than either cognitive or moral judgment (ie, it emerged from a more individual response). By the mid-nineteenth century the aesthetic was not only regarded as the appreciation of visual beauty, but sometimes as the exercise of good taste in general. Where such discernment is thought to be confined to a cultured elite, we end up with the notion of 'pure' value in art and life, a value which cannot be explained but which is somehow identified in the 'fine arts'.

The close association of the aesthetic lifestyle with beauty led to the accusation of sensuality, and in turn to the birth of the 'aesthete' (a term much used in the 1880s). This referred to individuals who indulged their physical senses; such gratification would include a highly charged (sometimes 'degenerate') interest in the 'beautiful'.

Modern approaches to the aesthetic have concentrated on the analysis of certain concepts within art, such as intention, meaning and representation. Marxist, feminist and other critics have long been concerned to give the aesthetic a moral or social framework. In addition, semiologists like Eco have identified 'aesthetic functions' in television and 'aesthetic codes' in a variety of media forms. Where the media use an aesthetic approach to representation, we encounter images which appear to have no immediate relationship with the content of the 'message'; for example, a police series might be more concerned with visual style than coherent narrative, while a television commercial could show images which would not normally be associated with the product advertised.

agencies (media) are organisations which provide a service for public or private industries. (See also *advertising agencies* and *news agencies*.)

agencies (social) are any human groups which affect the development or direction of a society.

agency is the operation of social power, located in the actions and behaviour of human individuals, groups or institutions. The action of human agents may reinforce existing social structures, but it is also able to produce a material change in the social formation.

agenda-setting: the practice of selecting and emphasising certain *issues* and/or events from among the various topics which form public discourses. Most definitions of agenda-setting state that the *media* are responsible for highlighting certain issues. For example, Watson and Hill say that the media (p. 3) 'set the order of importance of current issues' while O'Sullivan in 'Key Concepts' (p. 8) argues that the media 'wittingly or unwittingly structure public debate and awareness'. Gill and Adams ('ABC of Communication Studies', p. 6) mention 'the ways in which the media decide which information and which issues are most important for the public'.

McQuail ('Mass Communication Theory', p. 275) notes 'a correspondence between the order of importance given in the media to 'issues' and the order of significance attached to the same issues by the public and the politicians'. Caution should be exercised here; the idea that media, politicians and public may often share the same perception of what is important, does not prove that any one of the three are ultimately responsible for setting an agenda that all must follow.

agenda-setting (research): research into agenda-setting began in the USA after the Second World War. An early version of the concept was used by Paul Lazarsfeld in 1948, who talked of the power to 'structure issues'. He and two other researchers produced a short book on the 1944 US Presidential election campaign, called 'The People's Choice'. The objectives of the book were expressed as follows: 'to discover how and why people voted as they did'. Information was gathered using profession-al field staff and a locally recruited team of interviewers; the initial survey included some 3,000 householders in Erie County, Ohio, which had previously deviated very little from national voting patterns.

The results of the study showed that socio-economic status, religion, residential loca-tion, occupation and age, all affected the decisions of voters: social categories were shown to be linked to voting predisposition. The 'mediated propaganda' which vot-ers encountered did not produce a simple effect; votes were not secured just because the electorate read or heard political messages. Instead, a complicated relationship was observed, between what Lowery and deFleur (in 'Milestones in Mass Communication Research', p. 83) call 'the predisposing social characteristics of vot-ers', what they 'select and use from the political propaganda presented by the media', and '[voters'] ultimate choice'. The ability of politicians and the media to produce complete conformity was therefore called into question.

The term 'agenda-setting' itself was used by McCombs and Shaw in 1968, with refer-ence to the presidential campaign of that year. The problem they studied was the degree of influence exerted by the media over the electorate. Research took the form of a comparison between what a sample of voters said were the key issues, and the actual content of the news media over a 24-day period. Only 100 respondents, none of whom had decided which way to vote, were tested.

McCombs and Shaw found that the issues themselves and the order of importance accorded to these issues, bore a very close resemblance to the 'agenda' accepted by the sample of voters. The media (Lowery and deFleur, p. 270) 'had not indicated *what* the voters should think about the issues, but they did indicate *which* issues were to be thought about'.

The 1972 election provided McCombs and Shaw with an opportunity to widen their aims and to carry out a much larger study. Results suggested that there was little per-sonal or direct contact between voters and candidates, and that voters relied instead on the mass media, encountering 'only those aspects of national politics considered newsworthy enough for transmission through the mass media'. They confirmed that agenda setting, personal choice, and the 'gatekeeping' role of the media, form part of a complex relationship.

agony column: a feature in newspapers and magazines which offers advice about personal problems.

AI or *artificial intelligence* refers to two related areas of research; the first is the attempt to make machines behave 'intelligently', responding to their environment in a constructive and reasonably independent manner (demonstrating learning abili-ties, decision-making, or performing independent actions in response to stimuli). The second is concerned to develop machines which are able to mimic the process-es associated with the human mind. In this case, research is usually motivated by the desire to learn more about the intellectual abilities of humans. It is not, therefore, the study of computers as such, but 'the study of intelligence in thought and action' (Boden, 1987) which uses computer technology to test its theories.

The debate about how far it is possible to reproduce human intelligence, depends partly on how intelligence itself is understood. It is clearly more than just the ability to make calculations, for example, and must include consideration of human experience and behaviour. One of the tests set to determine the presence of artificial intelligence, is whether or not a computer, in the course of processing information, is able to produce new data through the use of inference (working out what new knowledge is implied by the relationship of established data). Popular representations of artificial intelligence in cinema, such as the HAL computer in '2001: a Space Odyssey', and the unseen 'Skynet' system in the Terminator films, examine the supposed threat to humanity posed by machine intelligence.

AIDA is a model which sets out the principal stages of advertising and marketing, as follows: A – create Awareness, I – secure Interest, D – create Desire, A – produce Action (a purchase).

algorithm: a prescribed set of rules or logical processes, through the application of which problems may be solved. The term originated as a corruption of the name of Al-Khwarismi, a ninth-century Islamic mathematician. The logical procedure involved in algorithms, lends itself to the construction of *flow charts* (see communication *models*).

alienation is estrangement from the social world; the origins of this term may be found in the Latin words 'alius' ('other') and 'alienatio' (meaning 'a state of estrangement'). Its subsequent use has varied over time, but has always included the notion of removal from a source of social connection or spiritual grace. The idea of alienation can mean estrangement from an original or essential human condition, from God, or from society. Theories of alienation are drawn therefore from psychology, theology and sociology. An individual's, or a group's 'separation' from a natural or desirable state, is variously explained. The problem is often seen as the necessary but harmful advent of civilisation.

In Marxist theory, alienation is the removal of the worker from the means of production, and his/her separation from the end product of labour. The distance capitalism creates between worker and tools/products, leads to a sense of alienation, in which the workers lose a sense of meaningful relationship to their own productive capacity. The capitalist system, in controlling production, and by appropriating the fruits of working class labour, denies people the opportunity to find satisfaction in their efforts. Instead of providing fulfilling activities, the capitalist mode of production treats individuals like commodities, to be bought and sold in the marketplace. Active commitment is impossible, and is replaced by various degrees of grudging compliance. Lawson and Garrod (see 'The Complete A–Z Sociology Handbook', 1996) write 'alienation is ... the totality of the objective conditions of capitalist production, which translate into subjective features of deprivation, loss of dignity ... and a feeling that one's life is controlled by impersonal forces'. (See also *alienative involvement, counter culture* and *anomie*.)

alienative involvement: drawn from the work of Etzioni (1964), alienative involvement is one of three types of attitude shown by employees to their role in the workplace. In this case, there is no commitment to the company beyond the need to secure a wage (see *alienation*).

alignment: a newspaper term indicating the correct levelling of the characters/illustrations in a line of text.

allocution: allocution is a formal address made by someone in authority, to his or her subordinates or followers; the original Latin term was 'adlocutio', meaning an address or exhortation (when someone is urged to do or think something). Early uses of allocution may be found in the address made by a Roman general to assembled troops, or a speech made by a religious leader (such as the Pope) to an assembly of followers.

The conditions essential for allocution are first, a leader whose authority is acknowledged by followers or subordinates, secondly an assembly of such individuals, thirdly the appropriate conditions for speech-making, and finally a speech which urges the audience to do, say, feel, or think something. For example, a general may wish to motivate his subordinates to perform some military action, perhaps by appealing to a sense of honour or reputation, while a religious leader might refer to the principles of conduct which should guide the faithful.

The concept of allocution has been revived by modern communication theorists to describe different types of 'information traffic'. Two telecommunications theorists, Bordewijk and van Kaam (1986), have used it to describe centralised forms of communication (the traditional mass media in particular) which deliver messages to large homogeneous audiences. Little sense of the relationship between sender and receiver found in true allocution, remains in this modern version.

Althusser, Louis: Althusser (1918–1990) was an influential French philosopher and teacher. He was a prisoner of war in Germany throughout the Second War; upon his release, he studied and then taught at the Ecole Normale Superieure in Paris. Towards the end of his career he suffered poor mental health and was incarcerated for killing his wife.

Althusser was opposed to the 'humanist' interpretation of Marx's works, which had argued in favour of human initiative and against *determinism* in social and economic life. He was more interested in the later Marx, identifying an 'epistemological break' between the early writings and the later 'scientific' theories.

Using structuralist approaches in his reading of Marx, Althusser argued that society is composed of a number of semi-autonomous structures, including political, legal, ideological, and cultural elements. One of his concerns was to analyse the systems of domination which allow the social order to be reproduced. His first book, 'For Marx', appeared in 1965. In 1969 he described the 'ideological State apparatuses' (such as the education system, political parties, the Church) which ensured that bourgeois *ideology* dominated industrial society. Thus Althusser addressed the problem of how ruling ideas help to maintain the class system.

In communication and media studies, most references to Althusser are focussed on his concept of '*interpellation*'. He thought that ideology (p. 47) 'hails or interpellates concrete individuals as concrete subjects.' Individual human subjects are 'interpellated' or called to order. Althusser argues that we 'constantly practice the rituals of ideological recognition.'

He gives the example of an individual who is hailed by a police officer. By responding to the call, the individual recognises the legitimacy of state power, and thus also their condition as a social subject. Althusser's picture of a necessary response to the power of interpellation, suggests that the influence of the dominant ideology is inescapable. In practice, individual subjects usually encounter more complex examples of authority, in which the message or instruction is couched in more persuasive terms.

Althusser's concept of interpellation seems rather inflexible, considering the variety of forms of address made through the media. However, it does recognise that there are power relations in society, relations which manifest themselves in the communication process. *Advertising*, for example, is one form which does attempt to 'position' its audiences, and may use references to their social location in order to secure sales.

ambient light: in film, this is the natural light which surrounds an object or a character.

Amiga: a brand name for computers manufactured by Commodore Business Machines Incorporated. The Amiga is used extensively in animation and computer graphics.

analogue: traditional media use analogue modes of reproduction, which transfer the physical arrangement of the original source, into a similar configuration in another form. For instance, representational painting depends on the transcription of the scene/figure chosen, into a similar arrangement on the canvas. The 'Cyberspace Lexicon' (p. 16) uses the example of 'the grooves on a gramophone record' which are 'similar to the soundwaves they reproduce'. Binkley, writing in 'Future Visions' (p. 95), explains that 'analogue media imbue objects with resilient marks perceivable either directly through the senses, or indirectly through a display process that carries out an additional transcription'. Photography is an example of direct analogue production, while video is indirect, requiring the translation of light patterns into analogue electrical signals and then their transformation back into recognisable images. *Digital* media, by contrast, convert the original source into an abstract form, changing physical quantities into numbers. *(See page 16 of this book for illustration.)*

analogue to digital converter: a device which converts continuous analogue signals to discrete digital units.

anchor: an American term for a well-known presenter who 'fronts' a news programme and provides a consistent reference point for the viewer.

anchorage: used by Roland Barthes to describe the way in which words or captions help to 'fix' the meaning of photographs, advertisements, or other visual displays. Visual material is supposed to be *polysemous*, or capable of generating a number of meanings. For example, a photograph of a man holding a pistol could suggest a number of ideas, including conflict, violence and so on. A caption reading 'sports day at Bluehill college' would suggest that a more mundane form of interpretation is suitable. The function of anchorage, according to Barthes, is ultimately ideological, narrowing the range of possible interpretations. (For an example of the way that captions anchor meaning see page 17.)

angle is a journalist's term meaning the perspective or 'slant' used for a particular story. For example, a news item on opposition to road-building could be presented as a study of alternative lifestyles among the protesters, as an indictment of government transport policy, or as an introduction to the history of civil disobedience.

Analogue

animation is the use of either stop–motion photography or computer-generated imagery to produce movement in cartoons, solid objects, or digital design. The stop–motion method depends on the shooting of objects or drawings frame by frame, with each individual element being moved or replaced by the next element. Thus, a continuous development of the scene or object is suggested. Where objects are photographed, and moved between frames before the next shot is taken, the process is known as '*pixillation*'. Animation, like all film-making, depends on *persistence of vision*.

A pioneer of animation was Georges Melies, whose 'Voyage à la lune' appeared in 1902. It featured a mix of live action and animated special effects. The first animated 'short' was Winsor McCay's 'Gertie the Dinosaur', of 1914. Walt Disney was probably the most successful corporate animator of the mid-twentieth century. (See also *cell animation*.)

Anchorage
The three front runners for this year's business award

Anchorage
Reporters question MP in corruption row

Annan: the Annan Commission report on the future of British broadcasting appeared in 1977. Led by Lord Annan, the committee was first set up under a Labour government in 1974. Its brief was to investigate all aspects of television and radio. The report it produced outlined four general principles which should characterise British broadcasting:

- accountability through Parliament to a public which is given more chance to make its voice heard
- diversity of services
- flexibility of structure
- editorial independence.

The Annan committee wished to move away from the duopoly represented by the BBC and the IBA (noting that broadcasting often seemed like 'a highly restricted club'), towards a more diverse approach which recognised the need to cater for minority interests. It argued that 'we do not need more of the same. There are enough programmes for the majority. What is needed now is programmes for the different minorities which add up to make the majority'.

Annan paved the way for the establishment of Channel 4, set up to encourage cultural diversity. The commission also favoured the introduction of Breakfast Television, a Broadcasting Complaints Commission, an Open Broadcasting Authority for the new commercial channel, and a Public Enquiry Board. The Labour government's response was mixed, but legislation was delayed because the Conservatives came to power in 1979. One of the report's legacies was Channel 4 (established under a Tory administration) which acted as a commissioning agent for independent producers.

anomie: the state of mind caused by the breakdown of established social norms ('anomie' was first used by Emile Durkheim, 1858–1917). In modern societies, according to Durkheim, traditional modes of behaviour have disappeared, but have not been replaced by alternative moral codes. The result is a feeling of disorientation and the growth of anxiety, leading to suicidal or homicidal tendencies. Merton (1957) used the notion of anomie to explain modern forms of deviance. He believed that great strain is placed on individuals when the opportunity to fulfil accepted norms of behaviour (such as the pursuit of material success), is denied by circumstances (the existence of deprivation, for example). Therefore, individuals are forced to pursue 'legitimate' goals by illegitimate means. (See also *alienation, counter-culture.*)

anti-narrative: a mode of film-making which works against the dominant *narrative* current, choosing instead to concentrate on *ideas* and themes, sometimes expressed through the repetition of sound and images, in other cases by rapid changes of scene and disordered editing.

anti-realist: a form of cinema which celebrates the artifice of film-making, in some cases avoiding claims to truth and referentiality, in others preferring to emphasise the mediation of camera between reality and social perception (the camera and other items of equipment sometimes appear on screen).

aphasia is a neurological term referring to language disorders which appear after an individual has suffered brain damage. There are different forms of aphasia, depending on the location of the injury, stroke, infection or whatever. Some types of aphasia are characterised by laboured speech and irregular word order. Other forms can manifest themselves as *semantic* difficulties. Studies of aphasia dating from the nineteenth century have shown that several areas of the left hemisphere of the brain are responsible for the production of *language.*

A-pictures: see *B-picture*

APL is the acronym for 'A Programming Language', a mathematically structured language developed by Kenneth Iverson in the mid-1960s. It was originally designed for IBM computers, and is used to solve difficult problems like linear equations.

Apple Computer Inc, founded in 1976 by Steven Jobs and Stephen Wozniak, was one of the first companies to manufacture 'microcomputers'. The company was started on capital of $100, but quickly established itself as a market leader in terms of design and ease of use. The 'Macintosh', developed by Apple, had enormous influence on computer and software design. Apple was reluctant to franchise its software, allowing Bill Gates' Microsoft to take the lead in this area. Despite these problems, Apple has established a strong 'niche' market in education and design.

archive: a file or store in which previously broadcast film/video/audio material is stored, sometimes including background notes.

Arendt, Hannah: Arendt (1906–1976) was profoundly influenced by the rise of fascism in Germany and wrote extensively about the nature of totalitarianism. She began her academic career in 1924 as a student of the philosopher Heidegger. In 1933, she fled Germany and established herself as an academic in New York. In 1951 she produced one of her most famous works, called 'The Origins of Totalitarianism'. This book analyses the historical precedents of fascism, tracing its bureaucratic character to the administrative practices of imperialism, where whole races were oppressed by racism and subject to 'administrative massacre'. Arendt's studies included a systematic investigation of totalitarianism, believing that it was completely removed from reality and founded almost entirely on *propaganda,* to the extent that the distinction between fantasy and reality became blurred and confused. Arendt wrote a number of articles on the trial of Adolf Eichmann, the Nazi brought to justice by the Israeli state. She discovered in Eichmann, not a monster but something worse, his complete ordinariness – what she called 'the banality of evil'.

argot: a *jargon* or *slang* used by a class or group (often based on occupation). Particular occupations, especially those which deal with technical issues, or are 'closed' or removed from the public, develop an argot. Members of armed forces represent one example.

articulation: the French linguist Andre Martinet argued that languages have the power of 'double articulation', creating sounds as well as meanings. In this system, the smallest unit of sound is called a *phoneme*, while the smallest units of meaning are called monemes.

artificial intelligence: see *AI*

Asiasat: in 1993 Rupert Murdoch purchased a 63 per cent share in Star TV, a Hong Kong company launched in 1991. Using a satellite called Asiasat, Murdoch was able to reach fifty-four Asian countries. Included amongst the nations in receipt of Star's programming was China, with a population of over a billion people. Star's 'footprint' (the area the satellite service covers) can reach 2.6 billion. However, the indiscriminate broadcasting of western programmes did not attain a mass market, so greater emphasis was placed on content which had a more local and regional appeal. (See also *News Corporation* and p. 20.)

aspect ratio: a cinematic reference, meaning the ratio between the width and height of a cinema screen. Silent cinema used a ratio of 1.33:1 (width to height) while modern systems use 2.2:1 or, for 35mm film, 1.85:1 in the USA and 1.66:1 in Europe.

Astra: a European television satellite launched in November 1988. In the 1980s, satellite broadcasting was strictly regulated. An American businesswoman, Candice Johnson, approached the Luxembourg government with the idea of making a private

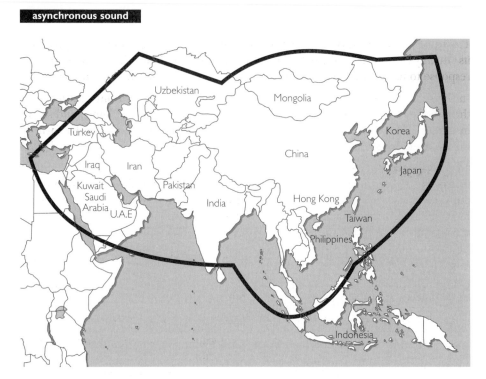

Asiasat – Star TV's footprint

investment in a European satellite. In 1985, her company, the Société Européene des Satellites (SES) won a twenty-two year franchise on the operation of a satellite system. The SES used the 'PAL' transmission system, thought inferior to the 'MAC' system favoured by the British government.

In 1986, a company called British Satellite Broadcasting won the Independent Broadcasting Authority's satellite franchise, but was prevented (by a European Community Directive) from using the established PAL transmission system. Therefore, BSB had to invest in the MAC system. BSB was committed to spending excessive amounts of money while its rival Sky (owned by Rupert Murdoch), invested in the Astra satellite and the PAL system. In November 1988, the Astra satellite was launched. Murdoch was ready to transmit his programmes in early 1989, putting BSB at an disadvantage from which it never recovered.

asynchronous sound is sound which is not produced in unison with the cinematic image.

attitude is a person's general evaluation of an object, person, event, institution, and so on. An attitude is a judgment of, or a reaction to, something. The psychologist Milton Rokeach calls it 'a relatively enduring organisation of beliefs around an object or situation' which predisposes an individual to act in a certain manner.

audience: the aggregate of individual listeners/viewers thought to receive public forms of communication. Audience is also used to refer to specific social groups, divided by class, sex, age, ethnicity and other characteristics.

The existence of two ways of conceptualising audience gives rise to what McQuail calls its 'duality', where it is formed ('Mass Communication Theory', p. 215) either 'in response to media' or where it 'corresponds to an existing social group or category'.

In the first case, audience is a sort 'temporary collective', brought into existence by the experience of listening to a concert, viewing a television programme, and so on; in other words, audience here is constructed both by the event and by the form of the event. The physical location of the audience, however, and its behaviour during the event, is different.

In the first example, the concert audience is composed of individuals who, for the duration of the performance, occupy one bounded space. They also experience the music in an identical format (live rather than recorded) and encounter the same musical sequence.

The audience for a particular television programme cannot easily be located; it is spatially displaced and may also be separated in time, if for example some members of the audience 'consume' the product at a later date, by watching it on video. Even where the majority of viewers watch the material during its designated period, research has shown that 'watching' includes a variety of other activities.

The difference in consumption, attitude and location has led some writers to ask if audiences actually exist in the way that media institutions describe them. For example, Ien Ang in 'Desperately Seeking the Audience' (1991) calls the audience 'an imaginary entity, an abstraction constructed from the vantage point of the institutions'.

Where audience is constructed in response to media, it can be split again, as either (in Ien Ang's words) 'audience-as-market' or 'audience-as-public'. She notes that (p. 170) 'audiencehood is becoming an ever more multifaceted, fragmented and diversified repertoire of practices and experiences'. The notion of audience as a number of practices, as a variety of meaningful social behaviours, avoids trying to arrange particular audiences into an unnatural sociological 'posture'. Rather than force audiences into a kind of frozen permanence, reflecting one 'moment' of their composition, Ang's concept of practice acknowledges the shifting nature of their arrangement, but still allows them to exist as concrete elements of social reality.

auteur: a label used for a film-maker whose work has a distinctive style. 'Auteur theory', brought into being by the French journal 'Cahiers du Cinema' credits certain directors with the status of 'author', distinguishing them from other film-makers whose work is thought less original.

authority: from author, the originator of something, comes authority, meaning the source of *power*. The two meanings, origin and power, come together in media and communication studies, in the sense that a message is often formed by a powerful individual or institution.

Etzioni (1964) divides authority into three separate types: the 'coercive' form, based on the use of force, the 'utilitarian' type which is exercised through legal and so-called rational authority and the 'normative', where relationships are based on the intrinsic value of the activities performed, or of membership of a certain group.

According to Etzioni, the 'coercive' form may include organisations such as prisons, concentration camps, and custodial hospitals. The 'utilitarian' form is supported by a system of economic reward, found in business, the armed services, and the civil service. Finally, Etzioni believed that the 'normative' form applied to hospitals, universities, and voluntary bodies.

In actual practice, all these forms will exist, to a greater or lesser degree, in every institution. Utilitarian approaches, for example, are quite easily reinforced by coercive features should the need arise. All powerful or ruling groups will possess the ability to mobilise any of the three types of authority, separately or in combination. Studies of authority also consider the reception of power, and the ways in which human subjects at times resist, and at other times co-operate with forms of public discipline.

autocue: the autocue or prompt is the roll of script reflected in front of the camera lens, so that presenters can look directly into the camera while reading news items for the audience.

babbling: sounds produced in the first months of an infant's life, thought by some to be 'pre-linguistic' and by others to exhibit some features of language. (See also *acquisition of language.*)

back issue: a magazine or periodical that is no longer current, though it may still be of interest to readers or collectors.

back lot: the rear area of a film studio which usually contains standing sets, such as urban streets, mock-ups of historical buildings and so on. These are used as a convenient substitute for location filming.

back projection is the projection of moving images onto a translucent screen, which can provide a background for a studio set. The projector stands behind the screen, unseen by the audience. In front of the screen, action is played out against the background and recorded by a camera. Camera and projector are synchronised, and share a common axis; at the same moment as each frame is projected from behind the screen, the camera in front records a frame.

Back projection

backbench: a newspaper term for the senior journalists who meet to decide which news items are important, and how each day's news should be shaped for public consumption. Their decisions will include the nature of editorials, the use of important pictures, and the choice of leading stories.

background has various meanings. In television, any backdrop, back-projection or other scene used behind foregrounded actors or objects. Also low-level music or sound effects used behind dialogue in TV or radio programmes. In animated features, the flat piece of artwork upon which cartoon characters are shown. In television, film and radio research, 'background' is information relating to a story or a person being interviewed.

backlist: a publisher's catalogue of books still in print.

backup file/disk: in computing and word-processing, a copy of a file or an entire disk, which acts as a guarantee in case work is lost.

BAFTA: British Academy of Film and Television Arts, a body which makes yearly awards for achievement in the field.

band: a group of frequencies which are set aside for radio transmission, eg. VHF, UHF, medium wave and so on.

bankroll: to 'bankroll' a media production is to put up money in order to support it.

banner headline: a newspaper headline that extends across the top of a newspaper page.

bar graph: a way of representing changes in data. A series of columns or bars, representing quantities, is set out along an axis.

BARB: the Broadcasters' Audience Research Board, used for audience measurement. Approximately 4,500 households have meters attached to their television sets which record, minute by minute, the channel being watched. BARB is owned jointly by the BBC and the ITCA (Independent TV Companies Association).

bardic function: a now-redundant comparison between the social function of television, and that of the traditional role of bard or storyteller in Celtic society. 'Bardic' television is, however, supposed to be reactionary because it attempts to create consensus about the meaning of unfamiliar events.

barn door: adjustable flaps on a studio light, used to direct the beam.

base/superstructure: an idea taken from Karl Marx, in which the economic foundation of a society is called the base, and the various institutional structures which grow from it (political, legal and social) are together known as the *superstructure*. According to Marx, changes in societies may be traced back to developments in the economic base.

Marx was careful to distinguish between 'forces' of production, which would include things like labour power, raw materials and the degree of technical development attained, and 'relations' of production, by which he meant the way that such forces are organised, managed and distributed. In a capitalist society, such relations are determined by the private ownership of production.

The idea of an economic base has been criticised because of the suspicion that Marxists believe the 'superstructure' to be entirely dependent on the economic base or foundation. In fact, Marx wrote that 'the mode of production ... conditions the general processes of social, political and intellectual life'. In other words, the base does not produce the superstructure as such, but determines the broad outlines of social development.

For example, we could say that digital technology is a 'force' of production which, organised as a capitalist enterprise, produces new conditions of life and reproduces specific power relationships. At the same time, the existence of certain discourses about digital technology (its social usefulness, its role in the workplace, and so on) depends on the existence of a superstructure which is flexible enough to at least allow such discussions to take place. Most left-wing theories do not suggest that culture is capable of being reduced to economic processes, and recognise that a superstructure or social sphere is just as real as the world of economic forces.

BBC see *British Broadcasting Corporation*

behaviour: the patterns of conduct which can be observed in human beings. Unlike actions, which are deliberate, not all forms of behaviour are consciously planned.

behaviourism: an approach to psychology which studies the observable actions of people, in the belief that this is the most reliable guide to understanding the human subject. Behaviourists believe that human behaviour is prompted by a process in which certain stimuli (events of some sort) are reinforced, while others are not. They reject as unreliable, any study of 'subjective' aspects of human conduct (such as emotional response). Behaviourism concentrates instead on empirical measurement, attempting to use scientific methods where stimulus can be compared with response. This often manifests itself in the use of controlled, laboratory-based experiments. Behaviourist approaches have also been associated with research into *persuasion.*

below the line: an advertising term referring to those sales activities, like demonstrations, exhibitions, direct mail, and the use of gifts, for which an advertising agency draws no commission. John Wilmshurst, in 'The Fundamentals of Advertising', notes that below the line activity has increased greatly since the late 1970s. Sales promotions are not welcomed in all countries, however; in Norway, for example, many techniques commonly used in Britain are banned. (See also *above the line.*)

Beveridge committee: this group, which submitted its report in 1950, carried out a wide-ranging and thorough enquiry into post-war British *broadcasting.* Lord Beveridge was anxious to ensure that the BBC should remain outside the direct control of government, and was not in favour of closer scrutiny by Parliament. His committee recognised the pitfalls of a broadcasting monopoly, but was hostile to the idea of a competitive structure; this, it was believed, would lead to a decline in quality, as rival institutions competed for audiences. The report also recommended that programme content should be overseen by the BBC's Board of Governors, that there should be a form of public representation, and that there should be reviews every five years and some devolution of the BBC's functions.

bias: a pre-disposition towards one particular viewpoint. The term is often applied to the attitudes and conduct of individuals, but is also associated with 'common sense' objections to lack of balance in media output. As a concept, bias is chiefly applied to those sections of the press and television which carry serious news stories. This is because news and documentary material is regarded as a matter of record; accuracy and truthfulness are the standards by which news production is judged, even though few people expect individual news reports to be completely reliable.

Bias is thought to manifest itself in various ways; in stories which are 'one-sided', in material which is incomplete, and in reportage which ignores entire events and/or alternative viewpoints. In all these cases, the end result is supposed to be the misrepresentation of the social world, based on the widespread conviction that the media play a significant role in the creation and circulation of public meanings. Various explanations are provided for the existence of bias, including the hierarchical structures of media ownership and control, the political allegiance of organisations, the commercial nature of most media enterprises, and the media's fear of authority.

The theory of bias is fairly simple, and depends on the idea that there is a balanced and reasonable point of view which is neglected in favour of a partisan approach. However, most commentators express reservations about the idea of bias, exactly because they think that its 'opposite' (an impartial view of the world) is impossible to achieve.

Watson and Hill for example (1997, p. 19), think that a person's outlook is always bound to be subjective or 'biased'. Gill and Adams (1992, p. 20) are convinced that 'it is quite impossible to report totally objectively about any event'. One danger in the approach of Watson and Hill, and of Gill and Adams, is that it may suggest the goal of accuracy and fairness is not worth pursuing, if only because an impossibly complete picture of events is being sought. Although selection (which is what these writers are describing), can contribute to bias, it does not always produce distortion. Selection is an inevitable part of *representation* and the *narrative* forms through which social exchange is often made (see *news values*). It is therefore possible to construct an impression of an event which an audience will judge to be reasonably well-balanced.

John Hartley, in 'Key Concepts in Communication and Cultural Studies' (1996), also criticises the notion of bias, arguing that it encourages the assumption that (p. 29) the world 'is endowed with an essential truth that can be rendered without bias'. Here, two ideas are being challenged; first, the notion that there is an essential truth which can be found and secondly, the belief that it is possible to re-present aspects of reality without bias. It makes sense to argue that there is no exact match between the world and the ways in which it is perceived, but this does not mean that reality is impossible to describe. Despite the limitations inherent in the concept of bias, it at least provides a reminder that media forms are capable of misrepresentation, and that media institutions should be subject to public scrutiny.

binary opposition: a term derived from *structuralism* showing how meaning can be created through the contrast between two terms. For example, 'public' and 'private' make a binary opposition which generates a range of meanings about the condition of social existence. Some theorists argue that binary oppositions suppress the ambiguities which exist in language, by providing only equally matched pairs. O'Sullivan notices the tendency in news reporting to create binary values, where one side of an argument is assigned a positive value and the other its negative opposite.

Binary oppositions are used in research, in the form of the *semantic differential* test. Subjects are asked how they would describe a product, event or any other phenomenon under study, by assigning it a value on a seven point scale. One half of a binary opposition is placed at each end of the scale, and the individual being tested is asked to select a point which matches his/her opinion most closely. For example, people could be interviewed about a product, and asked to mark a place on a scale which appears as follows:

Efficient — — — — — — — Inefficient

By using a series of paired oppositions for the same product (cold/hot, friendly/unfriendly, and so on) a fairly extensive overview of its attributes may be obtained. If a brand of consumer goods can be said to have a public image, then a semantic differential test will establish what kind of qualities it is thought to possess, and the degree to which each attribute is present. (See also *logical oppositions*.)

biograph: the American Mutoscope and Biograph Company, an early film company which gave its name to a type of camera.

biopic: a film which represents the life story of a prominent individual; from 'biography' and 'picture'.

bit: an abbreviated term for 'binary digit', which in computer language is either a 0 or a 1; a bit is the smallest unit of information in a computer.

bit-mapping: a computer technique for creating a graphics display, in which a unit of memory corresponds to a pixel (a 'picture element'). A pixel is the smallest element of a display space that can be manipulated.

black cinema: a term used of current African-American cinema, which has its origins in a series of films made in the 1970s. Melvin Van Peebles' 1971 'Sweet Sweetback's Baadaas Song', Gordon Parks Senior's 'Shaft' (1971) and Gordon Parks Junior's 'Superfly' (1972), began a successful genre which attracted Hollywood investment. The '*blaxploitation*' film had a brief flowering, until the genre was no longer deemed commercially viable.

In the later 1970s, black writers and film-makers began to widen the frame of cultural references used in the early movies, and moved beyond the stereotypes which had once served to raise black concerns. Charles Burnett's 'Killer of Sheep' (1977) is an example of realism in narrative and representation.

Mainstream success was achieved in the 1980s by stars like Eddie Murphy, though many other black actors had long worked in supporting roles that made them public favourites (Morgan Freeman and Danny Glover are two examples).

Spike Lee became a prime mover of black cinema, displaying a mixture of cultural insight and financial acumen which meant that his first production, 'She's Gotta Have It' (1986) earned $8.5m on an outlay of $175,000. Lee produced a consistently high standard of work, the best perhaps still the 1989 'Do the Right Thing', a study of a community at boiling point. 'Malcolm X', castigated as over-long, nevertheless contained some remarkable scenes, displaying Lee's extensive use of references to other films and disinclination to make features which follow the realist tradition. Lee also joined with Charles Burnett, Julie Dash, Charles Lane, and the Hudlin brothers to create the Black Filmakers Foundation. Other notable directors include Kathleen Collins ('Losing Ground', 1982), Heather Foxwood ('Trouble I've Seen', 1988), John Singleton ('Boyz 'n the Hood', 1991), and Julie Dash ('Daughters of the Dust', 1991).

blaxploitation is a term which was invented by the magazine 'Variety' to refer to exploitation films, usually made by white directors, but featuring black actors and aimed at black consumers. The genre emerged in the USA in the early 1970s, following the considerable success of Melvin Van Peebles' 1971 'Sweet Sweetback's Baadaas Song'. Van Peebles, a black director, produced a story which reflected the social frustrations of his time. The films which followed, often produced by Hollywood directors, concentrated on fairly simple plots in which black heroes (often private detectives) overcame the racism of white society. The best known of these are 'Shaft' of 1971 and 'Superfly' of 1972. By 1976, the genre was no longer seen as a safe commercial bet. Despite restrictions on the type of roles available to black actors, the blaxploitation genre had at least represented African Americans as resilient and successful. More serious black commercial cinema emerged from this beginning.

bleed: the part of an illustration extended beyond the area devoted to type; a bleed goes beyond the type to reach the outer edge of a page.

blockbuster: a film which is conceived, executed and promoted on a grand scale.

blue screen: in film, blue screen technique is used to produce 'matte' shots. A deep blue screen is placed behind the foreground action, and the entire scene is photographed. The film is then copied, using a filter to block out the blue area so that, at the next stage of production, a different background can be added. In television production, this technique is electronic and instantaneous, and is known as 'chroma key' (often written and pronounced as one word).

blurb is written copy used to advertise the contents of books and other printed material; an author's blurb is often produced in collaboration with an editor and appears on the back of his/her book as well as in leaflets and other advertising. Blurb is occasionally used, and sometimes even reproduced word for word by reviewers.

body language: the idea that a variety of non-verbal behaviours, deliberate or otherwise, create a communicative code which can be 'read' or interpreted by onlookers. Gesture, affective displays, facial expressions and other forms of movement all qualify as body language. Despite attempts to discover precise meanings for certain types of body language, it may be best described as an informal system which provides the context for speech. Michael Argyle ('Bodily Communication', p. 294), writes 'there is nothing like a verbal grammar ruling how the different kinds of units are to be combined'.

Judy Gahagen, in 'Non-Verbal Communication', says that there are two functions of non-verbal communication. The first is the expression of emotion, while the second illustrates and supports speech. Some theories of non-verbal communication stress the supposedly 'universal' meaning of certain types of gesture. There do seem to be some examples of body language which make a roughly similar impact across cultures.

bold is an abbreviation of 'boldface type' (the kind used for the initial word of this line).

boom mike: a microphone held on a long, telescopic boom.

B-picture: the Hollywood studio system (which lasted from the early 1930s to about 1950), was responsible for the introduction of the 'double bill'; two films which could be seen at one sitting. These were known as 'A' and 'B' pictures.

A-pictures had a relatively large budget and ran for at least 90 minutes of screen time, while B-pictures were cheaper, shorter, and did not feature major stars. Some companies, like Republic and Monogram, specialised in these second features. Although the double-bill system no longer exists, the term 'B-movie' or 'B-picture' continues to designate films which are not 'front rank' releases, but which nonetheless contain elements of interest. When 'Independence Day' was released in 1996, one critic called it 'the greatest B-movie of all time'.

brand is a term used in advertising to describe a commercial product; the process of 'branding' is central to marketing strategy, because a branded product acquires not just a name but a whole range of associations. 'Brand image' is built up over time, and may in the case of a car (for example) suggest to the consumer a range of qualities, such as 'reliability', 'style', and 'freedom'. One advertising executive, Larry Light, made the claim that 'as there is more focus on branding there will be even more focus on the psychology of persuasion' (see Price, 1993, p. 144). Related terms include 'brand loyalty' to describe the customer's adherence to a particular product, and 'brand recognition', the degree to which a prospective consumer is familiar with a particular brand.

bridging shot: a shot intended to show that there has been a change in location or a lapse in time; a 'bridge', therefore, connects two shots which show separate spatial or temporal sequences.

brief: the instructions or guidance given to a media worker; a reporter may be told how a story should be covered, a designer how a page should be set out, etc.

British Broadcasting Corporation: originally a private company (a consortium of radio manufacturers), the BBC received its licence to broadcast in January 1923. In its early days, it was controlled by six large companies which manufactured broadcasting equipment. Any British wireless group could join by purchasing one or more shares, producing a £50 deposit, and accepting the terms drafted by the Postmaster General and the manufacturing companies. The BBC licence fee cost ten shillings, and covered the ownership of wireless receivers.

The 1923 Sykes committee declared that the BBC should not be a commercial monopoly; two years later, in 1925, another committee produced the Charter of the BBC, which permitted the Corporation to broadcast for ten years from 1st January 1927. John Reith was the British Broadcasting Company's general manager, and was the Corporation's first Director General.

In 1926, during the General Strike, the role of the BBC was attacked by the political left. Although the Corporation remained independent, its reporting of the dispute gave undue weight to government propaganda. The General Strike revealed a great deal about the relationship between the government and the corporation. Churchill, then Home Secretary, wanted to take over the BBC for the duration of the dispute. Baldwin, the Prime Minister, advised caution. It was decided to allow the BBC to conduct its own affairs. However, Reith found himself in an unenviable position; he would be attacked by the trade unions and liberal opinion for what appeared to be his pro-Government reports, but was still not free of political pressure. He noted in his diary that 'they did not commandeer us, but they know that they can trust us not to be really impartial'.

Stuart Hood, in the second edition of his book 'On Television' (1983), described the composition of the first BBC Board of Governors as representing the interests and ideas of 'the most important groups within the British ruling class'.

The Seldon Committee reported on television in 1935, leaving the structure of the BBC intact, while the Ullswater report of 1936 was timed to coincide with the expiration of its first Charter on 31st December of that year. The number of BBC governors was increased from five to seven and the Charter extended for another ten years. The Corporation was praised for its impartiality, but criticised for the nature of its Sunday entertainment.

A single 'Home Service' was created in 1939. The BBC's development of television was interrupted by the Second World War, but radio broadcasting became an important wartime resource, carrying the British state's message of resistance to Nazi Germany, across occupied Europe.

In the post-war era, the BBC divided its radio network into the Home Service, the Light Programme, and the Third Programme. The Light Programme was devoted to the arts, serious discussion and experimental material. Television broadcasting was resumed in 1946. Four years later, the Beveridge Committee submitted the report of its enquiry into broadcasting. Lord Beveridge wished the BBC to remain outside direct government control. The committee, although aware of the dangers of a broadcasting monopoly, rejected the idea of setting up a commercial rival. The new Conservative government of 1951 was less hostile to the idea; its Television Act of 1954 created the Independent Television Authority. The first commercial channel was allowed an initial 'term' of ten years, but found itself criticised by the Pilkington committee of 1962.

The Peacock committee of 1986 looked into the question of public service broadcasting, examining the possibilities of alternative sources of finance for the BBC. In November 1992, the Conservative government published a Green paper called 'The Future of the BBC'. It proposed the following ideas:

- the BBC remain a *public service* broadcaster
- the licence fee should remain the central method of funding
- the Governors of the Corporation should not oversee management of programmes
- the BBC should become more efficient.

In 1994, a White paper appeared, called 'The Future of the BBC: Serving the Nation, Competing Worldwide'. It renewed the Corporation's Charter, ensuring that the BBC remained the main provider of Public Service Broadcasting. The Broadcasting Standards Council and the Broadcasting Complaints Commission were merged to form a new council which would monitor standards.

broadband cable: a transmission facility which can carry multiple channels and which permits the transmission of digital media products at high speed around the globe. Companies which control the cable networks will clearly be in a strong position to profit from increased markets for digital communications.

broadcasting is the institutionalised practice of sending television and radio content to large numbers of receivers. This form of media practice depends on the use of established genres and familiar codes. British broadcasting, in the days of the BBC's monopoly, depended on state regulation and public sponsorship through a licence fee. When commercial broadcasting began in the mid 1950s, the rules laid down for independent television were taken, by and large, from the standards already established for the BBC.

Although broadcast media operate in many different forms across the world, there is usually a framework of state regulation and control. The following characteristics, identified by Denis McQuail in 'Media Performance' (1992, p. 93), give an overview of the typical form of media organisation:

- monopoly or oligopoly market structure
- separation of editorial, production and distribution tasks
- an extreme diversity of product
- diversity of financial support, including advertising revenue, sponsorship, subsidy, subscription, and licence fee.

Marc Raboy, in his Introduction to 'Public Broadcasting for the 21st Century', argues that (p. 5) 'traditionally, public service broadcasting has been expected to represent the national as opposed to the foreign. It may be time to re-focus these conceptual categories in terms of the local and the global'.

broadsheet: a large-size newspaper like 'The Guardian' or 'The Times', as opposed to tabloid-sized newspapers like 'The Daily Mirror'. Some newspapers, like 'The Daily Express', began as a broadsheet and scaled-down to tabloid size, while others, like 'The Guardian', publish tabloid sections with the main newspaper.

Broadsheet

broken series is an American term for a television series which is cancelled by network television, but is then syndicated (passed on to other stations), often with the addition of new episodes.

browsing: a user's casual and non-sequential movement through the information held on a compact disc.

BSS: in the United States, an abbreviation for 'broadcast satellite service'.

buddy movie was originally an industry term for a film which centres on the friendship between two male protagonists. Some critics have suggested that these narratives carry a romantic subtext or even a more explicit eroticism. This may be true in some cases, but the charge of 'phallocentrism' which is sometimes made against these films (see Susan Hayward's 'Key Concepts in Cinema Studies', 1996) would imply that they are merely vehicles for continued male domination of the cinematic agenda. Alternatively, it may be argued that many of them reflect the complexity of male relationships, and that scenes which show 'male bonding' (although usually in the context of some perilous adventure), are treating a theme which requires exploration. In such a case, friendship, love, mutual respect and eroticism may indeed appear, but for a variety of purposes.

Much depends on how the film concerned presents its central relationship, and the kind of cultural and political environment in which such representations are received. Since Ridley Scott's 'Thelma and Louise' (a female 'buddy movie' of 1991), the agenda of these films has been re-appraised. However, 'Thelma and Louise' also helped to maintain the continued vigour of the whole genre, whatever the sex of the central characters. The 'buddy movie' will probably endure so long as friendship acts as a symbolic counterpoint to the cinematic representation of other, more destructive forces (greed, war, 'the system' and so on).

bulletin: a brief summary or overview of the day's news, lasting no more than five minutes.

bureaucracy: the existence of established administrative practices, overseen by organised groups of officials. These groups may function on behalf of a variety of institutions. However, bureaucracy is often seen as a subdivision, or even a central characteristic, of government or some other executive power. Max Weber saw bureaucracy as the dominant form of organisation in modern society. In this sense, it is a characteristic feature of *modernity* and not just a particular method of organisation.

Modern societies depend on systems, and on functionaries who are assigned to manage all aspects of organisational existence. Weber thought that bureaucracy was the most efficient form of organisation, and that it is a system in which rational action is seen in an institutional form.

It is worth noting that 'bureaucratic' organisations have come to be associated with inefficiency and wasteful practices, while bureaucracy has been charged with having a negative effect on the flow of organisational communication (see Walter Bennis, 1965). David Beetham, in his book 'Bureaucracy' (1996), sets out four uses of the term. The first indicates 'a type of political system' literally 'rule by the bureau'. The second refers to 'a system of administration' carried out by trained professionals. The third use maintains that bureaucracy should be understood as public as opposed to private administration. The fourth and last is taken from political economy, and identifies true bureaucracy as 'a non-market organisation' financed by a parent body.

byline: in journalism, the name of the individual who has written an article or feature. The byline appears with the article. Richard Keeble, in 'The Newspapers Handbook' (1994), mentions the fact that sub-editors sometimes refer to this kind of credit as 'the blame-line'.

C

cable: one of the earliest uses of cable for communication purposes was in Britain in the 1930s, when cable was laid for relaying radio broadcasts. In addition, cable was sometimes used to assist television broadcasts to areas which suffered from poor reception.

In 1982, the Conservative government's Information Technology Advisory Panel, advocated a speedy expansion of cable networks. This was at a time (the mid-1980s) when the conventional wisdom was that satellite and cable technology was about to transform the global market for television. The ITAP also advised that each network operator should be given monopoly control of the programmes transmitted. The problem was that the government had not carried out any research into the demand for cable.

What demand there is, appears to be largely confined to the sphere of entertainment; in the USA, 80–85 per cent of the material shown on cable, consists of feature films. It seems unlikely, however, that European uptake will reach American levels, where approximately two-thirds of homes have cable. There is a more than adequate supply, with well over a hundred European channels available on satellite. By 1993, however, only some 5.6 per cent of European homes were connected for cable reception. Germany and Britain had over two-thirds of this total. Hopes for massive penetration of previously untapped markets, such as Asia and India, have been subjected to more sober analysis, with the result that numbers able to receive cable appeared tiny by comparison with the millions of people living in these regions.

Cable and Broadcasting Act: an Act of Parliament, dating from 1984, which proposed the creation of a cable network for the United Kingdom. The Act created a Cable Authority but set up few rules for the laying of cable systems.

cable operator: any group or company that provides or owns a television *cable system*.

cable system: in America, a cable system is a facility located in any state or territory which receives signals from the licensees of the Federal Communications Commission. The cable system then makes secondary transmissions to its own subscribers.

cablecasting is the provision of television signals via a cable network rather than through a *broadcast* system.

CAD: see *computer aided design*.

Cahiers du Cinéma: a film journal founded in 1951 by Andre Bazin, Jacques Doniol-Valcrose, and Lo Doca. This was a tremendously influential journal which coincided with French 'new wave' cinema, advocating the primacy of the 'auteur' and 'mise en scene'. Many directors, such as Godard, Truffaut and Chabrol, produced articles for 'Cahiers du Cinéma'.

Calcutt Committee: this committee, led by lawyer and academic David Calcutt, was set up in 1990 to study press intrusions into the personal lives of individuals. The initial outcome of the enquiry was a report which warned the newspaper industry to avoid violations of privacy. In addition, a Press Complaints Commission was set up to monitor complaints against the industry. In 1993, Calcutt produced a second report, in which he called for a statutory code for journalists, a press complaints tribunal, and a new criminal offence which would cover the use of telephoto lenses and the planting of electronic bugs. The second report also criticised the Press Complaints Commission as ineffective.

calotype: an early photographic process from which modern negative/positive processes developed. An Englishman, William Henry Fox Talbot (1800-1877), had been attempting to perfect a system for fixing images. Although he had not declared his findings in public, Fox Talbot had invented the negative/positive process in 1835. Then, in 1839, *Daguerre* announced the success of his experiments in photography. Convinced that Daguerre's process was identical to his own, Fox Talbot made a presentation to the Royal Institution 18 days after the Frenchman's announcement.

The calotype, as the new process was called, was created by taking a sheet of good quality writing paper and immersing it in a weak solution of salt. It was then wiped dry and a solution of silver nitrate was applied to one surface. The drying process was then carried out in front of a fire. Thus prepared, the light-sensitive paper could be exposed in a camera; early negatives required at least thirty minutes of exposure time, though this was eventually reduced.

Positive prints were obtained from the negative by placing a second sheet of paper (sometimes waxed or oiled to increase transparency) in contact with the first, and allowing the action of sunlight to produce the new image. Fox Talbot described print-making in the following way; 'In the photogenic ... process, if the paper is transparent, the first drawing may serve as an object, to produce a second drawing, in which the lights and shadows would be reversed'.

In 1844, Fox Talbot produced the first book on the new process of 'photogenic drawing' or 'photography'. This was called 'The Pencil of Nature' because the pictures it contained were produced without 'the aid of any one acquainted with the art of drawing', as the author stated in his introduction. Each copy of the book required extensive effort; the first photographic 'production line' came into being to cope with the number of prints required.

In simple terms, the calotype (from 'kalos', Greek for beautiful) made pictures characterised by strong contrast between light and shade, grainy and 'artistic' in appearance. The Daguerreotype, on the other hand, produced images which revealed exceptionally fine detail. Its disadvantage was that it could not be used to provide copies whilst the Calotype could make any number of prints. (See *photography* and *Talbotype*).

camera: from the Greek 'kamara', meaning something with an arched cover, and the later Latin term for a vault, comes camera, a device (usually a box) used to record images by exposing light-sensitive film to a light source, or by allowing an artist to trace a picture onto translucent paper.

Originally a room, the *camera obscura* formed the 'hardware' for early experiments to establish a viable method of *photography*.

In 1676, the first reflex camera was produced. A reflex camera is one in which an image is reflected by a 45 degree mirror onto a focussing screen. A German monk, Johann Zahn, designed a portable camera in 1685, which used a lens mounted in an adjustable tube (the first 'single lens reflex' camera). John Wade notes (p. 9), that 'while the physics was now ready, the chemistry still had a long way to go'.

The production of the world's first permanent photograph, taken by Joseph Niepce in 1826, showed that the technical processes of photography have a close relationship to the *aesthetic* effect produced by individual pictures. Fox-Talbot made his own cameras (called 'mousetraps'), while Daguerre eventually patented and manufactured his daguerreotype line. The major processes in the mid-nineteenth century were the Calotype, the daguerreotype, and the wet plate process, invented by Frederick Scott Archer in 1851.

Various other inventions, like stereoscopic cameras and the rapid-fire 'pistolgraph' of 1858 were moderately successful, but it was not until the introduction of George Eastman's Kodak camera in 1888, that photography became a mass pursuit.

In the 1920s and 30s new, lightweight cameras like the Leica and Rolleiflex, encouraged a revolution in photographic practice, and sustained the growth of *photojournalism*. In the 1960s and 70s, the goal of simplicity was pursued relentlessly, with Kodak's 'Instamatic' 126 (a fixed focus camera) and the instant photography of the Polaroid (the SX-70 appeared in 1972). By the early 1980s, digital photography was introduced to the market.

In 'The Camera and its Images' (p. 68), Arthur Goldsmith argues that photographic technology evolved in response to four basic demands: to make it more convenient; to make it capable of recording any subject the eye can see; to improve the quality of the image; and to make the process less expensive.

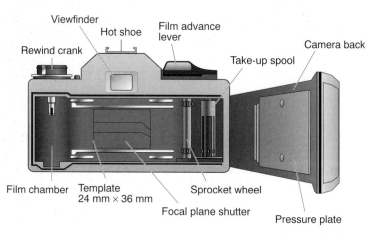

A modern camera

camera obscura: a dark box or chamber used for copying images. The origins of the camera obscura can be traced back to the Greek philosopher Aristotle (384–322 BC), who made a reference to it in his works. In the 10th Century, a Moslem scholar called Alhazen described a technique for indirectly observing an eclipse of the sun.

The camera obscura began as a darkened room with a small hole made in one wall; this provided the aperture through which light could enter – the scene outside could be projected onto the surface facing the hole. Whatever was projected, however, was upside-down and reversed left to right. The chief use of these early cameras was to follow the course of the sun through the sky and for the safe observation of solar eclipses.

In 1550 Girolamo Cardano, a physician and professor of mathematics, used a bio-convex lens to achieve a far brighter image. The scientist Giovanni Battista della Porta (who wrote 'Natural Magic' in 1558) experimented with a series of lenses until eventually he was able to invite an audience to watch a 'performance' given by actors. The performers stood outside the room and their image was projected onto the wall inside. The actors appeared upside-down and the reaction of the audience was not favourable; della Porta was charged with sorcery.

A 19th Century camera obscura

In 1569 another writer called Daniello Barbaro gave instructions for the use of the camera, 'close all shutters and doors ... until no light enters the camera except through the lens, and opposite hold a sheet of paper ... by holding the paper steady you can trace the whole perspective with a pen'. The use of perspective became an increasingly important issue; the world in mediaeval paintings had been flat – now it was shown in depth.

By the 17th Century, the camera obscura had become accepted as a scientific instrument and was used extensively by artists as an aid to drawing. The first reflex camera was produced in 1676. A reflex camera is one in which an image is reflected by a 45 degree mirror onto a focussing screen. The 17th Century version included a shaded structure at the top, into which the artist could insert his/her head and hand.

In 1685, a German monk called Johann Zahn designed a small camera which could be carried easily from place to place. This was in effect the first single lens reflex camera, and was the first capable of taking a picture, at least in theory. However, the chemical half of the technology did not exist. It was not until 1826, when Joseph Niepce used a camera obscura to expose a metal plate, that the first successful photograph was made.

camera-ready is a publishing term meaning copy and/or illustrations set out exactly as they will appear on the page; copy ready to be photographed for printing.

Campaign for Press and Broadcasting Freedom: a British organisation founded in 1979, it is devoted to making the media more accountable and democratic. It publishes a magazine called 'Free Press' and has produced a number of important reports, including studies of racism and homophobia in the press. Its work during events like the Gulf War, when news coverage was restricted, was particularly important.

canned: any electronic material that has been recorded and saved for later editing. Recorded film is said to be 'in the can', after the round canisters in which film stock is kept.

caption: information accompanying an illustration or photograph; captions are sometimes said to 'anchor' a picture, providing it with meaning. (See also *anchorage*.)

captive audience: a group which has no choice but to watch, or listen to some form of public or commercial material. Customers in restaurants may find themselves obliged to listen to recorded music, students in a lecture may have to listen to particular opinions, people queuing in a post office might have to watch a commercial video loop.

Carnegie Commission: an American body set up in 1964 to study non-commercial television. It led to the Public Broadcasting Act of 1967, which in turn set up the Corporation for Public Broadcasting.

cart (cartridge): a plastic case containing a loop of tape, which is used for playing pre-recorded inserts during television and radio programmes; carts are 'self-cueing' and often contain advertisements, jingles, and news items.

cartoon: originally, a preparatory drawing made by a painter. The term is also used of newspaper illustrations dealing with social and political issues. In film and television, cartoons are used in *animation*. In the twentieth century, the Walt Disney organisation dominated the production of cartoons. Mixtures of live action and cartoons have appeared in many films, from 'Mary Poppins' (1964) to 'Space Jam' (1997).

case study: the second part of the final examination for AEB Communication Studies is a case study. It is made up of two sets of papers taken from a wide range of sources; holiday brochures, newspaper and magazine articles, recruitment brochures, reports, books, job descriptions, promotional material, advertising, letters, and so on. The number of sources for each study will be limited, and will not cover all these examples. A number of days before the exam, the 'raw material' is given to each candidate. Individuals have to anticipate what kind of questions will appear. The chief principle is that the *content* provided, will have to be turned into a different *form*.

There would be no point, for example, in turning a series of magazine articles on personal identity, into another set of features cast in the same form. However, a radio script for a popular psychology programme, based on the magazine articles, would be an acceptable possibility.

The AEB gives the following information on the purpose of the case study: 'Questions will test the ability to adapt theories and/or models to practical situations, to adopt a mode or modes of communication appropriate to a particular role or roles, and to evaluate the case study materials'.

The reference to roles means that candidates must be prepared to assume the role of journalist, producer, educationalist, public relations manager, and so on, in response to the demands of the case study itself. For a thorough account of case studies, see Chapter 6 of Price, 'Communication Studies' (1996).

casual: a casual is a journalist who is employed on a temporary basis.

casualisation: the process of moving from full-time employment to patterns of part-time and short contract working. In the media field and beyond, it has become the practice of major employers to shed workers through early retirement and redundancy. They may then hire other employees (or to re-hire some of the original staff) at lower wages. Casualisation creates a pool of labour which can provide expertise for a specific project, and which can then be discarded at short notice. Not all employers carry out such practices, as some have agreed to minimum standards of training, but the media industry as a whole has neglected training and career development in favour of casual labour.

catchline: a term used in journalism; it is a phrase or word used to identify a story. For instance, 'strike threat' or 'safety fear' alerts an audience to the content of a particular news item.

categories: classes of things which have something in common. 'Plant', for example, is a category and may include dandelions, sunflowers and ivy. If, however, we consider the category 'flower', then ivy falls outside the category. (See also *categorisation*.)

categories of communication: see *communication* (*categories of*).

categorisation: the process of sorting objects, events or living things into a series of classes or groups. The *sense-data* collected by social groups is organised into systems of 'belonging.' Categories are used to refer to a variety of elements found in the world, from the fairly specific, to the more general features of experience. For example, the category 'cat' has a smaller range of reference than the wider category 'animal.'

Traditional approaches to categorisation assume that it divides human experience in terms of difference and similarity, so that clear boundaries exist between category types. Small variations are thought acceptable, provided they always share the same 'core' features.

Alternatives to the 'classical' approach were proposed by the philosopher Wittgenstein in 'Philosophical Investigations', where he used the example of the activities called 'games,' to ask what organising principle was actually used to assign various phenomena to the same category (p. 39). Instead of trying to find clear-cut boundaries between what is a game and what is not, Wittgenstein proposed the concept of 'family resemblances,' a series of relationships which exist between different examples, so that each share a number of features but do not possess all the possible criteria for membership.

In 1973, William Labov studied the linguistic categorisation of household objects such as glasses, vases, bowls, mugs and cups. In one experiment, he showed a group of students a series of pictures of various containers. Labov wanted to know if there might be any variations in the way each picture was named, once different uses of the objects were suggested to the students. He found that the context of use was an important part of the way in which objects were described.

Some theories of ideology assume that it is exactly the ordinary names given to aspects of experience, and the basic divisions made between 'things in the world,' which reflect a society's values and beliefs. For example, a 'descriptive' term like white, applied to people rather than to objects, has often promoted discrimination against certain groups and individuals.

cathode ray tube or *CRT*, a vacuum tube used in television sets. The cathode is a negative electrode. When placed in a magnetic field, the cathode sends out a stream of electrons to a screen, which appear as various forms of light and thus form pictures.

cause and effect in cinematic and televisual *narrative* cause and effect is a method of advancing a storyline. So, for example, one on-screen action can initiate another event. This, in turn, can produce a new action which continues to build the narrative. Branigan, in 'Narrative Comprehension and Film', called narrative 'a cause-effect relationship occurring over time'.

Notice that cause and effect must be represented in terms which an audience will understand. This means that narrative must be created through the use of certain film techniques; *editing*, for example, must show the relationship between events. If, for example, a protagonist is motivated by the desire for revenge, then some tangible reason must be given to justify that motivation. Therefore, an audience must be told about, or actually shown the cause (say, for the sake of argument, the death of a friend) which entails the effect. This could be done in an initial scene (shown before the viewer realises its later significance), through flashback, by allowing another character to recall the incident, and so on.

CD: stands for compact disc, a flat, 12 centimetre diameter disc which is covered with a highly reflective aluminium layer, then by a thin layer of clear plastic. CDs are used for the commercial production of music, while CD-I and CD-ROM are able to carry text and graphics. Laser discs, the analogue predecessor of the CD, carry video images.

In the case of the CD, the physical qualities of the original sound are converted into a series of binary digits. Each second of a musical performance is 'sampled' many thousands of times. Each sample is in turn inscribed on the optical disc, in the form of a series of reflective pits. These carry the digital codes which are read by a laser beam. The laser beam acts like the stylus on a gramophone, except that it does not actually touch the surface of the CD (the protective plastic coating is no hindrance because the laser shines through it to the reflective pits below). The beam reads the surface of the CD as 'pit' or 'absence of pit', a signal which corresponds to the of 'on' and 'off'of the binary code. A semi-conductor chip converts the digital information back into sound. Besides the advantage of a large capacity (a single compact disc can carry 650 megabytes of information), the CD is much less subject to wear than records and tapes.

CD-Rom/CD-I: CD-ROM is an abbreviation of Compact Disc-Read Only Memory. It first appeared in 1985, produced by Philips and Sony. Unlike audio CDs, which were aimed at the entertainment market, CD-ROM was intended for computer users, requiring the purchase of disc drives linked to PCs. An initial difficulty was the standardisation required, because the new product had to be accessible to all computer systems; Tony Feldman ('An Introduction to Digital Media', 1997) explains (p. 41) 'while CD audio demanded a physical standardisation, CD-ROM required a deeper level of standardisation affecting the logical structure of the data on the discs'. Eventually, a universal specification was agreed, called ISO 9660.

Early users of CD-ROM were largely confined to professionals involved in information retrieval, such as librarians. Initially, there were so few CD titles available for use, that there seemed to be little point in purchasing the disc drives. Feldman notes that there were only some 50 titles available by the end of 1986, while 'the installed base of disc drives was about 6500'. At the end of 1994, there were about 8000 titles and some 25 million disc drives worldwide.

The growth of a consumer, rather than a professional market for CD-ROM, meant that changes in the type of system used, and in the kind of material available, were inevitable. Philips forged ahead with CD-I, the Interactive version of the compact disc. The CD-I disc is digitally encoded, and can be accessed at random. The layout of information on the disc dictates which information will be interpreted as text, and which as audio or video.

The brunt of initial investment was borne by Philips, because other companies were reluctant to commit funds to an untried system. The first CD-Is were worthy productions which emphasised education and interactive learning, but most consumers did not want their leisure time filled with an activity that was too much like hard work. Feldman makes a similar point (p. 47); 'early CD-I titles ... which aimed to provide rich, interactive cultural experiences, were simply barking up the wrong tree'. The consumer market lay in computer games, a field which was exploited by specialists like Sony and Sega.

cell animation is an *animation* technique, in which individual 'cells' (sheets of transparent plastic) are used to produce cartoons. An image is first divided into a series of layers. The background, for example, need only be drawn once for a whole scene. Other details, such as middle ground, which requires some alteration throughout the scene, and foreground action, may need a number of separate illustrations to plot movement. When the cells are combined, they can be photographed to create single frames. Cell animation was the standard technique for studio animation until the advent of computer-generated imagery. (See p. 42.)

Cell animation

celluloid: cellulose nitrate, once used as a film base, but chemically unstable. Celluloid is sometimes used as a term for film in general.

censorship: censorship is the modern practice of restricting what may be said, recorded, published or otherwise disseminated, by laying down in advance rules which must be obeyed and subjects which must be avoided, and/or by intervening at a later stage, to remove or alter material which has already been drafted or recorded. In Ancient Rome the 'censor' was a magistrate who drew up a register or census of citizens, and supervised public behaviour.

Some issues of censorship often appear in public debate (for example, the issue of sex and violence in broadcast media). Other forms of censorship, such as the repression of civil liberties through laws like the Criminal Justice Act and the Official Secrets Act, receive rather less coverage.

Most commentators agree that informal and secret pressure is more effective than a direct assault on an individual or media outlet, but informal pressure is effective partly because the state has a formal power to which it can resort when needed. Paul Trowler ('Investigating Mass Media', 1996) reprints the words of a former Controller of BBC Scotland (p. 77), 'discreet government pressure or informal persuasion is more likely to succeed'.

Although power is not entirely concentrated in the hands of the state, certain events (like war) provide clear-cut examples of times when these interests converge. Liz Curtis' book 'Ireland: the Propaganda War' (1984) argued that the Army supplied news directly to media outlets, which reported biased and incomplete information. 'War and the Media', Philip M. Taylor's book about the Gulf conflict, describes a 'controlled information environment'. Taylor believes that 'the pluralistic media from mostly democratic societies were handled in a monopolistic manner that gave the appearance of being open'.

Centre for Contemporary Cultural Studies: the Centre for Contemporary Cultural Studies was established in Birmingham university in 1964. Richard Hoggart, who produced the highly influential book 'The Uses of Literacy' in 1957, was one of its founders, while Stuart Hall (later a professor with the Open University), became its second Director in 1969. The Centre represented both a move away from the traditional academic preoccupation with 'high culture', and a significant departure from Marxist orthodoxy. The cultural, as opposed to the economic sphere was given more prominence. The Centre studied the media, mass consumption, sub-cultures and a host of other areas and issues. It also produced a number of well-known writers and academics who went on to spread the influence of media and cultural studies in other institutions (Brunsdon, Ellis, Hebdige, McRobbie, Morley and Willis, to name a few).

In the 1970s, the Centre began to introduce a more feminist perspective in its work, emerging from the labours of the Women's Study Group. A new synthesis emerged, based on 'the site of oppression most commonly foregrounded in women's experience – the family and its economic, political and ideological determinants and functions' (David Harris, in 'From Class Struggle to the Politics of Pleasure', 1992). The experience of black people also helped to displace the primacy of class analysis which had once animated the Centre. In the early-1980s, the CCCS produced work on black experience of the police, and also material on the structure of the education system. Theories of *hegemony,* taken from the work of Antonio Gramsci, were particularly influential in the later studies produced by the Centre. It has now been re-formed as a department of Cultural Studies under the direction of Jorge Larrain.

certification is a term sometimes used to describe the process of film classification, in which a film is given a particular certificate according to how suitable it is deemed to be for particular audiences. The British Board of Film Censors awards U for Universal, PG for Parental Guidance, and 12, 15 and 18 certificates to specify the minimum age which will allow entry to an individual performance. (See also *censorship.*)

channel: a route along which a signal or message may be sent. Interest in channels of communication appears in most of the early work in the field, including the Lasswell formula of 1948 (where a channel is also known as a 'medium' of communication). Other references occur in the *models* of Gerbner and DeFleur (1956 and 1970 respectively). A channel may distort the message which it carries, if it is disrupted by 'noise' or physical interference. Certain types of channel are suited to carrying particular message forms. In some cases, the strongest feature of a channel of communication may cause that strength to be over-played. The producers of television news, for example, aware of its powerful visual representation of the world, may be inclined to use reports which contain 'good pictures' in preference to stories which require more elaborate forms of explanation.

character generator: an electronic device that produces letters or symbols, displaying them directly onto a tape and thus a television screen; used for producing titles in video films.

chequebook journalism: although newspapers often commission articles and features, chequebook journalism is a different kind of phenomenon; it depends on papers (usually tabloids) offering large sums to individuals for stories of scandal and intrigue. Where tabloids pursue the same story, they attempt to outbid one another. The practice has become an established feature of journalism, seeming to cause little public disturbance unless money is paid to individuals connected with certain types of criminal activity.

chiaroscuro: from the Italian words for 'clear' and 'dark' comes chiaroscuro, the technique of arranging elements of light and shade to create aesthetic effects in film.

Individual shots and scenes may be composed using chiaroscuro techniques. The term was originally applied to painting and drawings.

Chomsky, Noam: an American writer, born in 1928, who has had a notable impact on the study of language. In the 1950s, Chomsky redirected linguistic enquiry, moving from the dominant tradition (which had concentrated on phonology and morphology) towards the study of sentence structure. Chomsky was interested in the '*deep structure*' of language, and argued that the prime concern of linguistic theory must be to explore the underlying knowledge or competence of the ideal speaker–hearer.

Chomsky noted that all infants seemed to learn the rudiments of language in a similar way, though the actual data available to the child was limited and of 'degenerate quality'. This observation, together with the theory that all languages contain similar structures, suggested that the human species is genetically predisposed to acquire language systems and that, in Chomsky's own words 'the general features of language reflect, not so much the course of one's experience, but rather the general character of one's capacity to acquire knowledge' ('Aspects of the Theory of Syntax', 1965).

Most theorists now accept the 'mentalist' position expounded by Chomsky. If mental structures are geared to the acquisition of certain kinds of knowledge, including language, this suggests that the human organism is 'programmed to speak'. It may also suggest that people are innately predisposed to create meaning in general. As part of his notion of 'innateness' Chomsky proposed a theory of 'generative' grammar. Generative grammar is the basic system of rules that allows the production of an infinite number of sentences. It exists as part of the competence of the idealised speaker–hearer. Generative grammar 'may be said to generate a set of structural descriptions', incorporating 'a deep structure, a surface structure' and 'a semantic interpretation (of the deep structure) and a phonetic interpretation (of the surface structure)' ('Language and Mind', 1972).

chroma key: (sometimes printed as 'chromakey') this is a special effect in television which uses a blue background to allow the combination of two images. (See also *blue screen, matte.*)

chronology: the sequential ordering of events. Originally, chronology was the science of working out past or future dates (as in a chronological table, a diagram which shows events in their order of occurrence). In film and television narratives, chronological order is used to show how one event causes another.

However, the issue is more complicated than this suggests. In the cinema, for example, an event which is displayed at the beginning of a film may turn out, in the light of later developments, to belong to the end of the chronological narrative. It may have appeared at the beginning in order to draw an audience into a fictional world, to show what fate awaits the characters, to allow the viewer to see what led up to the event, and so on.

If we go a little further into this issue, the whole concept of definite beginnings and endings may be called into question by the narrative structure of film. Events are 'read' in the light of other events, and therefore qualified by the more complete knowledge an audience gains as the story unfolds. It is for this reason that Edward Branigan, in 'Narrative Comprehension and Film' (1992), distinguishes between chronological time and narrative time. Other media forms also disrupt chronological order. Television news, as Alan Bell notes (see 'The Language of News Media', 1991), reports the narrative climax at the beginning of each item.

cineaste: a film enthusiast.

cinema: as an institution, the cinema is composed of the film industry, the texts it produces, and the audiences it attracts. The beginnings of cinema (the word comes from 'kinema', the Greek for movement) lie in various traditions of public entertainment. Theatre, the *diorama*, the popular work of illusionists, and photography all contributed to its form. The growth of industrial production allowed the development of *cinematography*, contributing to the cinema's position as an entertainment industry run on capitalist principles, with the text as a commodity. (See *cinematography*.)

cinéma vérité is a French term which refers to documentary technique.

Cinématheque Française: the world's largest museum and library of film. Based in Paris, it houses a collection of over 60,000 films.

Cinématographe: a film *camera*, printer and projector made in late-nineteenth century France by the Lumière brothers.

cinematographer: in film, the person responsible for camera and lighting. Other terms for cinematographer include 'director of photography' and (the gender-specific) 'lighting cameraman'.

cinematography, origins of: the technical practices of creating film for public consumption. Magic lanterns, used in the seventeenth century, established the principle of projection. By the nineteenth, movement was introduced through a number of optical instruments. These included Henry Fitton's Thaumatrope (1826), Joseph Plateau's Phenakistoscope (1833), W.G. Horner's Zoetrope (1834) and Emile Renauld's Praxinoscope (1877).

All these inventions used simple designs or images, mounted in revolving drums and other devices, in order to create the impression of movement. They all depended, as do modern films, on *persistence of vision.*

The first cartoon show was created in 1877 by Emile Reynaud. Meanwhile Eadweard Muybridge, an English photographer, began to make images of human and animal movement. In 1878, he set up a row of twenty-four cameras, each worked by a trip wire, and thus obtained pictures of the individual movements of a galloping horse as it ran past each camera. Muybridge's work, consisting of strips or reels of film, was projected using the *Zoopraxiscope.* The magazine Scientific American reported that the viewer saw 'apparently the living, moving animals. Nothing was wanting but the clatter of hooves upon the turf'.

Between 1885 and 1887 in New York, Louis Le Prince projected moving pictures of horse-drawn traffic passing over a bridge in Leeds (where Le Prince kept a house). In 1895, an American called Woodville Latham invented a projector for large screen projection, as did the Englishman Robert Paul. In the same year the Lumière brothers began their famous series of public film shows in the Salon Indien in Paris. In the following year, Edison and Dickson developed their Vitascope and exhibited their films in a music hall in New York. Between 1896 and 1900 films grew in length and variety. The scale of production became increasingly grandiose. D.W. Griffith produced

'Intolerance' in 1916, a film made up of four stories linked together by a common theme. It took two years to make, ran for 115 minutes of screen time, and in one scene required 1,600 extras.

circulation: the size of readership of a magazine, journal or newspaper. The circulation of British newspapers is sometimes inflated by large numbers of copies distributed free through various outlets.

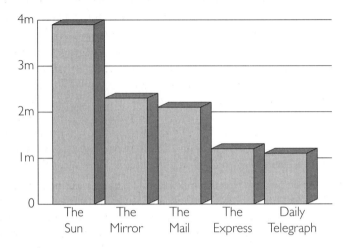

National daily newspaper circulation: papers selling above 1 million copies a day (adapted from an article in The Guardian, February 1997)

city edition: the final edition of a newspaper which serves a metropolitan area.

claptrap: a term investigated by Max Atkinson in his book 'Our Masters' Voices' (1984). A 'claptrap' is a rhetorical device used in public speech-making, designed to attract a burst of applause. It usually consists of a three-part list, combined with rising intonation. As the speaker gives emphasis to the final part of his/her words, an audience in sympathy with the message, will often deliver the required response.

Atkinson notes that (p. 6), ' ... large numbers of people ... react to public speaking in a more or less identical way.' This does not, however, confirm that an audience necessarily believes what it is told, or that certain *effects* will always be guaranteed.

Clarke orbit: another term for a 'geostationary orbit', in which a satellite placed at the correct distance from the planet, 35,786 kilometres above the Equator, and matching the speed of its rotation, will in effect hold a steady position above the Earth.

The Clarke orbit is named after the scientist and science-fiction author Arthur C. Clarke, who first proposed the idea of geostationary orbit in a paper published in October 1945. The first geosynchronous satellite was Early Bird, launched by the Intelsat agency in 1965. (See also *geosynchronous satellite*.)

classified advertising: small-scale advertising, usually confined to a few lines of text; also known as 'small ads'.

clip art: commercially prepared artwork which does not require copyright permission to use or reproduce; clip art is sold in books, but is increasingly available as part of the basic resource on a computer's hard-drive. Digital photo-banks are also a form of clip-art.

closure: closure in cinematic narrative is the resolution of the central conflict or problem. The 'causal chain' reaches its conclusion, in other words, the entire sequence of cause and effect has been played out. So a narrative which concerns the efforts of a police officer to catch a criminal, will eventually result in some outcome which not only marks the end of the story, but which also makes sense in terms of the entire narrative. As Edward Branigan says 'to narrate the end of a story one must do more than merely stop' ('Narrative Comprehension and Film', p. 115).

Criticism of film-makers' use of closure focuses on the practices of mainstream cinema. Susan Hayward, discussing mainstream cinema, feels that 'whatever form the closure takes, almost without exception it will offer ... a message that is central to dominant ideology: the law successfully apprehending criminals, good gunmen of the Wild West routing the baddies, and so on' ('Key Concepts in Cinema Studies', 1996). It is questionable if the dominant ideology in a de-regulated environment (where law and order is presented as 'ineffectual'), still promotes the values Hayward mentions. Many mainstream texts clearly offer quite different resolutions.

CNN: Cable News Network, a 24 hour cable news organisation started in June 1980 by entrepreneur Ted Turner. CNN began as a news programming service for the US cable companies, reaching less than two million homes in America. When Turner started the project, his intention was to serve the domestic market only, but he discovered that the channel had a wider audience. During a trip to Cuba in 1982, Turner learned that his host, President Castro, used CNN as a source of information. In India, he met leaders who complained that little of significance in Indian society ever reached the west, and that anything that was reported conformed to western *news-values*.

Some commentators, however, questioned Turner's conception of news. Richard Gilbert, for example (in a 'Listener' article of 16th October 1986) noted that 'what CNN means by news is very different from what the BBC and ITN mean. On CNN [it] means Hollywood gossip, sport, cookery hints, business ... and fitness breaks ...'

In 1987, however, CNN's 'World Report' began, providing uncensored news stories from across the globe, presented by journalists from various national broadcasting organisations. Turner, speaking in 1989, argued that the aim of 'World Report' was 'to bring the people of the world closer together' (see Flournoy's 'CNN World Report', 1991). Meanwhile, by 1991 CNN's 24-hour cable news was received in 58 million US households and, by satellite, in 140 countries.

Despite the generally positive response to the influence of CNN's international venture, Turner's approach to news has been criticised. Morley and Robbins ('Spaces of Identity', 1995), believe that (p. 16) 'CNN is having to recognise that the pursuit of further success will entail the production of different editions, in different languages, in different parts of the world'.

Code of Advertising Standards and Practice: a code drawn up in 1990 by the Independent Television Commission. The code covers the use of advertising and programme sponsorship. It applies to all independent terrestrial broadcasts, as well as to direct broadcast from satellite. The code prohibits the advertising of a range of products and services, including betting tips and the pools (though, strangely, adverts for the National Lottery are exempt). The code also prevents certain products, such as alcohol, being presented in a way which suggests that they increase attractiveness or ability.

codes: a code is a system which allows a particular culture to communicate through the use of *signs*. Although codes are usually described as 'systematic', in the sense that they are supposed to be organised collections of principles, not all display the same characteristics. In fact, there are such great differences between various types, that it is sometimes difficult to decide if certain examples really qualify as codes.

For instance, there are broad categories of code which describe quite different aspects of life; *linguistic* codes refer to the rules of combination in written and spoken language, while *aesthetic* codes concern artistic principles and matters of taste. Clearly, the two types are dissimilar. Do aesthetic codes, considering the highly subjective way they are worked out, really make up a coherent system? Even in the case of language, rules are not agreed in a formal sense; communication is possible because the established conventions of speech and writing are used in a flexible manner.

Codes are distinguished by the following criteria: they consist of a network of signs, forming a *paradigm* from which individual units of meaning may be chosen; the units selected are combined as a *syntagm* which conveys meaning within a certain cultural context; finally, the users of the code are in broad agreement about how the code is employed.

Various attempts have been made to identify the different types of code which exist. Pierre Giraud, in his book 'Semiology' (1975), distinguished between logical, aesthetic and social codes. Giraud produced smaller sub-headings using these three categories. His 'logical code' is split into 'language' (alphabetical codes, picture-writing, intonation and gesture), 'practical codes' (such as traffic control systems, or military signals like bugle-calls), 'knowledge codes' (such as algebra), and even 'codes used to predict the future' (like the Zodiac!). The 'aesthetic code' is composed of 'artistic conventions', while the 'social code' is made up of 'protocols' (clothes worn for various occasions), 'rituals' (ceremonies such as weddings), 'fashions' and 'games'.

There are problems with these divisions. Language, for instance, is only partly based on logic because the intuition of speakers is also a significant factor. The status of the Zodiac as a logical code is also questionable. Clearly, some codes can fall into more than one category. Fashion, for example, can be both aesthetic and social. Other writers have listed the various types of code, using terms like fixed codes, codes of conduct, binary, analogue, digital, logical, aesthetic, presentational and representational codes.

codes (formal/informal): one way of making sense of the various permutations of the term 'code', would be to ask to what degree individual codes depend on 'formal' rules or procedures. For instance, Morse code is only meaningful where those using it obey the system established by the code's founder; there is no room for improvisation. Morse code shows, therefore, a high degree of formality. Formal codes have clear rules, so that any deviation from their structure will lead to a breakdown in communication.

Other codes are much nearer the informal range of the spectrum. Some are so informal that their status as systems could be questioned, which would suggest that they are not really codes at all! It is worth noting that informal codes work in ways which are difficult to predict. They do not follow a prescribed pattern, depending instead on the context in which they appear.

An example may be found in the gestures and intonation which accompany speech. Gestures and intonation might be seen as supplementary codes, but they often provide essential clues to the ways in which an utterance is meant to be understood. An ironic tone of voice might undermine the 'official' meaning of an utterance, while a deliberate gesture is often used to reinforce an intended meaning.

codes (signifying): all codes are signifying codes; that is, they refer to ideas, objects, events and entities in culture and society. Signifying codes create meaning of one sort or another, whether through written signs, human behaviour, or artistic expression. A clear example of a signifying code is the English language. Successful communication depends on the ability of speakers and writers to recognise and produce various linguistic units. These units vary in size, from individual *morphemes* to complete sentences and/or utterances, but each will be used according to the language structure or *syntax* which prevails at any one time. In other words English, or any other language, is not just a random collection of written or spoken elements; it consists of conventional structures which are used by native speakers and writers to generate meaning.

Divisions may be made among signifying codes. First, we could describe those presentational codes which are observed during human interaction. These would include deliberate behaviour, gesture, posture, body language, intonation, and proximity. Next there are representational codes, the idea being that they 're-present' ideas at one remove. Representational codes may be divided into linguistic, logical and aesthetic forms. Linguistic representation takes place through speech, transcribed conversation,writing and so on; we used the example of language above. Logical representation includes systems like maths, binary and digital codes, and chemical symbols. Then there are aesthetic representational codes such as art, music, architecture, analogue codes and media texts. Both presentational and representational communication provide the means for the expression of social and cultural codes, including the rituals, protocols and ethical systems known to organised societies. The basic division between types of code could therefore be presentational, representational and social.

cognition: cognition is the action or faculty of knowing or understanding. Theories of learning and communication often study the process of cognition, in the belief that it holds the key to understanding many of the ways in which knowledge of the world is attained, retained and then used.

Research into understanding has included ideas about the existence of *schemas,* which are supposed to be cognitive frameworks or 'mental scaffolds.' Alternatively, schemas may be described as organised collections of information about objects or types of event.

A number of linguists, however, believe that supposedly 'internal' schemas are actually found in language. In 'Language, Interaction and Social Cognition', Fiedler and

Semin note (p. 79), that ' ... many psychological phenomena which are usually conceived as cognitive, motivational or emotional processes ... are permanently installed in language as an autonomous system above and beyond the individual.'

Another criticism of the cognitive tradition argues that 'information processing' suggests a passive model of human understanding. A turn has been made instead towards active models of cognition, in which the human mind does not simply process information, but concerns itself with 'explanation seeking' (Harré and Gillett, 'The Discursive Mind', 1994) and 'projective' thought (J.M. Moravcsik, 'Thought and Language', 1992).

Harré and Gillett argue that, rather than searching for evidence of actual processes, researchers imposed a framework of rules and logical structures on the study of human thought. However, cognition will continue to be an important field whenever studies are made of learning, thought and communication, especially where it is balanced with investigation of emotional responses.

columnist: a journalist who provides a regular column in a newspaper, either as a specialist in a certain field, or as a writer of general comment produced in a consistent style.

comics were originally a set or series of broadly humorous drawings which appeared in journals or newspapers. Comics grew from a long tradition of political cartoons, produced by artists like Hogarth (1697–1764) and Rowlandson (1757–1827). The 'Comic Magazine' of 1796, for example, carried a series of Hoggart prints in its pages. In the late nineteenth century, comic strips were produced in the American press, and spread rapidly to other newspapers. The US press magnate William Randolph Hurst, printed comic supplements for his newspapers.

The modern era began with the 'Famous Funnies' series of the 1930s, though comics eventually began to deal with more serious issues and appeared in their own right, as separate publications; thus the name 'comic' was transferred to a format, as well as being a description of the genre.

Modern comics have attracted academic interest, from George Orwell's 1939 study to Martin Barker's investigation of ideology and the effects tradition, 'Comics: Ideology, Power, and the Critics', which appeared in 1989. Barker began from the knowledge that (ix) 'comics have been lambasted with little hesitation, and with even less knowledge'. He was particularly successful in his re-appraisal of the ideological critiques offered by other writers. (For an introduction to comics and their history, see Price, 'Media Studies', 1993, pp. 389–400).

commentary: the descriptive narration (often given in voice-over) which presents or describes an event. In some cases, public commentary is largely (though never entirely) intended as a mere description. On a racecourse, whatever the drama of the event, the commentary must inform the enthusiast about the progress of the race and eventually the final outcome, since no individual will be able to see the entire event. The media is especially concerned with commentary, and it appears in a great many forms. The difference between the live, racetrack commentary and any televised sporting event, lies in the additional remarks which are made in the pauses between action or at the end of the event. Commentary becomes more than just what occurs, it becomes evaluative. Experts present arguments which they attempt to support through references to incidents, action replays, interviews with sportspeople, etc.

Television news is delivered as a commentary; the words of the *anchor* or presenter give context to, or 'frame' the items which are shown to the audience. Commentary here is always more than a mere description or lead-in, however, in the sense that it reveals how the media organisation imagines the relationship of the event to the value-systems held by an audience. Commentary, therefore, can be described as operating along a continuum from description to evaluation.

commercial: a film, television or radio advertisement that is presented during the 'commercial breaks' in other material.

commodity advertising is a form of advertising which promotes certain types of goods (cheese from a particular district, for example) rather than specific brands.

common sense is a category of practical knowledge, found in the ordinary exchanges of everyday life. Hostility to common sense is an established feature of much media and communication theory, and can be traced back to some of the Marxist perspectives which inform the subject.

Antonio Gramsci, for instance, calls common sense 'the 'folklore' of philosophy' and 'a conception which, even in the brain of one individual, is fragmentary, incoherent and inconsequential' ('Prison Notebooks', 1971, p. 419). The low status of common sense is, according to Gramsci 'in conformity with the social and cultural position of those masses whose philosophy it is'. The reason for this hostility can be found in Gramsci's attachment to a different outlook; 'at those times in history when a homogeneous social group is brought into being, there comes into being also, in opposition to common sense, a ... coherent and systematic philosophy'. This philosophy was, according to Gramsci, Marxism.

An equally negative appraisal of the concept is given by John Hartley in a contribution to 'Key Concepts in Communication', 1994. He argues that the media in particular 'have colonised this concept, and use it to 'prove' that the unequal distribution of wealth is ... actually only explicable as common sense' (p. 49). If it is true that the media behave in such a crude way, no example is given. The nature of common sense and its role in communication research may be due for reappraisal, as theorists look more closely at the ways in which people explain their reading of media texts.

communication: the exchange of meaning between human agents; Price, in 'Communication Studies', describes it as 'an activity in which *symbolic content* is ... exchanged between human agents, who interact within a shared situational and/or discursive context'. However, some forms of communication do not seem to depend on symbols (written language, for example) but instead appear to make a direct impact on the individuals or groups who receive 'messages'. For example, music, intonation and gesture all seem to act in a way which by-passes the symbolic route. 'Mass communication', on the other hand, does not share all the characteristics of interpersonal communication, since it is not primarily intended to be an exchange at all. There is no channel of two-way communication between media and public, though the media use forms of interpersonal address in many of their products, and the public have some limited *access* to public service media 'after the event' (once programmes have been broadcast).

communication (categories of): the five basic divisions between types of communication are:

- Intrapersonal communication, supposedly that which occurs within and therefore with the self. Most writers believe, however, that communication can be said to happen only when at least two individuals interact. The intrapersonal includes perception, cognitive and reflective thought processes, emotional responses, attitudes, values and beliefs, subjectivity and self-concept, and the creation and interpretation of meaning.
- Interpersonal communication, is that which occurs when two people are engaged in some form of communicative exchange. Interpersonal communication includes: mutual recognition, reciprocal exchange using available codes, the creation and interpretation of meaning, awareness of physical and social context, the assumption of personal and social roles, and some change of state, whether intellectual, emotional or physical.
- Group communication requires a collection of individuals who share some common attributes, goals or interests. The individuals concerned will interact within the context of the group and will share or at least display common values or norms of behaviour.
  All group communication must be include the following elements: a common perception of the group's identity, the ability to tell the difference between the group and its allies or rivals, a knowledge of aims and objectives within the group, participation in interpersonal exchange using available codes and channels of communication, and the assumption of formal and informal roles.
- Mass communication includes all the institutional practices of the mass media. Mass communication includes: high levels of industrial activity, formal centralised organisation, institutionalised values and practices, the mediation of authority, large scale of operation, a 'standardised' product directed to a mass audience, and the possibility of simultaneous reception of messages by audiences.
- Extrapersonal communication is communication between machines. It does not, strictly speaking, include communication between individual humans and machines, but between machines which are supposed to require little human intervention.
  The main feature of the extrapersonal is the processing of some form of potentially meaningful signal, between machines requiring human input but little supervision during the duration of the process itself.

communication (networks of): see *networks of communication*

community radio: community radio is based on the idea of encouraging local organisations to produce programmes for non-commercial purposes. The theory of community radio depends on local communities maintaining some control over the structure and output of individual radio stations, an entirely different concept to local commercial radio, which must maintain shareholders' profits.

commutation test: commutation is a form of substitution, and is used in media studies to demonstrate a point about the construction and meaning of media texts. If, for example, an advertisement shows the consumption of an expensive commodity in luxurious surroundings, how would the message alter if the product is removed and a cheaper brand substituted? Alternatively, could a new message be produced if the surroundings are entirely changed, or if the characters shown in the display are removed and other social types placed in the frame?

competence: a native speaker's underlying knowledge of his/her *language*, as opposed to the actual use of that language in real situations, which is called 'performance'. *Chomsky* is responsible for this distinction, which uses the notion of an 'ideal speaker/hearer', to represent the collective, intuitive understanding of language. He used an 'ideal' speaker as the representative example because he wanted to consider the rules and structures of language, eliminating from consideration real speech, since that was in his opinion always 'flawed' and therefore an insecure foundation for enquiry.

Chomsky's distinction between competence and performance is similar in some respects to *Saussure's* use of 'langue' (structure) and 'parole' (speech). Criticisms of Chomsky and Saussure appear in Bourdieu (see 'Language and Symbolic Power', 1991), who believes that both approaches create an illusion of a common language, ignoring past struggles and continued resistance to the construction of a dominant and 'legitimate' language.

composite: the term composite is used in a variety of ways. A composite shot is one which presents two scenes simultaneously. In cinema, a composite print is one which contains both sound and image. In video, a composite signal is a complete signal composed of picture, and colour synchronisation information.

compositor: another term for a typesetter.

computer aided design (or CAD): computer programmes created to help the production of various types of professional drawing, including architectural and engineering drawing.

computers: machines which are used to maintain data-bases, process information, produce graphics and allow desk-top publishing. Computer technology was used to decode German military information during the Second World War, but commercial use began to grow in the 1960s.

connotation is Barthes' second order of signification; what is suggested by or associated with an image, word, sound, phrase, and so on. A level of meaning that goes beyond the literal interpretation of *denotation*.

consent: voluntary agreement of a people to be ruled. There are various positions on the question of consent. Some thinkers, like *Chomsky*, believe that consent is manufactured by the state and its attendant media forms. Gramsci believed the process of domination was based on two principles ('Selections from Prison Notebooks', p. 12): '1. The 'spontaneous' consent given by the great masses of the population to the general direction imposed on social life ... caused by the prestige ... which the dominant group enjoys because of its position and function in the world of production. 2. The apparatus of state coercive power which 'legally' enforces discipline on those groups who do not 'consent' either actively or passively'. In other words, the oppressive apparatus comes into play when spontaneous consent has not appeared. Other writers, like

Goran Therborn, present a model in which modern states govern through a process called *subjection and qualification*. This means that individuals are given roles which ensure that the major relationships of power in the social order are not disrupted. Subjection is the need to repress or control, while qualification arises from the need to train capable, autonomous individuals. Therefore, both consent and refusal are built into the system itself. John A. Hall ('Coercion and Consent', 1994, x) believes that 'societies based on consent can generate great energies, including energies that allow them to coerce with mighty effectiveness'.

conspiracy theory is the idea that powerful forces in society, sometimes including elements of the media, exercise domination through secret agreements and behind-the-scenes manoeuvres. Most commentators regard this idea as an over-simplification of the way in which *power* operates. Despite the level of disapproval the theory attracts, it will continue to thrive wherever authoritarian modes of conduct persist and genuine examples of manipulation are discovered. The success of programmes like 'The X-files' can be explained partly as a reflection of American interest in state conspiracy, as well as evidence of the postmodern fashion for the irrational.

constituency: a body of customers, subscribers, or those who follow a particular belief or viewpoint; often used of newspaper readerships because papers have (at least at election times) a political stance with which their constituency is meant to identify. Constituency is also used to describe an electoral area which returns a member of Parliament.

construct: a construct is a cultural artefact which has been deliberately put together for a purpose; often applied to a media text.

construction/social construction: the theory that human ways of talking form social relations and thus social reality. Some social constructionists reject the idea that there are discoverable realities beyond what individual communities are able to describe (see John Shotter's 'Conversational Realities', 1993), while others remain realists, convinced that there is a real world besides 'social reality'.

consumer profile: a description of the habits of consumption, lifestyle, class, sex, etc. of a group which buys a particular product or service.

contact: an individual who acts as a source of information for a journalist.

contact sheet: a sheet of photographic paper on which is printed a whole roll of film, reproduced the same size as the negatives. Contact sheets are used so that photographers can gain an impression of the work, before selecting images that they wish to enlarge. (See p. 55.)

contacts book: a book or booklet used by a journalist to record contacts and sources.

content analysis: a research method which first identifies distinct types of content (in artefacts, speech events, media texts and so on), and then counts the frequency of their occurrence. In effect, a quantitative tally of content is produced. Content analysis is usually presented as an objective method, in the sense that it does not concentrate on one particular element, but simply records what it finds for the purposes of later judgment and comparison. However, as Leiss and his co-authors point out ('Social Communication in Advertising', 1990) 'although content

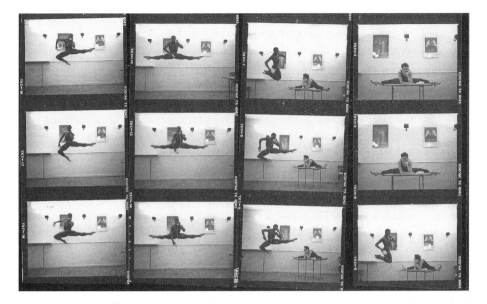

Contact sheet: Tony Nandi

analysis is considered an empirical approach, its starting point must always be theoretical'. This means that the beliefs which motivate researchers (the existence of bias in representation, for example) will colour their perception of content. Similarly, the act of making *categories*, or of making use of pre-existing ones, will help to influence what is found. Peter Langley ('Managing Sociology Coursework', 1993) identifies the tendency for values to influence results (p. 25): 'A research project concerning images of women in the media may well use content analysis as a method. A content analysis frame can be drawn which only includes counting instances where women are portrayed in stereotypical ways. A significant degree of stereotyping will inevitably be found'. Leiss et al. (p. 222) warn that 'in some situations, we simply cannot choose one from a number of categories'. The specification of ethnicity (Leiss' example) might require a number of categories, with each labelled either 'absent' or 'present', in order to avoid the danger that some ethnic groups will be ignored (which would happen in a less sensitive form of content analysis). Another method which helps to produce accuracy, is the use of 'ordinal' methods, where the relative strength of each item counted, is also estimated.

context: the specific conditions which provide structure for any act, statement, or event. The idea of 'context' is found in studies of literature, and is also used in the social sciences. In literature, context refers to those parts of a text which precede and/or follow an individual passage. The sections of text which 'surround' the passage being studied, help to establish its meaning. Of course, reference to context is required exactly because smaller units are often extracted from texts, for the purposes of detailed study.

In the social sciences, the idea of context becomes a little more involved. Context can be divided into a number of categories, each a factor in shaping an event. There are so many contextual factors at work, that it is difficult to say which are the most important in any one situation. To begin with, a simple example can be used – a speech event involving two people. According to the linguist Hymes, a speech event will be governed by the following aspects of context:

- structure, which is the form of the event (reunion, party, wedding, etc.)
- setting, the fact that all events occur in time and space
- participants, the addressor and the addressee
- purpose, what brings the participants together (to discuss something, to celebrate an event, and so on)
- key, the spirit in which the speech event is conducted
- topic, the subject matter
- channels, the choice of medium for transmitting messages
- message form, the speakers' attempt to present their messages in a way which will have a significant impact on the other people involved.

context (levels): the following is proposed specifically for this dictionary:

1 'functional context', meaning the purpose of an event and its subject matter, expressed through those human faculties which allow events to take place (the power of speech, organisation, gesture and intonation, etc).

2 'situational context', the immediate physical and temporal circumstances within which any event is played out. This first level of context, refers to the event's location in space and time.

3 'discursive context', which is the general range of ideas and opinions which the participants are able to draw upon when they interact. This will depend partly on the topic of conversation, and will often include ideological forms of discourse.

4 'social context' is the wider condition of the society itself, those forces and influences (or structures) which form the background to situated speech. These include inherited forms of language, social customs, and the state of political and economic development.

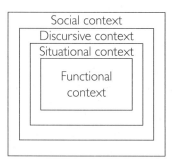

Context

It is important to realise that, in all studies of context, situation, functions, language, participants, and topic all play an important role; situation and discourse, for example, help to define one another. The interaction of participants creates the event itself, and is an essential contributor to the form it takes. The 'cultural range' of language presents a number of choices to the communicator. These choices are circumscribed first by what is grammatically meaningful and what is not, and then by the range of appropriate meanings which may be generated in the context of interaction.

contextual intention: the idea that individuals produce meaning appropriate to the context in which they find themselves, and that their intention to communicate cannot be separated from that context. Price, in 'Communication Studies' (1996), argues that (p. 99) 'if we accept a view of expression as social, then 'what we meant to say' (or our intention), will be influenced by our knowledge and expectation of various situations. 'What we meant to say' will become, in most circumstances, what it is possible to say'.

continuity editing: continuity is the state of being continuous, while editing is the technical procedure of arranging and reshaping content. In mainstream film, the relation of a continuous *narrative* is an important consideration for a director. The script supervisor oversees this aspect of production, making sure that individual details in each scene (costume, angle of shots, etc.) remain consistent.

Continuity editing, then, is an established practice in mainstream cinema, designed to produce a smooth transition from shot to shot and from scene to scene. Over the years, certain rules of editing evolved, including the following:

- an individual section of a film will require the use of an *establishing* shot
- conversations are represented by alternating between shot and reverse shot
- cross-cutting between separate events will be used
- the '*180 degree*' rule will be obeyed
- *dissolves* and mixes will signify changes of screen time.

contrapuntal sound: a sequence of sounds (especially musical sounds) which run counter to or against the images they accompany. Contrapuntal sound is able to provide an ironic commentary within a narrative. The idea is that an audience will 'read' an image in the light of what they hear. So, for instance, a scene which shows a tranquil landscape could be qualified by a musical interlude which suggests the onset of more disturbing events. Monaco, in 'How to Read a Film', comments on earlier attitudes to the use of sound, when it was employed to support the emotional inflection of the narrative (p. 182); 'the Hollywood sound style was strongly parallel'. He goes on to illustrate this statement, noting that 'the programmatic music of thirties movies, nudged, underlined, emphasised, characterised, and qualified even the simplest scenes, so that the dullest images as well as the most striking were thoroughly pervaded by the emotions designed by the composers of the nearly continuous music track'. More contemporary film-makers, and 'modernist forms' in general 'problematise the transparency of discourse' (Claudia Gorbman, in 'Unheard Melodies', 1987, p. 3).

convention: conduct or practice governed by agreement, tradition, rules or any combination of these elements. Where convention relates to behaviour, participants will recognise established modes of public conduct. Whether or not they follow these social codes precisely (bearing in mind that such codes are themselves inexact), is less important than the fact that they are seen as appropriate. Convention is re-established (and gradually re-invented) whenever interactions take place within any recognised public context.

Where convention relates to forms of expression like writing, the creative impulse must work within a rule-governed system (language). In 'Communication', (p. 6), McQuail argues that 'communication necessitates the conscious manipulation of physical forces and objects according to agreed rules and conventions.'

This still allows great varieties of individual choice to be made within broad conventions. All communicative forms, including speech, gesture, writing, graphic design, music, film, broadcast talk and so on, have codes and conventions which have become established through use.

Convention is closely related to role. The production of meaning always takes place within a specific *context*, a situation which may actually help individuals to produce coherent messages, rather than limit their freedom to act.

convergence: the theory that media 'platforms' are beginning to merge into a single, computer-based form. Watson and Hill (1997) cite the work of Everette E. Dennis, which argues that 'the nearly universal integration of systems that retrieve, process and store text, data, sound and image' is the most important feature of contemporary media development.

conversational analysis is the academic study of ordinary speech exchanges. Various criteria are used to describe the structures of everyday conversation. According to William Labov (1970), the range of possible speech acts within an exchange are: question and answer, challenge and response, and invitation and acceptance. Susan Hunston (see Coulthard's 1992 'Advances in Spoken Discourse Analysis') proposes no less than thirty-two identifiable acts of everyday speech.

In 'Everyday Conversation' (1991), Robert E. Nofsinger recognises that certain types of conversation (exchanges in a courtroom, for example) have formal goals, so that the participants must understand what 'moves' (social or communicative actions) are needed to reach that goal. The criteria which shape each individual response are: what has been done so far, what needs to be done, what each utterance seems designed to do, and what alternative actions might have been performed at each point in the conversation. The existence of shared knowledge of the world, and not just shared rules of language use, is essential to co-operative speech.

What Nofsinger calls (p. 1) the 'immense power of everyday talk,' includes the following functions: ' ... to contact and influence other people: to enlist their help, to offer them companionship, to protect ourselves from their demands, to establish important relationships with them, and to present ourselves as having the qualities they (and we) admire.'

Research into conversation has discovered recurring patterns of interaction, structures which occur despite the change of personnel or situation. Heritage, writing in 1984, found that: ' ... organised patterns of stable, structural features ... stand independently of the psychological or other characteristics of particular speakers.'

In all studies of conversation, attempts to apply theories of conventional, or 'rule-defined' meaning, often fail to explain the material studied. In Nofsinger's view, this is because researchers (p. 33): ' ... underestimate the extent of meaning that goes beyond what has been said in so many words (or is even contradictory to it).' Nofsinger argues that participants in a conversation often supply meanings which are only implicit in what speakers say.

Conversational analysis carried out by Zimmerman and West (1975) seemed to suggest that men and women use different interactive styles; men were more likely to interrupt and overlap the speech of women. A study of gender and conversation appears in Jennifer Coates' 1993 'Women, Men and Language'.

copy: copy is the written material (articles and particularly editorials) to be edited and published in newspapers; it can also refer to any written work which is to be submitted for publication. 'Hard copy' is material which is typed or word-processed onto paper.

copy desk: in a newspaper office, the section of the organisation which deals with the editing of copy; headlines are added and the general presentation of the material is handled.

copy editor: an editor responsible for ensuring that copy is properly written and tailored to the space to which it has been assigned.

copywriter: a writer who composes advertising copy, intended as information and/or as persuasion.

corporate speech: a term imported from the USA referring to the public discourses which corporate business groups use to intervene in the public sphere. As Watson and Hill point out ('A Dictionary of Communication and Media Studies'), 'corporate speech in the USA is classified as having the same right as the speech of individuals ... thus, a tobacco company cannot be restrained from propagandising, through public advertisement, its products'. An important field of research, as yet little attempted, is the analysis of the features of corporate speech.

correspondent: a journalist working in either a specialist field (such as an 'environment correspondent') or in a particular physical/conceptual location (eg. 'Washington correspondent').

counter-culture: the general term for those groups which express their opposition to mainstream values and lifestyles through cultural forms and practices. Oppositional culture can assume many forms, depending on which aspects of the dominant system are disliked. In a capitalist society, rejection of consumerism and the 'acquisitive society', together with distrust of the political system, has become apparent among travellers, roads protesters and urban squatters' movements. In many cases, counter-cultures are created when economic policies exclude individuals from the political system.

crab: the sideways movement of a film or video camera across a scene. Cameras are sometimes mounted on a 'crab dolly', a four-wheeled device, or on tracks which are laid down for a trolley to run along.

crane: a large camera platform which holds both camera and camera operator. The term 'crane' also refers to the elevation and depression of the camera boom.

crash: the failure of a computer system.

credit: the use of someone's name or 'byline' on a newspaper story or a photograph.

critical pluralism: a theory of society and culture which recognises the existence of a variety of power structures in society, but unlike traditional pluralism is prepared to acknowledge that some interest groups have greater access to social power than others. References to critical pluralism appear in the work of writers who either wish to move away from leftist forms of analysis (but are reluctant to shed all vestiges of radicalism), or who are aware of the shortcomings of established pluralist thought. The theory represents an uneasy compromise which, increasingly, may be offered to students as a 'watered-down' alternative to the left-wing tradition which gave birth to media and cultural analysis.

cropping: removing unwanted areas of a photograph in order to achieve a more aesthetic or balanced composition; sometimes used to censor or distort the appearance of material regarded as sensitive.

Cropping

cross-cutting: in film, a technique for cutting back and forth between shots, which allows an audience to follow two or more separate spheres of action, in the knowledge that the separate events shown in each scene are taking place at the same time. Cross-cutting is used a great deal in action movies, where the activities of (for instance) a group of bank-robbers, are inter-cut with shots of the police officers planning their capture.

crossing the line: see *one hundred and eighty degree rule*. A rule established in mainstream film-making which prevents a camera moving across a line of 180 degrees; to do so gives the impression that the actors have changed position, whereas in fact the camera has made an 'unjustified' move from one place to another. (See p. 61 for figure.)

CRT: see *cathode ray tube*

crystal set: an early type of radio receiver, which used a crystal detector, a tuning coil, and earphones.

cultural competence is the idea that access to culture in a capitalist society is determined by the 'competence' of the individual; this competence is constructed along class lines, so that individuals will use those cultural products with which they feel most familiar. The theory was advanced by the French sociologist Pierre Bourdieu (b.1930) who also studied the school system as an agency of 'cultural reproduction'.

Crossing the line: Shot b) can follow a). Shot c) cannot follow a).

culture is the process through which public discourses and material practices are conducted, and the end product of that process; a specific, (e.g. national) culture is found in those beliefs, values, and ideas which make up the 'shared bases of social action' ('Collins Concise English Dictionary').

The word comes from the Latin 'cultura', which had a range of meanings including 'inhabit, cultivate, protect, honour with worship' (Williams, 'Keywords', 1983, p. 87). These Latin meanings evolved separately so that, for example, 'inhabit' became 'colony' and 'honour with worship' developed into 'cult'. In fifteenth century England, culture meant domestic and agricultural management, as in 'cultivation'. Some dictionaries continue to print 'cultivate' or even 'cultivated land' before offering other definitions (see the 'New Shorter Oxford', 1993).

The notion of husbandry and management (what Williams called 'the tending of something, basically crops or animals') came to include the cultivation or improvement of human minds. This, in turn, led to a more general and abstract use, in which culture referred to the sum total of the ideas, values and practices common to a particular *society* or social group.

Culture can be the artistic and social pursuits of a society/social group, and the 'enlightenment or refinement resulting from these pursuits' ('Collins Concise English Dictionary', 1992). Williams (p. 88) describes this difference in meaning as 'an abstract process or the product of such a process'. In eighteenth century German usage, culture (or 'kultur') referred to a nationalist and imperial strain of civilisation, suggesting the promotion or export of one form of social organisation.

Elitist definitions of culture as the pinnacle of artistic and literary expression were challenged in the late 1950s, by writers like Raymond Williams and Richard Hoggart. They began to reformulate culture as a term denoting the whole range of activities which take place within a society. Once the concept had been used to describe general social processes, instead of the activities of a minority of critics, a more democratic perspective was the outcome.

culture of deference: a term applied to the tendency of editors, journalists, and other media professionals, to treat established authority with respectful subservience, so that the opinions of the powerful remain unchallenged. It was used in an article published in 1991 in the '*Index on Censorship*', (written by Richard Norton-Taylor).

cut and paste: in computing, an electronic process that allows text to be highlighted, removed, and reapplied in another position. The term comes from the physical practice of cutting out and pasting text, a method used before electronic processes were available.

cutaway: in film and television, a brief shot which is inserted in a scene to show an important detail, or action which takes place somewhere else besides the main location. In many cases, a cutaway is used to disguise breaks in the main 'take' or master shot.

cutting room: the facility used for editing film. Until quite recently, rejected material would end up quite literally 'on the cutting room floor'.

cybernetics: 'cyber' is taken from the word 'cybernetics', first used by Norbert Wiener in the 1940s. Cybernetics meant the science of control and communications in animals and machines. Since its first use, the prefix 'cyber' has come to indicate computers and 'machine intelligence'.

cyberspace: is a term originally coined by the American author William Gibson in 'Neuromancers' (1984), to refer to the electronic 'space' created by all the connected databases, telecommunication links and computer networks. 'The Cyberspace Lexicon' (p. 56) speculates that cyberspace might 'constitute a new space for human communication and action'. Cyberspace also includes the concept of 'virtual reality', where the user puts on a headset and data-glove in order to enter a computer-generated world. This world may be a room, a landscape, or some other location, and contains three-dimensional objects which can be manipulated by the user's electronic hand. Fictional treatments of the virtual reality industry, including books and film, often experiment with the idea of human interaction within this artificially created environment. Cyberspace is, in the last analysis, both a literal electronic channel of communication, and a metaphor for a new dimension of human experience.

D

DAGMAR: the acronym for 'Defining Advertising Goals for Measured Advertising Results', a book written by Russell Colley in 1961. Colley decided that all commercial communications must take the prospective buyer through four stages: awareness of the product, understanding of what the product is and what its properties are, conviction that he/she must buy the product, and finally the decision to act. The advantage of the model is that it takes account of the potential customer's responses. Its weakness lies in the fact that it does not acknowledge that a great deal of advertising is devoted to reinforcing brand awareness, rather than persuading a consumer to buy new brands.

Daguerre, Louis (1789–1851) was a celebrated early nineteenth-century photographer. He worked with another French pioneer, Joseph Nicephore Niepce (1765–1833) to produce photographic images renowned for their clarity and fine detail. The *daguerreotype*, as it was known, consisted of an image fixed on a metal plate, the surface of which was coated with silver oxide. The drawback of the daguerreotype process was the fact that no prints could be made from the image, and it is for this reason that the process was essentially a 'dead end' in the technical development of photography. William Henry Fox Talbot's *calotype*, by comparison, was a negative–positive process which could reproduce prints. Daguerre's other contribution to the history of public communication, was his elaborate development of the *diorama*, a form of popular entertainment which flourished in the early nineteenth century.

daguerreotype: a photographic process pioneered by Louis *Daguerre* and first revealed to the public in Paris in 1839. A modified *camera obscura* was used to capture an image, which was focused on a ground-glass surface. A photographic plate, made from a sheet of copper coated with silver, was inserted. Exposure time in the latter part of 1839 was approximately six minutes. The exposed plate was then placed in a box where mercury was heated to produce fumes; exposed areas of the plate absorbed mercury atoms and produced an image, which was fixed with hyposulphate. The process was capable of creating finely detailed pictures.

dailies: in journalism, the term refers to a *newspaper* or *bulletin* that appears on weekdays (sometimes including a Saturday). In America, when film-makers refer to 'dailies' they mean the prints of the previous day's shooting, which are studied for quality, continuity, etc. (also called *rushes*).

daily rate: the amount a newspaper charges for advertising space per day.

darkroom: a light-proof room equipped for processing photographic materials.

data is the term used to refer to facts, figures, symbols, observations, measurements, or information in general, used to describe things, people, situations, or events. Data of various kinds may be held on a *database* until they are ready to be analysed and used. 'Raw' data means information which has not yet been used or processed.

A distinction is sometimes made between data and *information*, where information is described as timely or valuable knowledge acquired through experience or study. In media and communication research, different types of data may be collected.

Primary data are original items (interviews, for example) collected for a research project, while secondary data are materials which have already been compiled and which can be found in a variety of public sources (books, *CD-rom*, reports, etc.)

data processing means the application of a computer program to a store of information so that a particular aim may be achieved (e.g. classifying, sorting and storing data). For instance, if a database, such as a list of names and addresses, needs to be sorted into alphabetical order, a program can be used to achieve this outcome.

data protection is the framework of legal measures designed to control access to data stored in computers. The fear that personal information may be abused, has led to legislation in a number of countries, including Denmark, Sweden, Norway, France and West Germany. In Britain in 1978, the Lindop Committee produced a report which argued that individuals should be able to exercise control over personal information held on computers, within the context of the 'efficient conduct of industry, commerce and administration'. The *Data Protection Act* was drafted in 1984 and came into force in 1987. In Canada and the USA data protection only applies to the public sector and compliance with it is not compulsory. Besides the use of legal means, private information can be guarded using *cryptography*; information is 'scrambled' before it is saved on a computer's memory. The issue of data protection has sometimes caused conflict between individuals and the state.

Data Protection Act, 1984: this British act allows individuals to check if any public or private body holds information on them, and to see any personal data which may have been gathered. Any complaints may be directed to the Data Protection Registrar (a watchdog set up under the Act). In certain circumstances, where the individual has suffered as the result of inaccurate or damaging information, or because of unauthorised disclosure of data, compensation claims can be made through the courts. There are seven exemptions to parts II and III of the Act: personal data held for domestic or recreational purposes; information which the law requires to be made public; personal data which may be retained in the interests of national security; data used for payroll, pensions and accounts; unincorporated members' clubs; and mailing lists.

database is any organised store of information, especially where that information is kept on an electronic file which can be '*accessed*' by computer. Software programs are used to arrange and retrieve the stored information.

Datanews: the digital news service offered by UPI (United Press International).

day for night: a film-making process which uses filters to make daytime scenes appear as though they have been shot at night.

daybook: a collection of news stories which may be useful in the creation of features or news assignments.

daytime television: the period of television programming from early morning to approximately 5 pm.

DBS: see *direct broadcast satellite*

deadline: the latest practical time at which news material can be received for use.

deaf aid: a slang term used in the TV industry for the inconspicuous ear microphone worn by presenters; it enables them to hear cues from a director.

decibel: this is the standard measure of relative sound intensity or power, and is one tenth of a bel.

decisive moment: this is the brief instant in time when all the elements of a scene come together to provide the best possible opportunity for a photographer. The 'decisive moment' has been called 'an interplay between form and content caught at its revealing climax' (see Peter Turner, 'History of Photography', p. 152). It is a term coined by French photographer Henri Cartier-Bresson (b. 1908) which describes his approach to making images, though he said that few of his own pictures were true examples. At the start of his career in 1930, Cartier-Bresson was influenced by the surrealist movement. Although he found *photography* exciting, it was not until he began to use the unobtrusive Leica camera that he gave full expression to his talents. His subject-matter stands within the 'human interest' tradition, but is regarded as one of the high points of artistic achievement in twentieth-century photography. Cartier-Bresson was also one of the founders of the *Magnum* photographic agency, which was registered with the County of New York on May 22nd 1947.

decoding: the process of interpreting communication which has been 'encoded' in some form, such as the symbolic *code* known as *language*. Stuart Hall (following the work of Frank Parkin) proposed that texts are 'de-coded' (or re-interpreted) by audiences in a variety of ways which do not necessarily suit the powerful institutions which create public messages.

Hall (1980) believed that the ideological content of texts can be accepted, rejected or modified by its audience. He described these three possibilities as 'positions', and named them preferred, *negotiated* and oppositional. A preferred reading would fall into line with the type of interpretation favoured by the text itself, the idea being that the text would contain a bias towards one viewpoint. The preferred reading, according to a later statement by Hall (1987), 'is the point at which power intersects with the discourse'. A negotiated reading would accept some, but not all, of the text's values. An oppositional reading would reject the text's whole approach, favouring instead an interpretation which opposes the 'preferred reading'.

The *active audience* thesis, however, depends in the first place on the idea of resistance to ideologically inflected messages; or, in Justin Lewis' words (p. 265) 'the assumption that there is already a preferred meaning ... which we can then negotiate with, agree with, or oppose'. Returning to the idea of the preferred reading, Hall (1987), described it as 'an attempt' to get an audience to accept a particular set of ideas, which would make it a feature of the encoding process, and not really part of audience response at all. In addition, it seems that very few readings of a text are either completely 'preferred' or entirely 'oppositional'. Isolated oppositional readings, where they do occur, do not necessarily qualify as 'acts'.

decoding (research): as research into audience developed, the model proposed by Hall began to be modified. The division of responses into three broad types seemed a little inflexible. Eventually, particularly through the work of David Morley, new elements were introduced. Morley decided that the crucial factor in audience response lay with (1980, p. 18) 'the range of discourses at the disposal of the audience'. Such work led to the development of the concept of 'interpretative communities', a phrase used by Stanley Fish to describe those groups which shared social ties and thus cultural perspectives.

Jane Roscoe and her co-authors (see 'The Television Audience', European Journal of Communication, 1995) set out to test the concepts of active and critical audiences, basing their research on a variety of group responses to a television programme on the Birmingham Six. They discovered that the preferred reading of the programme was fairly liberal but ultimately inadequate, presenting the men's imprisonment as a 'miscarriage of justice', and leaving unchallenged the 'legitimacy' of British policy in Northern Ireland.

Roscoe argues that *agenda setting* remains strong, and that the Birmingham Six programme was (p. 105) 'transmitted during a time when ... miscarriages of justice were being debated in the public sphere'. Therefore, most viewers interpreted the programme within the agenda current at the time. It appeared that the groups selected for research did not 'go beyond the parameters set by the text'. Very few adopted the oppositional perspective, which is so often regarded as the hallmark of the 'critical' viewer. Roscoe's work points to the need to study audience response within the context of the agendas current at the time of reception.

deconstruction is an attack on the European tradition of thought and reason. It first appeared in 1966 in a lecture given by Jacques *Derrida*, an influential *post-structuralist* writer. Derrida believes Western philosophy to be full of logical contradictions. *Structuralism*, for example, seems to Derrida an attempt to establish a core of meaning (or 'centre'). This provides stability and clarity, but ignores the 'play' of meaning, allowing one interpretation a privileged position above all other possible readings. Furthermore, Derrida considers that no author has absolute control over language and so cannot be sure that the intended meaning will be accepted or even recognised by readers.

Instead of arguing about questions of principle, deconstruction aims to produce a free and active interpretation of the literary and philosophical text, using what Derrida once called 'blind tactics'. Deconstruction is essentially a refusal to play by established rules. Supporters of deconstruction believe that it allows a fresh and creative approach to language and meaning, despite the fact that it is still forced to use the old systems of thought and writing it seeks to expose. Its opponents argue that deconstruction concentrates on trying to prove what cannot be known or understood, leading to inaction and disengagement in a world where language has real effects on human lives.

deep focus: a technique in cinematography which keeps all the elements of a scene in focus, from the near foreground to objects in the extreme distance.

deep structure: is the underlying framework of sentence organisation (the 'surface' structure of a sentence or phrase is known as *syntax*). Deep structure allows a reader to identify differences in meaning, in those sentences which have identical syntax. It also ensures that sentences which have different surface forms, but the same underlying meaning, will be recognised.

As an example of the former consider the sentences 'The woman saw the boy' and 'the man saw the dog'. An example of the latter type might be 'It is dangerous to drive at high speeds' and 'Driving at high speeds is dangerous', in which both sentences express the same meaning. Deep structure is discovered through the process of *transformation*. The linguist Noam *Chomsky*, who is most closely associated with the concept of deep structure, argued that the relationship between deep and surface structures provides the foundation of human *language*.

degradation: the gradual loss of image or sound quality when tapes are copied from copies; each 'generation' takes the product one step further away from the quality of the original.

demo: a 'demonstration' tape or CD, used to promote an individual or a group of musicians, etc. Demo tapes are used as a kind of electronic audition.

democratic-participant: a theory which rejects the highly centralised, market-led model of media practice which exists in most liberal democracies. It states that media should serve the interests of the people, offering opportunities for participation and control based on libertarian principles. In the democratic-participant model, the needs of a variety of social groups, rather than the demands of media *bureaucracies*, dictate policy and shape content. The practical evidence of democratic-participant theory is found in a variety of small-scale publications and in some community organisations, but it is not an idea which has attracted widespread support in a media landscape which remains dominated by large corporations. Democratic-participant theory is one example of a normative theory of the media (one which describes the way media ought to operate 'if certain social values are to be observed or attained' See McQuail, 'Mass Communication Theory', p. 4).

demographics is the study of the characteristics of populations, including birth and death rates, age, sex and ethnic characteristics.

denotation: in *semiology*, denotation is the first order of meaning of any *sign*. It is the obvious, or surface meaning of a word, image, object, sound, etc. For instance, the word 'red' may signify one among a number of colours. *Connotation* is the second order of meaning, in which a greater series of meanings and associations may arise. The connotative meanings of 'red' might include danger, heat, sexuality, and so on.

depth of field: the distance, taken from the nearest to the furthest point from the camera, within which any object remains in focus.

deregulation: the dissolution of rules and regulations which restrict but also protect the status of public services. The Broadcasting Act of 1990 ended the existence of the Independent Broadcasting Authority, and created the Independent Television Commission, which was to exercise a 'lighter touch' over the commercial television sector. The ITC is responsible for licensing and regulating commercial television, including ITV, Channel 4, satellite and cable services. In each ITV region the ITC awards a fixed term licence to a body responsible for providing the ITV output for that area. The present licence period began in January 1993 and will run until 2002. At that time, the ITC has an opportunity to redraw regional boundaries or alter licence requirements. The ITC has no direct responsibility for the content of commercial television.

Companies bidding for broadcasting licences had to satisfy a 'quality threshold' and then present sealed bids to the government. The quality threshold consisted of three key requirements; to provide regional programmes, to broadcast high quality news programmes at peak viewing times, and to provide a wide diversity of programmes to cater for 'a variety of tastes and interests.' In 1993 four television companies lost their licences and were replaced by new groups; the new stations were Carlton, Meridian, Westcountry and the breakfast TV station GMTV.

Derrida, Jacques: (born 1930) is an important *post-structuralist* thinker, whose 'Of Grammatology' (1967) influenced a number of writers on media, language and culture. *Deconstruction*, though it was originally just one term among a number used in Derrida's early work, has become one of the most significant 'buzzwords' in media and cultural studies. Derrida's chief objection is to the 'fixed' *categories* which exist in western thought and philosophy, which he believes hide contradiction and confusion. His particular interest lies in written texts, which he regards as 'impure', arguing that the written word is never fully present (it stands in for the idea or thing to which it refers) nor entirely absent (it is visible on the page as a graphic system). Derrida uses the term 'différance' to indicate this quality of language. In French, the verb 'différer' means both to differ from, and to defer (or 'put off'). Derrida believes that meaning is always scattered or dispersed along the 'chain' of linguistic *signification*. The *sign's* relationship to a present reality is therefore always deferred because reality is always mediated by language.

descriptive grammar is the linguist's attempt to describe what native speakers unconsciously know about their language, including the units, structures and rules revealed in linguistic expression.

desensitisation: an 'effects' theory which states that repeated exposure to media representation of anti-social acts, can lead to indifference (lack of sensitivity) to such acts in real life.

desk-top publishing: known as DTP, this is the combination of word-processing with software packages offering a variety of graphic design features. The production of high quality copy, with high standards of typography and text which flows around scanned images, makes professional standards more accessible.

determination: determination refers to the factors which shape or direct any phenomenon, or which bring it to a definite conclusion. It comes from the word 'determine', which means 'to set bounds to' something, to limit in scope or to define. In some uses, determine means to bring something to an end, as in settling the future of an event or the fate of a person. Determinants may be internal elements or external forces. For example, a substance like steel will behave in a certain way, depending on its chemical composition (an internal determinant) and the various forces which are allowed to act upon it, such as heat or compression (external determinants).

determination (cultural): in media and communication studies, determination refers to the way that any *communication* event (a television programme, a conversation, etc.), takes place within certain social, political and economic conditions. External forces, combined with the structure of the event, set the boundaries within which the event may develop. So, to take one example, the type of article printed by a magazine will be determined to some degree by a number of factors:

the magazine's financial resources, the magazine's editorial policies, the market it intends to capture, the personnel it employs, the laws relating to media ownership and publication, the discourses which circulate within a society, the political and social climate, and so on. The difficulty lies in deciding which factors are most influential at any given time, or in any particular situation. In addition, it is clear that communication and *culture* are not simply the products of a society, but that they in turn influence the wider social context; the cultural sphere is also capable of determination, as when, for example, a newspaper article on a controversial film sets an *agenda* for public debate.

determinism is the idea that certain of the major forces which affect human life (variously thought to include biology, technology, and economics), ultimately direct the fate of the human species. Determinist beliefs are criticised for their tendency to emphasise the power of impersonal forces at the expense of free will or autonomy.

dialect means those forms of speech characterised by a particular vocabulary and pronunciation, used by people who belong to an identifiable region, class or social group. A dialect was once seen as subordinate to standard English, but it is now more usual to describe all types of speech, including *received pronunciation*, as forms of dialect. (See also *argot, slang, jargon*.)

dialectic: a method of philosophical enquiry which comes from the Greek for 'to converse'. As used by the ancient Greek philosopher Socrates, dialectics meant a method of debate, in which truth would be investigated through discussion or reasoned argument. A number of different opinions are expressed and, through questions and answers, a conclusion eventually reached. Aristotle believed this method of enquiry to be flawed, because it started with ideas with which participants in a debate could agree, rather than from ideas which are widely accepted in society as a whole. In the Middle Ages, the dialectic continued to be associated with the public exercise of logic, and remained a method of discovering truth through formal argument.

In the hands of nineteenth-century philosophers like Hegel and *Marx*, the contradiction previously located in argument, became a dynamic force which existed in the real world. Hegel believed that thought (which he regarded as the true reality) passes through contradiction to resolution. The social world is therefore created through a process of thesis, antithesis and synthesis. Marx, on the other hand, regarded the material world, not thought, as the fundamental aspect of reality. Marx's collaborator Engels advanced the idea of 'dialectical materialism' in which matter itself is dynamic and subject to alteration, rather than fixed or static. Human existence is therefore forced to adapt to changing circumstances. Dialectical materialism as a 'law' of existence, was applied both to the natural world and to historical processes. In recent years, there has been a move away from the notion of dialectical laws, and an increasing use of 'dialectics' to describe the interaction between opposite forces. However, the old notion of dialectic as argument also continues to be used.

dialogics: a term used by the Russian theorist Bakhtin (1895–1975) to indicate the idea that every speech act or written expression must be seen in the context of previous communication events. Therefore, communication is not simply one-way but part of an extended dialogue between a number of individuals and groups. This also means that language is social. Some forms of expression, in Bakhtin's opinion, are 'dialogic' (the novel, comedy, speech) while others are 'monologic' (traditional forms like epic verse, tragedy, and lyric forms).

diaspora: a term describing the dispersal of communities to various parts of the world; the culture in which the victims of slavery, war, and economic deprivation exist. 'Diaspora cinema' is an art form which deals with the cultural and social alienation of such dispersed groups.

diegesis: the narrative content of a film, including speech, actions, and events; everything which is on-screen and clearly part of the fictional environment. Some writers, like Metz, go further to include the fictional space/time dimensions suggested by the narration. Diegetic sound is that which can be attributed to an on-screen source (that which seems to belong to the narrative) such as the speech of an actor. Non-diegetic sound comes from 'outside' the cinematic world, such as voiceovers and musical passages with no obvious on-screen source. However, non-diegetic sound also belongs to the fictional environment.

diffusion refers to the spread of innovation across sub-groups and, in some cases, across a social system. An early example of diffusion study is found in the work of the American researcher, E. Katz (1957). He investigated how doctors made decisions on adopting new drugs. Katz collected demographic information (age, medical school attended, etc.), but also examined attitudes, exposure to information sources, and how his respondents prescribed medicines. The doctors were asked to name the three colleagues with whom they were most likely to discuss cases, the three from whom they were most likely to seek advice, and the three with whom they were most likely to socialise.

From this information, a 'map' of interpersonal relations in the medical community was constructed. In addition, the study followed the progress of a new drug as it gained acceptance among the community. A number of conclusions were reached, the most important being that interpersonal influence in primary *groups* is effective in maintaining a significant degree of conformity of opinion and action within that group. Doctors tended to prescribe the same drugs as their closest colleagues, especially when faced with illnesses which were difficult to diagnose. (See also *opinion leaders*.)

diffusion of innovations: in 'Diffusion of Innovations' (1983), Everett Rogers examined more than 2000 diffusion studies, discovering that different channels of communication play different roles in the diffusion process. Media channels reach large audiences rapidly, spread information, and change weakly held attitudes. Interaction between individuals, on the other hand, is more important in overcoming resistance or lack of interest on the part of the receiver.

digital technology: the use of separate numbers or characters to represent data, as opposed to the *analogue* systems used in earlier forms of technology. A digital signal is composed of binary digits (0 and 1) which can be compressed and stored on optical discs like *CD-ROM*. All forms used in media (graphics, music, text, animation, video, photographs etc.,) can be 'digitalised'.

Analogue systems of reproduction are similar to their source, though the reproduction can be made in a number of variable forms. Digital systems do not resemble their source. While analogue media transcribe information (reproducing the arrangement of the physical properties of what is being copied), digital media convert information into 'formal relationships in abstract structures' (Timothy Binkley, in 'Future Visions', 1993). Digital video, for example, converts light or sound into numbers. In doing so, it strips away the physical property of the source, imposing a grid-like system which removes the 'rough edges'. In the case of sound at least, digital reproduction is based on sampling the original source. Numbers, which are abstract qualities that have no physical existence, have to be represented in some form. Binary digits (0 and 1) are the 'tokens' which represent, in various combinations, specific numbers; these numbers, in turn, represent the original information.

The difference between analogue and digital reproduction

digital video interactive (DVI): an interactive system that can display any type of audio-visual material.

digital video recording (DVR): the recording of digital rather than analogue video.

diorama: a large-scale translucent surface, painted with an imposing scene and used in public performances to create dramatic 'special effects'. Through the use of lighting effects and backdrops, scenes could be made to alter; for example, cities would seem to be consumed with fire, a fall of snow could be produced, or dawn would break in the sky. The diorama was a popular public entertainment in the eighteenth and nineteenth centuries.

direct broadcast satellite/DBS: any geostationary satellite that broadcasts directly to receivers, without having first to go through a ground or earth station.

direct cinema is a style of documentary film-making pioneered by Albert Maysles in post-war America, in which film was shot with minimum intervention from the director. A close relation of 'cinéma vérité', direct cinema used lightweight cameras and improved sound equipment to capture a sense of the real.

direct input is the composition of stories by writers or reporters, working directly onto computer files which can then be edited and set on screen.

directional microphone: a microphone which has a limited range of 'acceptance', and thus needs to be pointed in the direction from which a specific sound is made. The advantage is that unwanted noises are reduced.

disclaimer: a term used in newspaper, book and magazine publishing to refer to a printed announcement which asserts that a story has no connection with certain persons or organisations.

discourse: at its simplest discourse means verbal expression. In studies of everyday language, it refers to a unit of speech which can be subjected to analysis (the 'unit' must be larger than a sentence or a single utterance, because meaning is difficult to discover in small elements). The term discourse is also used to indicate a specialised form of language, in which certain rules and conventions are observed and typical statements or phrases are employed in a structured way; for example, there is supposed to be a 'discourse of the law', in which lawyers, judges and others use a special type of professional speech.

So far, 'discourse' has been used to refer to the form and content of human speech. More recent studies use the term to indicate the social process of creating meaning, through the use of language and other *symbolic forms*. This approach has two advantages: first, it reminds us that linguistic expression has an impact on the social world, shaping ideas and actions. Second, it allows us to study the creation of meaning through other 'systems' (or symbolic forms), such as visual communication, intonation, body language, music and so on.

discourse analysis is the study of speech. Discourse analysis is employed by linguists to examine the ordinary modes of speech used in conversation, as well as the more formal utterances used during public events like elections, trials, and various types of ceremony. The analyst will examine the form of the speech event and the meanings which emerge from that form. The overall system of meaning to which words contribute is known as *semantics*. It is our innate ability to create meaning in general, rather than a knowledge of 'correct' examples, which allows both the recognition of meaningful sequences and the creation of new examples. Quite apart from semantics, the discourse analyst must also study the 'moves' used in conversation (such as greeting, enquiry, response and termination), and the devices used in formal speech (such as repetition, 'rule of three', and assertion) to understand the strategies deployed by speakers.

discourse analysis (ideological): the study of the ideological references found in all forms of public expression. As the term 'discourse' has evolved (becoming the social process of creating meaning, as well as the end product of that process), 'discourse analysis' has increased the scope of its reference, to include the study of ideological expression. Inevitably, the types of material thought suitable for analysis have also multiplied. Advertisements, films, radio programmes and other examples drawn from mass media forms are investigated. Discourse analysis in this area refers not only to the study of language and linguistic patterns, but also to images, sounds, and design used in the presentation of media *texts*. A search is made for coherent patterns of meaning, for the 'typical' representations and narratives found in texts.

discourse and power: writers like Michel *Foucault* have suggested that *discourse* is a major factor in the exercise of *power*. This has encouraged some thinkers to characterise discourse as the expression of a particular viewpoint or *ideology* (though Foucault himself believed that the operation of power was more diffuse, and conflict more general). The media are often identified as sources of ideological discourse, since it is clear that television, radio, film, etc., are not simply outlets for neutral information. For example, a television news report on a government scandal might, through its choice of certain terms and images, suggest to its audience one particular interpretation of the event. The danger lies in imagining that a 'pure' form of discourse can be constructed, one which exactly represents a particular system of belief. Although a certain discourse may be used to impress or influence an audience, it can only do so by taking into account the beliefs of the target group. The point is that all 'ordinary' forms of communication already contain a variety of discourses; it is the use of these discourses in context which reveals the attitudes, values and beliefs of speakers and/or communicators.

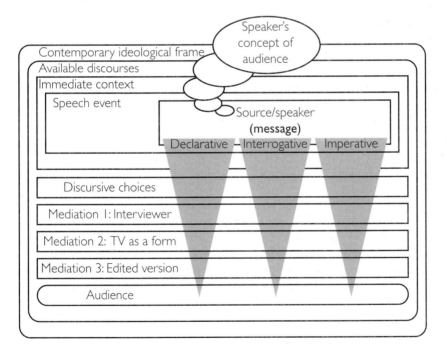

Discourse and power
'Model of a politician's discourse mediated by television' after S. Price, in 'Media Studies' (1993)

Discourse has therefore evolved from its original, speech-based meaning, to become a concept which refers to the structured *representation* of events in human and mass communication; in other words, events are presented in a certain light, sometimes in order to persuade or deceive. Gunther Kress (1985) writes 'a discourse provides a set of possible statements about a given area, and organises and gives structure to the manner in which a particular topic, object, process is to be talked about'. When a topic is given structure in this way, it often takes a narrative form. Established discourses may therefore be described as 'social narratives,' stories which offer broadly plausible explanations for events in the social world (see Price, 'Communication Studies', 1996). The use of a particular discourse often involves deliberate selection and choice, but also occurs where an institution or individual is forced by circumstance to use statements or narratives which will be familiar to an audience.

disinformation is the deliberate use of false and negative information, in order to discredit political opponents, and mislead and confuse the public. The KGB (the former Soviet Union's secret police) used 'dezinformatsiya' against a variety of targets. Disinformation was much in evidence during the Gulf War.

disorientation is a technique used in cinema to make an audience question their relationship to the spatial/temporal world created by a particular film.

display advertisement: a large-scale advertisement which appears in newspapers or magazines.

dissolve: a dissolve is an effect in which one shot is faded out, while the next is simultaneously faded in.

distanciation: used in film studies, this idea emerged from radical practices in the theatre and from early Soviet cinema. The German writer Brecht (1898–1956), who composed a number of plays in close collaboration with other authors, believed that audiences needed to adopt a critical perspective on theatrical narratives. To this end, he used various devices to remind them that they were watching a performance (direct address to the spectator, 'educative songs', actors seated amongst the audience, and so on). Writing in 1940 about one of his plays, 'The Threepenny Opera', Brecht noted that 'the educative elements were ... not an organic consequence of the whole, but stood in contradiction to it; they broke up the flow of the play and its incidents, they prevented empathy, they acted as a cold douche for those whose sympathies were becoming involved ... the play has a double nature. Instruction and entertainment conflict openly' (see 'On Experimental Theatre'). In sum, Brecht argued that 'artistic understanding' could be encouraged by *'alienation'*.

In the case of film, distanciation can be achieved in three ways: through editing, narrative, and characterisation. Distanciation through editing includes the use of jump-cuts, on-screen titles, and unmatched shots. In narrative terms, it might involve the creation of an 'empty' story in which little happens, or perhaps the construction of a narrative which is 'over-filled' with meaning. Characterisation may be used to alienate an audience by providing very little with which to identify, or by making all the film's protagonists equally unappealing.

distribution rights: the licensing of films, television programmes and other types of media content, to companies which then exercise the right to distribute the material to exhibitors.

D-notice: a 'defence notice' which is issued by the British government's Services, Press and Broadcasting Committee when it wishes to prevent the publication of 'sensitive' information. The D-notice carries no legal force, and is not a form of public instruction. It is a request to an editor of a newspaper, and uses the power of secrecy in order to secure its goal. No one can be certain how many D-notices are issued and it is clear that other, less formal means of influencing the press are employed. Richard Keeble, in 'The Newspapers Handbook' (1994), describes an incident which occurred during the lead-up to the Gulf War (p. 51); '[when] details of the 'allied' strategy were stolen from a Defence Ministry official's car, a D-notice banning newspapers reporting the event was issued ... news of it leaked to an Irish paper. Thus it became public knowledge and London-based newspapers went ahead and carried their own reports. National security did not appear to be seriously damaged'.

documentary: a type of film or audio production which regards reference to aspects of the real (through the use of location-based *actuality*), as the guiding principle in its formation, and an important feature of its subsequent mode of address. A document, strictly speaking, is supposed to be a record which provides evidence of some aspect of real life. The documentary is motivated by an attachment to 'actual' references, but it is often the case that individual examples of 'real' events shown in the documentary format, turn out to be unreliable (sometimes being restaged, decontextualised or over-emphasised). In addition, the editing and re-assemblage of actuality is itself often regarded as an 'artificial' formation which counts against claims to represent 'truth'.

John Grierson (1898–1972), the founder of the British documentary movement (and the first, in 1926, to use the term itself), did not make simple claims for the transparent truthfulness of the documentary. He distinguished (in Hardy, 1979) between (p. 20) 'descriptions of natural material' and 'creative shapings of it'. Grierson's view of documentary was of a form which does more than describe (p. 22–23) 'the surface values of a subject', using instead a method which 'explosively reveals the reality of it'. He went on to argue that 'you photograph the natural life, but you also, by your juxtaposition of detail, create an interpretation of it'.

John Corner chose 'The Art of Record' as the title of his 1996 book on documentary, pointing out that it is (p. 2) 'meant to indicate what is by now a widely recognised and problematic duality in documentary work – its character as both artifice and evidence'. He objects (p. 4) to the 'failure to recognise the continuing need of public culture for a cinema and a television of non-fictionality', a form which 'despite its recognition of the problems of representation, continues to regulate its activities by a discipline of principles and codes of practice'.

documentary films: the first film shown in public, the *Lumière* brothers' 'La Sortie des Usines Lumière' of 1895, falls within the scope of the documentary. It recorded the departure of workers from the Lumière factory at Lyon.

The early Soviet Union produced a number of individuals who recorded the industrial and agricultural advances of the state, as well as film-makers dedicated to more straightforward propaganda. In the 1920s, Dziga Vertov made educational documentaries for 'Kino Pravda' (Film Truth), displaying a great interest in the aesthetic qualities of the image (representing part of an avant garde far removed from later Soviet 'realism'). Robert Flaherty achieved renown for his 1922 film 'Nanook of the North', a famous early documentary which has since been criticised for its manipulative direction. In the late 1930s, Humphrey Jennings produced a number of outstanding films based on the sights and sounds of ordinary British life, including 'Spare Time' (1939). He went on to make documentaries about life in the industrial north, and also shot material for the Mass Observation Unit. In the 1950s, Grierson's principles came under attack from the film-makers associated with 'Free Cinema', who argued that documentary films should be (in Susan Hayward's words, p. 133) 'free from all commercial pressures' and needed 'to be inflected with a more humanist and poetic approach'. Lindsay Anderson, Tony Richardson and Karel Reisz formed the vanguard of this group and were associated with the film journal 'Sequence'.

A fashion for 'drama-documentary' (drama-doc) emerged in the 1960s with films like Ken Loach's 'Cathy Come Home', in which actors were used to dramatise real social problems. John Corner also describes developments in the 1980s, when documentaries like Connie Field's 1980 'Rosie the Riveter' used archive material to (p. 6) 'explore the experience of women in industry during the Second World War'. According to Corner, this was an 'attempt at popular feminist historiography'. The 'Griersonian spirit' returned in 1986 with the Black Audio Film Collective's 'Handsworth Songs', which explored black identity through a study of the Handsworth riots in mid-1980s Birmingham. Corner also recognises 'hybrid' forms such as the 'camcorder format' encouraged in the 1990s by the BBC's 'Video Diary' series.

dogma: from the Latin for 'opinion', dogma has come to mean a complete doctrine, and furthermore one which is rigid and narrowly-focused, as in 'dogmatism'. Also sometimes used in a religious context.

dominant discourse: if a *discourse* is a way of 'talking' about something, or even explaining events, then a dominant discourse is one which takes precedence over other explanations. So, for example, there may be various explanations for the existence of poverty, but one view may dominate.

The first question to ask is, how does it dominate other perspectives? Is it more convincing, so that everyone recognises its superiority? Or is it simply more widespread, like some kind of superstition? The second question is, from where does the dominant viewpoint come? From the media, from opinion leaders, or from cultural traditions which pre-date mass communication?

These questions are answered in different ways by different schools of thought. A Marxist approach, to take one example, would suggest that discourses emerge from struggles between classes 'rooted, in the last instance, in the relations of production' (Diane Macdonell, 'Theories of Discourse', 1986). Therefore, it may be that a dominant discourse is most likely to come from the dominant class in society. Watson and Hill make a similar point in their dictionary (p. 70) when they say that 'the dominant discourse is usually that which emanates from those dominant in the social and cultural order'. Notice, however, that Watson and Hill are not suggesting that social and cultural dominance is the same as, or grows directly from, economic leadership.

When it comes to the second point, there is little doubt that some discourses which achieve a 'dominant' position, do indeed come from powerful sources. It is also clear that such discourses may be circulated by the media; however, all discourses have to compete for attention and credibility.

domination: the exercise of a commanding influence over someone or something. Weber used it to mean the likelihood that an order which is given, is obeyed. However, domination does not have to be exercised in such an obvious way. It is also found in the structures of society, in the unequal relationships which are not marked as 'controversial' and do not always draw attention to themselves.

The work of Jurgen Habermas is important in this respect. In 'Theory and Practice' (1986) he argues that power in the modern, 'technocratic' society represents a different type of domination from previous forms. 'Technocratic consciousness', he writes (p. 255) 'is less ideological than all previous ideologies' because it does not simply falsify reality. It transforms practical – moral and political – questions (freedom, equality and so on) into technical ones. Again from Habermas we hear that 'the depoliticization of the mass of the population and the decline of the public realm as a political institution are components of a system of domination that tends to exclude practical questions from public discussion'. In such a situation, domination continues because it is difficult to identify its existence, let alone question its function.

dot matrix: a computer printer which forms letters from dots; it is efficient, but output is not of the highest quality.

drive refers to any mechanism that moves a playback or recording system, including the disc drive in a computer.

DTP: see *desk-top publishing*

dummy: in magazine and newspaper publishing, a mock-up issue which allows adjustments to be made. Dummies are often planned on pages of reduced size.

DVI: see *digital video interactive*

DVR: see *digital video recording*

Early Bird was the first *geosynchronous* satellite, intended for intercontinental telephone services; it was launched in June 1965. Owned by the US Communications Satellite Corporation (COMSAT), it had the capacity for 240 voice telephony circuits, the equivalent of one television channel. Although not designed for the transmission of television signals for direct reception by viewers, Early Bird was put to this use.

earth station: a communications centre, usually on the earth's surface, which receives or relays information from satellites, space stations, or other earth stations.

ECU: in film and video production, an extreme close-up.

edit control unit: an electronic device, sometimes called a remote control unit, used for editing video tape. The unit is linked to two monitors. Two video tapes are required, a master and an edit tape. Images from the master tape are displayed on the left-hand screen, while the edit tape is viewed on the right. There are circular dials at left and right (the control knobs) which are used to find the correct place on the tapes. Moving the control knob to the centre position brings a tape to a halt. There is a 'window' on each side of the unit which shows the time settings for both source and editor tapes. When the start of the scene on the source tape needing transfer has been found, the IN and SET buttons are pressed (simultaneously) for the source unit. The scene will be transferred from master or source tape to the edit tape. The process may be repeated any number of times, until the task is completed. Sound may also be transferred from source to edit tape.

edit point: the 'in' and 'out' points of a scene within a video film, which is to be edited onto another tape.

editing: is the process of making adjustments and corrections to texts; video editing is an electronic rearrangement of pictures and sound, either by organising material in sequence (assembly editing), or by placing new shots within sequences which already exist (insert editing). Two VHS tapes are required for editing; the master tape containing the source, and the edit tape which will retain the edited material. The edit tape must carry a signal at the beginning, lasting at least 30 seconds, so that the electronic image may have something to 'hook' onto at the start of the tape. The place at which an edit is to be made, is known as the 'edit-in point'.

editor: on newspapers or magazines, a person who edits material for publication. A sub-editor is responsible for editing journalists' copy, while the chief editor is effectively the chief executive, responsible for the publication but answerable to a proprietor if there is one (some newspapers are owned by trusts). In film and television an editor is someone who edits tape to broadcast standard.

editorial: a statement about some matter of public importance, appearing in a newspaper and otherwise known as a 'leading article'.

editorial policy: the principle followed by a television or radio station, a newspaper, magazine, etc., which governs the way that news, entertainment, features or any other material is sought, assembled, and circulated.

effects: the various types of impact made on audiences by media content. 'Effects' is a term which can be used in one of two closely related ways. The first is a reference to the argument that media forms and/or media content have a measurable impact (whether direct or indirect) on the behaviour, attitudes or actions of audiences; these actions/attitudes/behaviours are supposedly altered or reinforced (often for the worse) by the 'messages' media forms produce.

The second usage refers to the tradition of mass communication research devoted to identifying media effects in general, and describing examples (real or imagined) of message impact on audiences. Shaun Moores ('Interpreting Audiences', 1993, p. 5), notes that 'ever since the emergence of industries for the large-scale production and distribution of cultural goods, academics have asked about the effects of those products on consumers'.

The immediate problem lies in the fact that investigations of media influence have sometimes assumed that the media are guaranteed a successful impact on their 'target' audience. McQuail (in 'Communication', 1975, p. 191), writes of the 'inappropriateness of many formulations of the process of mass communication, a failure to acknowledge that this is a subtle and complex process, a matter of bargaining, interaction and exchange'.

effects (types): it is important to distinguish between broad categories of effect and how effects in general are thought to be produced. Types of effect include the following:

- socialisation, where the media is thought to 'initiate' groups and individuals into the social framework (socialisation may be considered a 'long-term' effect)
- social control, in which the social system (based on class, gender and ethnic divisions) is supposedly reinforced by the media (partly through *agenda setting* and *moral panics*
- attitude change, supposed to take place among vulnerable sections of the population
- behavioural change, where exposure to a media stimulus results in some form of change in individual or group conduct.

If we turn to the ways in which effects are thought to occur, these can be described as follows:

- *hypodermic* effects, a model in which there is a direct relationship between stimulus and response (the media message is 'injected' into audience members)
- *inoculation* theory, where (as a result of long exposure) individuals or groups becomes *desensitised* to particular types of content
- *two-step flow theory*, based on the idea that *opinion leaders* pass on their response to other members of the community
- the *uses and gratifications* model, where people choose how to be affected, in the sense that they have their own pleasures and purposes in mind
- psychodynamic models, in which the degree of effect is dependent on individual psychology
- subcultural interpretation, where audience response is made from within

a like-minded group (based on class, age, gender and other perspectives), sometimes agreeing with the general approach of the media source, sometimes rejecting it, and most often reaching a *negotiated* position.

The focus in the hypodermic model is on the power of the media. Here, the media produces a clear message with a strong effect. Moving onto two-step flow theory, messages are mediated by opinion leaders, so the notion of direct effects begins to look less convincing. By the time we reach subcultural interpretation (called 'structured interpretation' by Trowler in 'Investigating Mass Media', 1996), it seems that the balance of power has shifted, with the audience able to negotiate the message it receives.

effects (research): Stuart Hall (1982) pointed to the limitations of effects studies, criticising their focus on immediately observable behaviour. Moores (1993) describes the transition from pure 'effects' research to the 'critical paradigm' which began in the 1960s. He notes (p. 6) that 'cultural theorists drew on *semiotics* and began to talk about the message as a 'text', as a complex and structured arrangement of signs rather than an empty vehicle for the transmission of information or opinion. In this jargon, receivers became 'readers'.' Combined with the encoding/decoding model proposed by Stuart Hall, this development implied that direct effects are only possible in certain conditions, where the media are strong, the message unambiguous and the audience particularly susceptible to suggestion. Some theorists, notably Fiske (1987) used the 'turn to audience' to argue that the media have relatively little power. The emphasis on audience led some writers (notably Bennett and Woolacott in 1987) to argue that there is actually no text at all, just a variety of 'reading formations'!

More recent research into the media has moved away from the struggle to quantify effects, towards a greater concern with the ethnography of media consumption. Researchers like Pertti Alasuutari, who produced a study of viewing habits in Finland (1992), have tried to discover the values attached by audiences to the programmes they watch. Instead of looking for behavioural change, Alasuutari constructed a 'moral hierarchy' of television programmes, based on how viewers explained what they did and did not watch. (See also *audience, active audience, ethnography.*)

elaborated code: a form of speech identified by Bernstein (1971). Bernstein carried out research into the the language use of children, arguing that there are considerable linguistic differences between the speech of the working and the middle classes. He formulated a hypothesis which stated that there were two distinct codes, 'elaborated' and 'restricted'.

The concept behind the two types of code is essentially one of necessity. The use of elaborated code is found among the middle classes, who are often placed in social situations where participants are unable to draw on shared understandings, and thus have to resort to highly individualised forms of *discourse*, generating speech based on complicated *syntax* and an extensive vocabulary. 'Elaborated code' is supposed to be relatively independent of the context in which it is used, dealing in generalisations and abstractions. It is associated with formal education.

The restricted form, by comparison, is used in contexts where the participants know what to expect, and can draw on shared experiences and meanings. Restricted code is supposed to be simpler in construction, requiring a smaller level of vocabulary. In Bernstein's view, the working classes do not have access to elaborated code; their discourse is therefore characterised by a greater dependence on context. The middle classes, however, have access to both codes.

Bernstein's work has been read as valuing elaborated code more highly than its counterpart, but his work can be used to argue that access to middle-class society is restricted by established discourses.

electronic mail/e-mail: the system which permits the sending of text/letters via a local area network, wide area network or even the Internet. Electronic mail originates in an 'editor', a simple word processor system, and is then interpreted by mail reader software.

electronic media: the electronic media include radio, television (cable and broadcast), direct broadcast satellites, etc., as opposed to the print media (newspapers, magazines, books).

electronic news gathering: see *ENG*.

electronic newsroom: a newsroom system which depends on computer-based news composition and editing.

electronic publishing: the publishing of textual and pictorial material in electronic form, as opposed to print. Electronic publishing includes CD-ROMs, teletext, video cassettes, databases and video discs.

ellipsis: in language, the omission of words from a sentence, or larger elements from a passage (often marked by three dots to indicate where the missing element would have appeared). In film, ellipsis means those sections of narrative a viewer might expect to see,which are passed over. In most cases, some form of editing (fades or dissolves) are used to indicate that time is moving on. A *jump-cut* is a form of unannounced ellipsis, in which the viewer is disorientated by a cut which shifts the action from one time and place to another.

E-mail: see *electronic mail.*

embargo: a date or time on a news release, before which the information it contains must not be published. An embargo is designed to control public knowledge of certain news stories, and is used on documents like Budget papers. In 1996, the 'Daily Mirror' obtained full details of that year's Budget, but dutifully handed the documents back to the Conservative government without publishing anything.

emblematic shot: in some examples of early cinema, a shot would be presented at the very start of a film, representing the *genre* and revealing something about the *narrative* content which an audience could expect to encounter. For instance, if a film was about a robbery, then a shot of a robber about to enter a bank might appear. Emblematic shots seem to be an early equivalent of the *establishing shot,* or other introductory sequences used by modern film-makers, except that they are more clearly thematic than the spatial/temporal signal which is the function of most establishing shots.

emotions are feelings and responses associated with certain types of stimuli. Much communication research has focused on intellectual or cognitive processes, to such an extent that some writers feel that the emotional factors in human understanding have been neglected. Jaak Panksepp (see 'Gray zones at the Emotion/Cognition

Interface' (p. 289)), argues that; '... emotions have a power of their own in directing and disrupting behavioural options, thinking processes, and bodily states ...'

Emotions, according to Panksepp, are created from the activities of 'specific types of neural circuits' in the brain which are quite different to the centres of intellectual processing. Panksepp sees human emotions as 'instinctual' operating systems of the brain which promote a coherent individual response to 'basic survival needs.'

This accords with Gerald Edelman's study of the limbic system, which lies at the base of the brain, and is traditionally regarded as the seat of the emotions. The brain stem is thought by Edelman to contain structures called 'value systems,' which are supposed to have evolved to recognise beneficial events and occurrences (such as actions taken in order to eat, to seize objects, etc.). The value systems are thought to select only those firing patterns which, through experience, produce useful actions. The idea here is that every useful action is suffused with value, so that even the highest and most abstract levels of human thinking are based on more than intellectual processes; they are also founded on emotion. Such studies are useful when certain types of human communication (through music, for example) seem to depend largely upon emotional response.

empiricism: from the Greek for experience; empiricism is a form of social enquiry which works from quantifiable and observable evidence about the nature of reality and the world. 'Classical' empiricists (such as Locke, Berkeley and Hume) argued that concepts come from sense experience. The world of ideas is therefore a 'weaker' copy of impressions gained from the senses. David Hume, writing in 'An Enquiry Concerning Human Understanding' (1777), addressed this notion; 'all our ideas or more feeble perceptions are copies of our impressions'. John Locke believed that; '... our knowledge of our own ideas is more than just our own imagination, and there is a conformity between our ideas and the real nature of things ... all simple ideas represent something real.'

In later empiricist accounts (see John D. Greenwood's account in 'Realism, Identity and Emotion', 1994), this 'developed into the doctrine that a concept or its linguistic expression is meaningless unless it can be defined in terms of observable phenomena'. In this scenario, concepts are 'validated' by measurable scientific evidence. Ultimately, any crackpot theory about life could be regarded as valid, provided it referred at some point to some form of quantifiable evidence.

Empiricism was used in a derogatory sense from the seventeenth century onwards. The problem lay in the rather unfair notion that empiricists were really only interested in observable phenomena, and were not concerned with theory at all.

In recent years, following the rise of postmodernism, scepticism about the validity of scientific and/or empirical method has again be expressed. The charge of 'empiricism' has thus sometimes become a term of abuse, and has been aimed at related, but distinct philosophies such as realism, which opposes traditional empiricism as well as the various forms of modern 'scepticism' (*postmodernism,* social constructivism).

encode/decode: communication depends on the accurate use and successful recognition of *codes.* In order to create meaning, concepts can be 'encoded' by choosing a system which organises signs into meaningful patterns. These systems include writing, speech, graphic design, and so on. The idea of encoding depends on the notion that most messages are not 'direct'; that they must be changed into another form and then 'translated' back into the original form once received.

encryption: the creation of *codes*; hence the practice of protecting computer information by encoding data, so that access is only possible through the use of the correct code or 'key'. In the US, security on the Internet follows a particular pattern. The client and the server he/she contacts, are protected by Netscape's 'secure socket layer' (SSL). A key symbol appears on the client's screen, showing that the exchange is protected from outside interference. A large prime number is generated as a one-off token for the duration of the session. The client sends the number to the server via a secure third party – in America, a Certification Authority such as the private company RSA Data. The number is used during the exchange and discarded at the end of the session. Tony Feldman (1997) notes that strong encryption algorithms 'are classified by the US authorities as munitions'.

ENG: electronic news gathering, a system which relies on the use of lightweight or portable video cameras as opposed to the use of film cameras and stock.

enlarger: a device used in darkrooms to produce enlarged prints from negatives (rather than contact sheets which are printed at the same size as the negatives).

Enlightenment: a period in history, beginning in the eighteenth century, during which scientific experiment, rationality and the use of reason were used to dispel the ignorance and superstition previously thought to have clouded human judgment. Enlightenment rationality allowed the development of ideas about human equality, but also led to the kind of thinking which produced 'total institutions' (like modern prisons). For many *postmodernists*, the Enlightenment stands as a symbol of monolithic power, producing a form of social organisation which led only to tyranny. Many Enlightenment philosophers at the time were aware of the contradictions which the new era embraced. Moses Mendelssohn (1729–86) for example, argued that Enlightenment was difficult to define, because it was a process which was still unfolding. He also thought that the unlimited development of reason in individuals could undermine the political, religious and social order, leaving people in a state of intellectual egoism. Similarly, Immanuel Kant (1724–1804), who called Enlightenment 'man's release from his self-incurred immaturity', was careful to distinguish between the public use of reason and the more negative private employment of the same process.

enunciation: a proclamation or definite expression of some sort (such as the 'enunciation' of a theory), this term was used by Emile Benveniste (1971) and then adopted by film theorists. Enunciation in this sense is a form of speech act, the time-bound act of making an address. During the course of a film, the spectator is addressed by the action, and is thus the enunciated. In making sense of the narrative, he/she becomes the enunciator.

epics: from cinema, a reference to films which are conceived on a grand scale, require extensive financial and material resources, and feature a 'cast of thousands' as well as boasting well-known stars in the central roles. Epics usually deal with historical themes. D.W. Griffith's 'Birth of a Nation' (1916) a racist chronicle of

American society after the Civil War, is thought to have started the trend in epic cinema, which reached its height in the 1950s with films such as 'The Robe' (1953), and began to decline with films like 'Cleopatra' (1963). However, many Hollywood films still retain epic qualities.

EPOD: the European Platform for Optical Discs, a trade clearing house involved in marketing video discs and CDs. Formerly the European Laser Disc Association, it publishes sales figures for discs in the European marketplace.

equilibrium/disequilibrium: part of the narrative theory propounded by the theorist Tzvetzan *Todorov,* who described the structure of the 'fantastic'. According to his theory, the narrative environment begins with a state of order, in which all aspects of the fictional world are as they should be. What follows is a disruption of that state, followed by a recognition of the disequilibrium which ensues, then by an attempt to repair the damage of disruption, and finally a return to some new form of balance or equilibrium.

escapist: a term applied to film or television entertainment regarded as lightweight, designed merely to take the viewer away from the everyday world. The use of the term implies that more attention should be given to the real. The argument has also been applied to advertising.

establishing shot: a shot used to establish certain ideas about a scene, so that an audience can orientate itself to the action with regard to space, time, events, characters and so on. Location is the most obvious example; a building is shown, then a close-up of one window is featured, so that an audience assumes that the action which follows takes place in a room in the building.

Establishing shot

estrangement: the idea that an audience should be kept at a distance from the otherwise involving spectacle of artistic performance, so that intellectual faculties remain unclouded and the individual is roused to action. It was an effect used by Brecht in the theatre, and was subsequently applied to film theory.

ethics is the science or study of moral behaviour in society. The study of ethics is undertaken in order to describe situations which might challenge the integrity of media workers.

ethnography is the study of the way of life of a people or culture, usually involving some form of direct or participant observation. 'Ethnographic' approaches came from anthropology, but were taken up by sociologists. In turn, media studies has used the principles of ethnography to observe groups in their natural or usual settings. David Morley and Roger Silverstone, in their contribution to Jensen and Jankowski's 'Handbook of Qualitative Methodologies' (1991), define ethnographic approaches as (p. 149) 'the analysis of multiply structured contexts of action, aiming to produce a rich descriptive and interpretive account of the lives and values of those subject to investigation'. Television viewing, the aspect of culture which interests Morley, would therefore require close study of the domestic environment. Ann Game, in 'Undoing the Social' (1991), draws attention to the idea that all forms of such research can be seen as forms of 'writing' rather than the objective 'reports' they appear to be. The whole question of the relationship between author/researcher and the subjects of the investigation (the individuals or groups under study), is central to what Game sees as (p. 32) 'the self–other relation' and the 'constitution of the other in research practices'.

etymology is the study of the history of words.

European Broadcasting Union: an association of western European broadcasters, but also including some associate members from other countries.

evaluation: a critique of academic or practical work, including (in communication and media studies projects) consideration of the suitability of textual form, content and address to the chosen audience. Evaluation is often carried out as a form of self-assessment, and covers all aspects of an individual's efforts. Questions which should be posed for a successful evaluation/self-assessment include:

- Was the project chosen relevant to a particular audience?
- Was the project enquiry focussed through the use of a problematic or hypothesis?
- Had all relevant sources of information been identified and edited?
- Were the most suitable methods of textual research used?
- Were the most useful forms of audience research selected?
- Were appropriate methods of design selected?
- Were all alternative decisions and courses of action analysed?
- Was the social and ideological context of the communication process understood?
- Was the project tested on an audience?
- Was a synopsis provided for the guidance of the reader?

exchange: the reciprocal movement between two or more parties, of ideas and concepts (in speech or some other communicative form).

exclusive: an exclusive is a news item which a print or broadcast medium claims as a unique scoop; a story which no other outlet has used.

ex-nomination: the theorist Roland Barthes used this concept in 1973 to describe how the economic conditions of a society remain absent from the representations made of that society. Barthes used the example of capitalism, which he described as the social system which did not want to be named. As Hartley writes ('Key Concepts', p. 86) 'it is uncontroversial to say that we live in a capitalist economy ... however, Barthes points out, the situation is not so simple in political discourses. There are no capitalist parties as such'. In other words, political parties do not name themselves as capitalist but as 'democratic', 'liberal', 'conservative' and even 'socialist'.

explication: in communication theory, a form of definition which attempts to link empirical research with conceptual understanding, discovering the meaning of a concept by testing it in a real context. Explication works at the denotative level, discarding a term if its connotations lead away from the concept which the theorist wishes to use. (See also *denotation* and *connotation*.)

exposé: a news item which exposes information of a sensitive or secret nature, which some individual or group had previously kept out of the public realm. The story has to fulfil the *news values* of those organisations which discover the information, usually concerning personal scandals or institutional wrong-doing.

expression: expression is the representation by individuals of their internal apprehension of the world, whatever form that takes (speech, writing, graphics, gesture, or any other recognised mode of communication).

The purpose of expression has been variously described; it may be used in order to change an individual's circumstances, but is often engaged in for its own sake. Among the problems raised in studies of expression, is the relationship between a person's intention, and the degree to which this intention can be accurately expressed. In the case of public communication, there are various contextual pressures on individuals which often results in the production of certain 'genres' of speech to meet the occasion. Individuals may only really find an exact meaning when they come to express the various ideas and emotions which they experience.

In Irving Goffman's view, some forms of behaviour are regarded as 'natural' (an expression of the unconscious), while others are thought to be deliberate. In 'The Presentation of Self in Everyday Life', Goffman writes (p. 2); 'the expressiveness of the individual ... appears to involve two radically different kinds of sign-activity: the expression that he *gives,* and the expression that he *gives off.*' Goffman argues that 'the first involves verbal symbols or their substitutes' while the second covers a wide range of action that others treat 'as symptomatic of the actor.' Since deliberate expression may be mistaken for natural expression, Goffman calculates that the individual is able to convey misinformation through speech and other patterns of behaviour.

expressionism: in film it is a style in which emotions are demonstrated on-screen through the use of dramatic lighting, characterisation, sets, etc.(See also *German expressionism.*)

extra-personal communication: 'the processing of some form of meaningful or potentially meaningful signal, between machines requiring human input but little supervision during the duration of the process itself' (Price, 'Communication Studies', 1996, p. 14). Communication between human individuals and computers is really a form of intrapersonal processing, while communication between two opera-tors at different terminals may actually be a form of interpersonal communication using an electronic *channel.* Research into 'artificial intelligence' covers a number of fields, listed by Geoffrey James (see 'Text, Context, and Hypertext'), as robotics, lan-guage processing, vision and speech, and expert systems. Expert systems (p. 15) 'simulate the behaviour of an expert, reproducing the logic that the expert applies to a routine situation.' (See also *artificial intelligence.*)

eyeline: the direction in which a subject appears to be looking, from the perspec-tive of the *camera.*

eye-witness reporting involves the presence of a professional reporter or *journalist* at a newsworthy event, producing copy from his/her own observations.

F

facsimile/fax: a form of telegraphic communication in which printed material is transmitted along 'phone lines, the copy appearing as an exact reproduction of the original.

Fairness Doctrine: a requirement stating that US broadcasters presenting controversial issues, should allow reasonable opportunities for conflicting views to be aired. The Fairness Doctrine is often referred to as a 'regulation', but was actually an interpretation of communications policy made by the *Federal Communications Commission*. It was then assumed, in retrospect, that the Doctrine was added to Section 315 of the 1959 Communications Act. In 1964, an FCC document called the 'Fairness Primer', attempted to clarify the Doctrine, while another report in 1974 (the 'Fairness Report') provided further details. Ellmore (1991) argues that the most important statement of the 1974 document, is the one which reads 'We regard strict adherence to the Fairness Doctrine – including the affirmative obligation to provide coverage of issues of public importance – as the single most important requirement of operation in the public interest'. The deregulation of broadcasting in the 1980s led eventually to the idea that the marketplace, rather than government regulation, would ensure equal treatment of public issues. In addition, the political right (which appropriated the notion of fairness in organisations like 'Fairness in Media') attacked the networks for setting a liberal agenda. This agenda was supposedly achieved by covering issues which made right-wing causes look bad and liberal causes good. As a result of the political climate, the FCC abandoned its commitment to the Doctrine.

fairytales: following the work of the Russian writer Vladimir *Propp*, film theory has taken up his structuralist explanation of the Russian folk-tale and applied it to film. According to Propp, there are a certain number of situations which recur in such tales, and a limited number of roles which can be acted out in the course of the *narrative*. Propp insisted that character was in fact a function of the narrative, and not individual or psychologically valid.

family resemblance: a term used by the philosopher Wittgenstein, with reference to *categorisation*. Traditional approaches to the subject argued that categories exist because there are clear boundaries between classes.

Wittgenstein (writing in 'Philosophical Investigations'), challenged the received wisdom by asking what organising principle was actually used to assign various phenomena (objects, events, living things) to the same category. He used the example of 'games' (see 'Linguistic Categorisation', p. 39), including: 'board-games, card-games, ball-games, Olympic games, and so on'. He asked 'what is common to them all? ... If you look at them you will not see something that is common to *all*, but similarities, relationships ... ' Instead of trying to find hard and fast credentials, or clear-cut boundaries between what is a game and what is not, Wittgenstein used the example of 'family resemblances,' where a series of relationships between the members exists, each sharing a number of features but none having all the possible criteria for membership. Family resemblance solves the problem of trying to find hard and fast categories.

fashions of speech: a term used by Price (1993), to refer to the use of convenient and popular phrases which provide plausible explanations for actions and beliefs, allowing the speaker to avoid a close engagement with an issue.

feasibility test: in project and research work a feasibility test is a number of practical and theoretical questions used to find out if a certain line of enquiry is both intellectually sound and physically manageable within the time set. It may include the following questions:

- Is there an accessible audience which can be tested?
- Is a reasonable amount of secondary data available?
- What are the advantages and disadvantages of the methods to be used ?

Federal Communications Commission: the governing body for US broadcasting (See also *Fairness Doctrine.*)

feedback: a minor term associated with the US tradition of linear communication models; it simply means the response of a 'receiver' to a message, which the sender then uses to help construct a fresh message.

feigning: Erving Goffman's term for the manipulation of one's own behaviours, in an attempt to mislead an onlooker as to one's true character and personality.

feminism: a theory of social action which begins from the premise that women suffer from various forms of discrimination, both private and public. Although feminists hold a number of different views about the precise nature of patriarchy (a society dominated by men), and are divided about the type of action required to improve the condition of women, all feminists recognise the existence of gender inequalities.

The areas in which feminism has had an impact on media studies, are listed by Gail Dines and Jean Humez in 'Gender, Race and Class in Media' (1995). These are: making visible the male domination (both economic and cultural) of media industries, criticising 'male bias' within the field of media study, bringing previously undervalued 'female genres' to the foreground of academic enquiry, beginning the examination of women's experience as media consumers and encouraging female practitioners to experiment with new themes and approaches.

Such achievements have not prevented mainstream feminism from being criticised by those who feel their own perspective has been neglected. This is particularly true of black and 'third world' scholars, whose theories of feminist practice are strongly influenced by experience of class and race, as well as gender.

A number of writers have identified different currents in feminist critiques of society. The divisions most often recognised are set out in 'Channels of Discourse, Reassembled' (1992), in which Kaplan points to the difference between political and philosophical approaches to feminism. The latter includes 'essentialist' and 'anti-essentialist' approaches. Essentialism regards the difference between the sexes as biological in origin, while anti-essentialism is more concerned to investigate how notions of 'the feminine' are constructed in patriarchal society. Kaplan divides political feminism into four types:

- bourgeois feminism, aiming to achieve equal rights within the political system

- Marxist feminism which sees the oppression of women from a class perspective
- radical feminism, separatist in nature, seeing patriarchy as unable to be reformed and men in general as an oppressive group
- post-structuralist feminism, which investigates the structures of language to discover how women are excluded from the 'symbolic order' (leading in some cases to attempts to correct the bias of 'man-made' language, in others to the use of Lacanian psychoanalysis).

Some writers, notably van Zoonen in 'Feminist Media Studies' (1994), have objected to the continued use of such divisions. Among her reasons are the conviction that such an approach stresses divisions at the expense of similarities, that it overlooks national variations, that it concentrates too strongly on issues of importance to industrialised countries, and that it implies that certain types of feminist are only interested in specific issues.

feminism (research): media or communication research undertaken from a feminist perspective. Despite acknowledging van Zoonen's objection to the division of feminism into schools of thought, Trowler ('Investigating Media', 1996) still repeats similar divisions as a guide to feminist media scholarship.

In his view liberal feminism is concerned with the accuracy of media representations, and the relationship between women's position in society and their treatment in and by the media. Radical feminism is interested in identifying male domination of media institutions, and arguing that women must set up their own media structures. Finally, socialist feminism examines the economic structure and its role in the exploitation of women as workers, consumers and domestic labourers. These positions provide only the briefest overview of a complex situation, and are not a reliable guide to the kind of media research which feminists are likely to undertake.

Feminist research has included Diana Meehan's study of women's roles and actions in television, Lillian Robinson's empirical research into the difference between women's work roles and television's representation of female labour, Jennifer Coates' study of gendered language use, Janice Radway's study of romantic fiction, Janet Lee's work on 'subversive sitcoms', Tania Modleski's investigation of 'women's genres' such as soap opera, and Laura Mulvey's famous description of 'the male gaze' and theories of spectatorship in films.

fibre-optics: a type of communications technology, in which digitalised information in the form of light impulses, is sent along fine-spun glass fibres. Fibre-optic cables are capable of carrying thousands of television channels along a single pair of glass strands. Tony Feldman ('An Introduction to Digital Media', p. 72) writes that 'it is hard to properly illustrate the leap in capacity which fibre optic technology offers ... imagine that the entire population of the world decided simultaneously to have a conversation with itself ... and then double the amount of information this mega-conversation would generate ... the amount of information could be transmitted along a single filament of optical fibre no bigger than a human hair'. In practice, high capacity fibre systems are used where demand is greatest, such as large telephone systems in major urban areas. Where consumer need is less intense, copper is still used to carry telephone communications.

Feldman notes that 'most of the advanced communications networks in the world are today a hybrid mix of fibre and copper.'

fill: a light used to fill in shadows.

floppy disc: now often referred to simply as a disc (or disk), this was the original term for the thin, flexible material coated with magnetic oxide which carried computer data. Discs were held within protective sleeves, within which they could be rotated. Modern discs are more robust inside a harder casing and smaller than their earlier counterparts (3.5 inches as opposed to 5.25 inches).

flow chart: a diagram which, by means of symbols, statements, directional arrows and interconnecting lines, shows how a certain objective may be achieved.

folk devils: a term used by Stan Cohen in 1972 to describe the way in which certain groups are identified as a threat to society; such groups are then castigated by the media. The negative reaction supposedly caused among law-abiding citizens, is used to reinforce social norms and to ensure continued support for strong policies on law and order.

foreknowledge and expectation: the film theorist Stephen Neale pointed out that film genre is not a hard and fast structure, with considerable overlapping between types of film. He advanced the idea that *genre* was not entirely textual; that is to say, it depends also on the foreknowledge of an audience. Audiences would expect to see certain generic elements at work, based on their experience of other comparable material. The film-maker could therefore introduce certain 'signals' to an audience, so guiding their expectations.

forensic discourse analysis: in 'Advances in Spoken Discourse Analysis', Malcolm Coulthard describes forensic discourse analysis as the practice of testing the authenticity of interview records or statements (taken from suspects by the police). Coulthard describes the aim of forensic analysis as follows (p. 243): 'discourse analysis can say nothing at all about the truth of what is said *in* the disputed text, but can sometimes comment usefully on the truth of diverging claims made by both sides afterwards *about* the text.'

Coulthard argues that a faked interaction is (p. 244) 'the work of an amateur dramatist.' Forensic discourse analysis is based on the idea that such fictions can be discovered by identifying 'non-authentic features' in the record of the exchange. What are these 'non-authentic' features? One example is the difference between the content of a statement and the form in which that content is expressed.

There is evidence to suggest that human beings do not remember *semantic* and *grammatical* information in the same way. Sachs (1967), showed that the meanings of sentences are easier to remember than their precise 'grammatical shapes'. Therefore, it is usually the case that people will forget the exact grammatical form of a sentence, but will remember the information it contains.

forensic discourse analysis (evidence): in studying evidence, the difference between an original utterance and a subsequent report, allows the analyst to question any material which shows an exact similarity between the two. Coulthard cites the case of the Birmingham Six, who were imprisoned for an IRA bomb attack they did not carry out. Parts of one defendant's interview, and the statement which followed it, were identical. The police claimed that the accused, William Power, had retold the story in the same words. Power, on the other hand, insisted that the police had copied the second text from their record of the first.

Using the principle of difference between form and content (where the same experience is 'encoded' in different forms), and the idea that people cannot, as a rule, remember the exact form of their utterances, Coulthard demonstrated that two statements were unlikely to be exactly the same. He produced contrasting versions of Power's testimony while police evidence, by offering identical versions of Power's experience, looked unconvincing.

During the Birmingham Six trial, the evidence presented was covered twice, because the defence disputed the admissibility of part of the prosecution case. As a result, Coulthard had access to two versions of the events described by the defendants, each different in form but essentially similar in content. Extracts from the two versions supported the observation that an individual could not, contrary to police evidence, reproduce identical accounts.

formal organisation: a human collective which is created to pursue an explicit purpose or goal. It is governed by rules and usually managed through a hierarchical system of control. Its characteristics can be listed as follows:

- it is established by an individual or, more usually, a group of individuals
- it has a set of official or public objectives, concerning which its members show different levels of awareness, and towards which they display varying degrees of commitment
- it allocates roles to individuals and sets up a division of labour based upon various tasks
- it institutes methods of control over individuals and groups
- it sets up specialised departments or sections
- it uses both official and unofficial systems of communication
- it develops formally structured relationships, together with unofficial networks and working practices
- it operates within broad 'areas' of influence (controlling part of a specific market, for example)
- it manages resources (successfully or otherwise).

All organisations have the ability to exert some measure of influence upon people inside and outside their boundaries. The degree of influence and the kind of power exerted depend upon the role of each organisation in society. A few will play a significant part in early socialisation –schools are the obvious example. Others have less direct or prolonged contact with individuals, but have the potential to wield some power over the individual. People create organisations as *formal* and not personal entities, but few people who work within organisations have the chance to make up or influence the rules.

Foucault, Michel: (1926–1984) a French post-structuralist who produced books on a wide range of subjects, including imprisonment, sexuality, mental illness, history and language. His impact on media and communication studies comes from his work on *discourse* and *power*. Foucault was hostile to systematic forms of academic enquiry, believing that they neglected the peripheral and provisional aspects of human experience. He also objected to traditional ways of understanding the past, in which events are placed within a grand or 'totalising' discourse.

Technical rationality was another target. In Sarap's words (1988, p. 76), 'Foucault reiterates the fears of Nietzsche and Weber: science uncovers the mythology in the world; but science itself is a myth which has to be superseded'. However, despite his dislike of scientific rationality and his demonstration of the 'impersonal' nature of power, Foucault did not attack the exercise of power. He often stressed its positive aspects and its role in the production of new capacities. Power did not, in Foucault's view, emanate from the state, but was to be found in all social relations.

fragmentation: a theory of power put forward by David Tetzlaff in 1991. He argues that mass produced culture helps to maintain the dominance of the capitalist system, not by centralising control (the traditional Marxist model), but by fragmenting the cultural outlook and political beliefs of subordinate groups. Media messages do not attempt to persuade individuals to believe in the capitalist system – instead, they are likely to have little relationship to the real conditions of power in society.

fragmentation (in computing): the 'presence of small increments of unused space spread throughout disk storage' (Webster's Dictionary of Computer Terms, 1992). This phenomenon occurs when files are deleted and new ones created.

frame: in linguistics, a frame marks the boundary of a transaction; Malcolm Coulthard (1985), writing about classroom interaction, notes that (p. 123) 'the boundaries of transactions are typically marked by frames whose realisation ... is largely limited to five words – 'OK', 'well', 'right', 'now', 'good' – uttered with strong stress, high falling intonation and followed by a short pause'.

frame grabber: a device used in computing to select and store individual frames from video footage.

Frankfurt School: founded in 1923 in Weimar Germany, the Frankfurt Institute for Social Research became the focal point for a number of Marxist academics known collectively as the 'Frankfurt School'. The School's leading thinkers were Max Horkheimer, Theodor Adorno, Erich Fromm, Walter Benjamin and Herbert Marcuse.

When the Nazis came to power, the group was dispersed, its members seeking refuge in the United States. It was later re-established in post-war Germany, some 30 years after its founding members had begun work.

Although they pursued separate projects in a variety of fields (philosophy, sociology and social psychology, amongst others) the individual theorists shared certain preoccupations. Their work is distinguished by hostility to bureaucracy and authoritarianism in general, including the capitalist and and communist varieties. In attempting to explain the defeat of working-class radicalism and the triumph of fascism in Europe, they produced a perspective known as 'critical theory'. This emphasised the ideological power of monopoly capitalism and the birth of a 'mass culture' industry. The class system had survived through the ability of the 'culture industry' to propagate a myth of equality and classnessness, incorporating those tendencies which had once opposed the ruling class. In addition, capitalist economies had successfully provided material goods, which helped to secure the pacification of the working-class.

Sometimes attacked for pessimism, the early context of the School's work was a society in which mass communication had propagated fascist ideology, using cinema, radio, and stage-managed rallies. Believing the working-class to be naturally combative, these 'neo-Marxist' thinkers believed the media to be a manipulative tool. Despite their over-estimation of media influence (Marcuse referred to its 'hypnotic' power), the Frankfurt School made some important observations about the limits of freedom in modern societies. Its distinction between real and simulated contentment (the 'euphoria of unhappiness' is one description of modern life in a consumer society), anticipates both situationism and the more radical currents in *postmodernism*.

functionalism is a sociological approach to the study of communication and society which had a significant impact on American social theory. It is based on the notion that societies are cohesive systems. The various features of a society, including public communication, political traditions, public institutions, and so on, are understood as serving clear purposes within society as a whole. They contribute to the overall balance and well-being of the larger system. Anthony Giddens (see the second edition of 'Sociology', p. 711), writes that the purpose of studying the function of a social practice or institution is ... to analyse the contribution which that practice makes to the continuation of the society as a whole.' Influential American functionalists were Emile Durkheim and Talcott Parsons. Robert K. Merton, whose research in the late 1950s included studies of large scale industrial societies, modified the traditional structural functional perspective to take account of those factors which produced social conflict rather than cohesion. He noted that a practice which served a positive function for some, could very well have a negative effect on other groups, calling those social activities which threaten to de-stabilise society, 'dysfunctions'. Merton believed that traditional functionalism had wrongly applied to large societies, the lessons learned from the study of smaller, more closely-knit communities. Price (1996) writes that 'other shortcomings [of functionalism] include its attribution of 'purposes' to a society, and its relative lack of interest in the meanings that human actors give to the events in which they participate'. Hanno Hardt, in 'Critical Communication Studies' (p. 16), argues that the preoccupation with functionalism in the United States emerged from 'a Western utilitarian culture' which defines communication 'in terms of its effectiveness or efficiency.'

G

gaffer: an electrician working on a television or film set, usually the person in overall control of lighting.

galley: a shallow tray which holds type after it has been set. Also a word for the proofs of printed pages.

Gallup poll: a public opinion poll, associated with the American Institute of Public Opinion, set up by George Gallup in 1935.

game show: a television or radio programme devoted to a contest between individuals or teams; the term usually refers to shows where members of the public, supervised by a host, compete for prizes, though some game shows contain regular *celebrity* appearances. In 'TV Games: People as Performers', (see 'Television Mythologies', 1984, p. 42) Bill Lewis studies the spatial relationships set out in the studio, and claims that movement 'from the desk to another playing space' reinforces 'complex and powerful myths of social and educational mobility'! He thinks that game shows demonstrate 'the larger ideological of the mass media: persistently concealing social inequalities behind an unquestioning celebration of highly selective cultural and material values'.

gangs: organised groups which carry out activities on or beyond the threshold of legality; gangs may be 'territorial' (aiming to control a particular space), concerned with the monopolisation of a particular form of activity (illegal sale of drugs, for example), or preoccupied with a certain kind of lifestyle (expressed in consumption, appearance, etc.). In many cases they display all three attributes.

Research into gangs and youth 'cults' like mods and rockers in the sixties, football hooliganism in the seventies and eighties, and studies of motorcycle gangs, has labelled such groups are 'deviant,' in the sense that the gang or criminal association is thought to hold values which run counter to those valued by conventional society. According to the sociologists Shaw and McKay, however (in 'Sociology', Haralambous, 1990, p. 596), crime in low income areas is: ' ... one of the means employed by people to acquire ... the economic and social values generally idealised in our culture.'

Price ('Communication Studies', 1996) studies the *discourses* of Los Angeles gang members (p. 219); 'using one speech-genre, Scott [a gang member] is able to refer to his role as a 'community activist,' and makes a point of justifying the possession of weapons in political terms ... when Scott speaks of gangster activity, he uses military phrases to describe the drive-by shootings which he leads'.

Gangs often feature in media accounts of deviancy, leading to what some regard as a vicious circle in which deviance is amplified by media reports (see *amplification of deviance*).

gangster movie: a film genre which takes as its subject matter the social phenomenon of gangsterism. The first gangster film, according to Susan Hayward (see 'Key Concepts in Cinema Studies', 1996), was 'Fantomas', made by the French director Louis Feuillade in 1913/14. In America, the genre started to appear in the late 1920s, developing in the next decade into a powerful form. Dealing with conditions of life in the 1930s, gangster movies used as a backdrop the effects of prohibition (when the manufacture and sale of alcohol was forbidden by law) and the economic hardship brought about by the depression. Hayward writes (p. 146) 'gang warfare and criminal acts became part of the popular press's daily diet and soon became transferred to film'. Early successes included 'Little Caesar' (1930), 'The Public Enemy' (1931), and 'Scarface' (1932). By 1934, however, the Motion Picture Production Code acted against the portrayal of gangsterism in film, with the result that film-makers turned their attention to the adventures of plain-clothes police and private eyes.

gate: the total sum taken by the promoter of an event; the box-office takings, which depend on the number of people who attend an event like a film performance. The term comes from the physical entrance or 'gate' through which patrons enter to see an event.

gawkocracy: a slang term, used in America to refer to the television audience in general.

gazette: originally, a news-sheet or periodical (some believe it came from 'gazeta', a small Venetian coin).

gel: gel stands for 'gelatin', thin sheets of transparent material which may be dyed different colours and used in the lighting of theatre film and television productions.

gender: the social category based on behaviours thought appropriate to an individual's biological sex. Sex refers to the anatomical or biological differences, while gender refers to the psychological, social and cultural differences between men and women.

The distinction between sex and gender is the starting point for many critiques of representation in the mass media. If gender differences are socially constructed, and society itself is based on unequal relations of power, then we can see why many writers argue that mainstream representations will be biased against subordinate groups. Dominant ideology is supposedly used to keep the downtrodden in their place. Dines and Humez, in 'Gender, Race and Class in Media' (1995), take this position (p. 7); 'Ideologies of gender promote sexist representations of women ... ideologies make inequalities and subordination appear natural'.

The purpose of gender-based and especially *feminist research* into the media is to identify and attack those power structures which sustain patriarchy's financial and ideological dominance of culture. Research into media representation may include studies of male as well as female roles, but the majority of work has been carried on the role of women.

A book edited by Kath Davies ('Out of Focus', 1987) studied media representations of women, comparing these with how women perceived their own identities. Diana Meehan made a study of women's roles and actions in television (see 'Ladies of the Evening', 1983) which identified no fewer than ten different female roles.

In recent years, opposition to theories of gender-specific pleasure in the cinema (see *scopophilia* and *spectatorship)* has come from authors who argue that audiences can make identifications across gender boundaries.

general release is the national exhibition of a major film, through the simultaneous release of multiple copies to numerous locations.

generation: when an audio or video tape has been copied, each copy of the original tape is 'first generation'. If tapes are reproduced from the first set of copies, then they become 'second generation' tapes, and so on. Quality declines with each generation.

generation of meaning: the production of content in the communication process which has the potential to be understood. Meaning may be generated through symbolic forms, such as spoken and written language, or other more informal modes of communication (gesture, intonation, etc.).

generic forms: the major forms of mediated communication; television, newspapers, film, radio and so on.

genre: a specific type of film, radio, or television production. Examples of genres are action films, musicals, love stories, Westerns, etc. However, it is difficult to say where one genre begins and another ends, quite apart from the idea that some films are said to 're-define' their genre.

Stephen Neale, in his book 'Genre' (1980), proposed a solution. He thought that the best way to understand genre is to see it as a system of (p. 19) 'orientations, expectations and conventions' which circulate between 'industry, text and subject'. This means that an audience participates in the creation of genre, through expectations created through previous contact with similar texts.

geostationary: the position held by a satellite relative to the earth, if it travels through space at the same speed as a point on the earth's equator; because it revolves at the same speed, it appears in a fixed position above the earth.

geosynchronous: see *geostationary*.

German expressionism: a film style which followed the expressionist art movement; these artists were dedicated to conveying inner emotional states in dramatic and unusual forms. Its cinematic variant (existing between 1919 and 1931) was highly stylised, with unsettling camera angles, dramatic sets, and severe contrast in lighting effects. The narratives themselves were often nightmarish, with horror stories featuring in many of the tales. Famous expressionist films include 'The Cabinet of Dr. Caligari' (1919), 'Destiny' (1921), 'Dr. Mabuse, the Gambler' (1922) and 'Nosferatu' (1922). These films influenced the development of the film-noir style which became popular in France and America in the 1940s.

gestalt: an organised whole in which each element affects every other part. The psychologist Ehrenfels (1890) proposed the idea that some types of stimuli (shapes, for example), have a 'pattern quality' which creates something which becomes more than the sum of its parts. The example used in Gross' 'Psychology' (1992), is a square. A square is more than merely four lines, it has an 'emergent property' called 'squareness'.

Gestalt theory is found in psychology, where it is used in studies of perception and for certain types of therapy. The best known examples are the 'figure and ground' designs used to show how certain forms are reversible.

gesture: any significant movement made with a limb or part of the body; the deliberate use of movement to convey meaning, which can include facial expressions. Gestures have been studied since at least the seventeenth century, when Francis Bacon called them 'a kind of emblems'. Charles Darwin's 'The Expression of the

Emotions in Man and Animals' (1872) proposed the notion that physical expressions might be inherited. Although some psychologists believe they have identified a number of facial expressions which are universal (creating the same meaning across all cultures), modern studies of gesture have emphasised gesture as 'the product of social and cultural differences' (Keith Thomas in Bremmer and Roodenburg's 'A Cultural History of Gesture', 1991).

Some writers, notably those who write popular anthropology, use the term '*kinesics*' for the study of communicative gesture. However, body language is to a large degree ambiguous. It is often difficult to tell if there is a direct correlation between a particular stimulus and the observable outcome. Michael Argyle ('Bodily Communication', p. 294) gestures towards the importance of context in determining what deliberate bodily communication really signifies; '... to make the meaning of an ambiguous non-verbal signal clear the sequence of events and the structure of the situation needs to be shown'.

ghost writer: a writer whose contribution to a work is unacknowledged, and whose name does not appear on the finished product.

Glasgow University Media Group: the Glasgow Group set out to investigate British television news, and monitored every news bulletin broadcast over a six month period, between January and June 1975. The group's first publication (produced by eight authors) appeared in 1976, entitled 'Bad News'. It combined detailed quantitative analysis of industrial reporting, and mixed this with semiotic analysis of the cultural significance of news stories.

It produced many straightforward but significant findings which confirmed what had long been suspected; that the news was highly generic in content, showing a strong link between type of content and the duration of each item. Overall, the central thesis was that the news was biased in its treatment of trade unionism and the working class.

Further publications emerged from the Group, encompassing 'More Bad News', 'Really Bad News', and 'War and Peace News', which appeared in 1980, 1982, and 1985 respectively. The last of these volumes dealt with the Falklands War, the miners' strike of 1984–5, and the war in Northern Ireland. The Group proved both influential and controversial; most academics welcomed its work while news organisations were keen to defend their integrity.

In the later 1980s and 1990s, the work of the Group became largely topic-based, concentrating on news treatment of AIDS, industrial disputes, sexual violence, and Northern Ireland. In this period, research methods included quite creative approaches, using group discussion but also in some cases, the reconstruction of news items and the use of scriptwriting exercises, all designed to reveal the common themes and ideas which the media had helped to circulate.

glass shot: a camera shot taken through glass, on which a scene has been painted or titles written. (See also *matte.*)

global village: Marshall McLuhan's 1964 term which described the effect on the world of the increased speed and reach of communications technology; the human sphere of experience becomes global, and the global becomes intimately known. In McLuhan's words 'with electricity we extend our central nervous systems globally, instantly interrelating every human experience'. Thus he declared the 'new world of the global village' in which 'electric circuitry has overthrown the regime of time and space' (see 'Understanding Media', 1964). Although McLuhan has been criticised for over-emphasising the breakdown of more traditional forms of society, and failing to substantiate some of his claims, his concerns have anticipated many of the debates currently taken up by *postmodernism*.

globalisation: a worldwide socioeconomic process characterised by the increasing interpenetration of cultural and political forms, which some theorists maintain is leading to a 'global society'. Martin Shaw, writing in 'Global Society and International Relations' (1994) declares (p. 3) 'for the first time since human beings inhabited this earth, it is possible to describe comprehensive networks of social relationships which include all people'. In support of this view, Shaw identifies a global economy, elements of a global culture, and the possibility of co-ordinated political action.

Anthony Giddens ('Sociology', 1993, p. 528), writes that 'the world has become in important respects a single social system, as a result of growing ties of interdependence which now affect virtually everyone'. The growth of Western media, in terms of cultural influence, is another feature of this process.

Other commentators sound a note of caution, including the sociologist Paul Hirst, who believes that the nation-state is still an important factor and has not been assimilated by a global 'authority'. The view that Western culture is overwhelmingly powerful has been challenged by Liebes and Katz, whose 'The Export of Meaning' (1993) studied the reception of the American programme 'Dallas' in three different countries. They note that (ix) 'having begun with the problem of the authenticity of culture', they found themselves observing struggles between 'national cultures, cultures within a nation, and between the sexes within families'. In this study, globalisation does not appear to homogenise individual or sub-cultural response.

graffiti: the plural of the Italian word 'graffito', meaning a drawing or words scratched or otherwise inscribed on a wall. It has a long history – graffiti appears on the walls of the ruined city of Pompeii. It is often used as a form of political comment, appearing extensively on billboards. In addition, the 1970s and 80s saw the development of an illegal and artistic form of expression in many American cities. At first, simple 'tags' or names appeared, written in pen in public places, often accompanied by a number (which turned out to be the house number belonging to the person named). Gradually, graffiti tags became more elaborate, using special styles and using colour paint available in aerosol cans. While some practitioners concentrated on covering blank spaces in simple 'throws' (an outline of their tags), others began to develop style to such an extent that some of the best pieces were regarded as art. In some cases, a graffiti artist would abandon the hazardous practice of painting on the side of subway trains, and would turn instead to making canvases for sale in art galleries. True graffiti remains, however, an underground activity.

grammaticality: the condition of knowing what kind of sentences and utterances are grammatically correct.

graphic: an illustration or visual motif or device, which can be decorative (like an ornate border round a letter), informative (an iconic symbol on a lavatory door), or symbolic (in the sense of standing for something else, like the Christian cross).

grip: a studio worker in a production crew, whose responsibilities may cover the movement of dolly-mounted cameras, pulling cables, and general duties on set.

gross receipts: the total sum of money received by a distributor of films, before any subtractions for costs and overheads are made.

ground station: a station which receives television signals from a *satellite* and transmits them to subscribers.

group: a group is a number of persons classed as belonging together; if the group is identified from the standpoint of those belonging to it, it may be described as a human collective which recognises the distinctive qualities of its own criteria for membership, including a shared perception of aims and objectives, available roles, and certain codes which demonstrate conformity.

Group theory recognises divisions between large and small groups, between formal and informal groups, and also between groups which are joined voluntarily and those to which individuals belong without advance consent. The latter includes groups such as family and class. There are always difficulties in drawing boundaries between some of the sub-divisions (small, large, formal, informal, mentioned above).

When groups are actively chosen by individuals, they are selected for a variety of purposes which may vary widely; the drive to achieve forms of social solidarity, involvement in leisure activities, and so on.

Some studies describe the collectives to which people belong as 'in-groups' and 'out-groups'. An 'in-group' is the collective with which the subject identifies, while an 'out-group' is a body which possesses contrasting and supposedly less desirable characteristics. This leads to the notion of *social identification*, where active attachment to chosen groups depends partly on making a strong differentiation between the 'in-group' and those collectives seen as different.

McQuail (see 'Communication', 1975) describes the idea of belonging as follows; 'to belong to a social group, a society, a culture is to share a common denominator of frames of reference, significant objects, systems for describing the world and facilitating interaction with each other.' The question of who defines the criteria for group membership is of particular significance, because groups are often categorised by people or institutions which observe them from the outside.

group communication: this form of *communication* requires a collection of individuals who share some common attributes, goals or interests. Such individuals will interact within the context of the group, and will share (or at least display) common values or norms of behaviour.

Some argue that group communication exists only where participants are able to address one another face to face, which implies that there is a point at which group communication breaks down. It is possible, however, that forms of communication take place within wider social groups, which exist without requiring contact between individual members. All group communication must be founded on the following elements:

- a perception of the group's identity, broadly common to its members
- the ability to tell the difference between the group and its allies or rivals

- a knowledge of aims and objectives within the group, whether those aims are agreed or imposed
- participation in exchange using available codes and channels of communication
- the assumption of formal and informal roles.

group identification is the tendency of a group to describe itself in ways which contrast with other groups, or which resist or incorporate the descriptions assigned to it by 'outside' forces. Groups are not necessarily permanent, and are constituted by the need to achieve certain aims, so that identification can change as circumstances alter, giving rise to the use of sometimes quite contradictory positions. The need for each individual to identify him/herself in a reasonably positive way, is a social need, expressed as a wish to find something in common with groups thought desirable. The group need not be physically present, because close physical proximity is not required in the process of categorising the self.

Gutenberg: Johannes Gansfleisch zur Laden zum Gutenberg (1400–68) ranks with the earliest inventors of print, beginning his work in 1450. One of his great achievements was to print a Bible which, in the words of J.D. Bolter (see 'Communication in History', 1995), 'can hardly be distinguished from the work of a good scribe' because 'early printers tried to make their books identical to fine manuscripts', using the same thick letter forms and page layout. As *printing* evolved, letter-forms became thinner and layout changed so that more print could be seen on each page.

gutter: in newspapers, the space between pages in a centre spread, also used to describe the space between columns.

H

hacker: an individual who gains access to a computer system without authorisation and proceeds to read or otherwise use confidential files. In 1997, a schoolboy in Britain was charged with gaining entry to closed files, including some held by the United States Department of Defence. Although hackers do not always demonstrate political motives, reaction to their actions from official bodies illustrates how the 'secret state' guards its security.

halftone: a method of reproducing pictures by photographing them through a screen. The screen is made out of glass or plastic, and is covered with fine vertical and horizontal lines which cross one another at right angles. This breaks continuous-tone artwork into dots; the final image is composed of dots of various sizes and density, which can then be easily reproduced in a newspaper or magazine alongside text.

hand-held: any filming technique which relies on hand-held methods, rather than the use of a tripod, Steadicam system or other mechanical support. Hand-held shots are used to create a sense of realism in film and television, and were used in the 1980s and 90s in a number of US-based dramas. The much vaunted use of hand-held shots in the police series *Hill St. Blues,* was largely confined to the opening shots of the drama, while the shaky image associated with *NYPD Blue* was a deliberate technique used within the framework of a rather slick and mainstream production.

hanging indentation: a style of typesetting in which the first line of each paragraph is printed at full width, and the rest of the lines are indented on the left.

Hankey Committee: a 1943 committee charged with preparing plans for the development of television after the end of the Second World War. The report produced by Hankey characterised television as a medium of *actuality.*

hard disc/drive: a rigid computer disc that is either mounted in its own case, or permanently fixed inside a computer. A single hard disc has a storage capacity of several million characters, or *bytes* of information.

hard sell: this is usually thought of as a particularly aggressive or insistent form of advertising message, but was originally a description of advertising content; messages which contained a lot of information about the product (especially where that was 'scientific') were examples of 'hard sell', while more general modes which focussed on product image, were known as 'soft sell'.

hardware: the permanent stock of equipment used in TV stations, radio studios, computing facilities, etc., such as cameras, editing suites, consoles, microphones, computers and other material (contrasted with software, the data on video tape, computer discs, etc.).

Hays Code: a series of rules about screen violence and decency that was introduced in 1922 when an organisation called the Motion Picture Producers and Distributors of America (MPPDA) was founded. This body soon became known as the Hays Office, after its first president. The MPPDA, in lieu of direct government censorship, applied pressure to the motion picture industry to regulate its own affairs. However, certain forces on the American right, including the Legion of Decency, began to make increased demands on the MPPDA, with the result that by 1934 the Motion Picture Production Code had become mandatory. Watson and Hill ('A Dictionary of Media and Communication Studies', 1997) reveal that 'political as well as moral attitudes were subject to severe censorship. The Legion of Decency, for example, supported the Fascists in the Spanish Civil War and generally opposed any production with leftward leanings'. The code continued to operate until 1966.

HBO stands for Home Box Office, the first cable service in the United States to be offered by satellite. It provides films and sports coverage for its subscribers.

HDTV: high definition television, a system which offers enhanced picture quality to the consumer. What actually constitutes 'high definition' depends on when and where the term is used. It is first discovered in 1934, when the electronics company RCA mentioned the concept in its report. In 1936, the BBC began the first 'high definition' service, when television pictures were made up of 405 lines.

It was in 1968, however, that the modern notion of HDTV began to take shape. The Japanese company NHK began research, using projected 35 mm film as a guide to the quality desired. The recommendation eventually made was that 1125 lines should be used. The first experimental use of the system was undertaken in 1979. By 1989, NHK was offering a limited service, increased to an eight-hour daily broadcast two years later.

HDTV pictures are made up of as much as five times the amount of information required for a conventional TV picture, and so require a much greater bandwidth. In Japan, a standard was agreed; 1125/50 Hz Multiple Sub-Nyquist Encoding (MUSE), a bandwidth compression technique that allowed the signal to be carried by existing frequencies allocated to satellite services.

Attempts by Japanese industry to get their HDTV system adopted as the universal standard were rejected by European interests, on the grounds that the Japanese system was incompatible with that used in Europe. The real motivation lay in a marked reluctance to allow the Japanese to dominate another sector of the international electronics market. European research into HDTV was co-ordinated by the 'EUREKA' programme. Over three years, from 1986 to 1989, this body developed all the equipment necessary for high-definition television. It uses a 1250 line picture and a wide-screen 16:9 aspect ratio. In the United States, no fewer than five separate contenders lined up in 1990 to develop the new system.

In the meantime, because HDTV requires the use of satellite systems (they can carry the large bandwidths required), terrestrial broadcasters are unable to carry high definition television. In opposition to HDTV, some broadcasters are working on 'enhanced definition' TV. As a result, confusion about the competing systems has spread. Some companies in Britain, however, are building up a 'catalogue' of programmes shot in high definition, in Super 16 film, or on 35 mm stock, in anticipation of the growth of HDTV in the future. Powerful American–Japanese consortia are presently working to develop high definition technology.

headline: a heading set in large type, which appears above any important story in a newspaper. Headlines are not always simply informative, they often attempt to present a particular view of the news.

hegemony: from the Greek 'hegemon', meaning leader, comes hegemony or lead-ership; it was a term used by the Italian Marxist Antonio Gramsci, to describe the general dominance which one group or alliance exercises throughout society. How is dominance over subordinate groups achieved? Gramsci said that 'social hegemony and political government' ('Prison Notebooks', 1971, p. 12) is made up of 'the 'spon-taneous' consent given by the great masses of the population to the general direction imposed on social life' and 'the apparatus of state coercive power which 'legally' enforces discipline on those groups who do not 'consent' either actively or passively'.

How is consent achieved? Gramsci argues that it is caused (p. 12) by the 'prestige ... which the dominant group enjoys because of its position and function in the world of production'. In other words, it is built on recognition of productive (economic) power. The power of the dominant group impresses the subordinate ones; this could only happen if both sides shared certain values. The actual work of domination is car-ried out, not by the ruling individuals themselves, but by their 'deputies', that group known in society as 'intellectuals'.

For Gramsci, the condition known as hegemony comes about when a ruling group or class has managed to persuade other groups to accept its own cultural and moral values. Some modern writers add that hegemony is a form of domination which is made to appear both natural and legitimate, but Gramsci spent more energy on exploring the longterm preparation that was required to establish the 'moral' or cul-tural leadership he had in mind.

In using the concept hegemony, Gramsci was not simply analysing the ruling class, but trying to prepare the ground for a Communist hegemony. This required a patient 'war of position' which demanded (p. 238), 'enormous sacrifices by infinite masses of people'. During this struggle, the ruling groups would require 'an unprece-dented concentration of hegemony' and, as a result, not just more 'cultural' leadership (as many modern commentators suggest) but in Gramsci's words 'a more 'interventionist' government, which will take the offensive more openly against the oppositionists'.

heliography: Joseph Niepce's term for the type of photographic process he invent-ed in the early years of the nineteenth century, (from 'helios', the Greek for sun). The world's first permanent photograph is reputed to be one taken by Niepce in 1826. It shows a scene from his window at Gras in France, and required an exposure time of approximately eight hours, using a pewter plate (said to be about as light-sen-sitive as a stove-lid).

hermeneutics: from the Greek verb 'hermeneuein', meaning to explain or expound, or to make something clear, comes hermeneutics, a form of analysis which studies *texts*, actions, institutions and other spheres of human life. Hermeneutics began as a method of study during the Reformation when protestants challenged the interpretation of biblical scriptures. In the nineteenth century, Wilhelm Dilthey believed that cultural phenomena, such as texts, were 'objectified' expressions of life. Another major figure in this field was Martin Heidigger, who proposed the idea that human beings are able to interpret texts by anticipating the structure of the whole.

In hermeneutics, *textual analysis* tries to interpret both the structural meaning of a text and its reference or context. Its larger purpose is to understand the historical context and the human subjects whose actions and understandings cannot be separated from that context.

HICT project: the 'Household Uses of Information Technology project', set up by the Economic and Social Research Council. A number of media and other researchers (all at one time associated with the Centre for Research into Innovation, Culture and Technology at Brunel University), undertook a study into the uses of household media technologies. A central notion in the whole exercise was expressed in an early paper by Roger Silverstone and his colleagues, which used the concept of a household's 'moral economy'. The paper went on to explain 'we want this notion to refer to ... families' own way of working with the social, economic and technological opportunities which frame their world' (1989, p. 1–2). In a later essay, the authors argue that 'to understand the household as a moral economy ... is to understand the household as part of a transactional system, dynamically involved in the production and exchange of commodities and meanings. At stake is the capacity of the household ... to create and sustain its autonomy and identity ... as an economic, social, and cultural unit'. Technology is appropriated by the household and changes its character from commodity to domestic object, while the precise use and status of each object is a matter of negotiation and sometimes conflict.

hidden agenda: a concept which appears from time to time in studies of media and communication to describe the masked intentions that are supposed to lie behind a range of communication acts. Such acts may include interpersonal exchanges, mediated communication, or any event where true intentions are kept hidden.

hierarchy: a graded structure of authority within an organisation or social system. In communication and media research, the study of hierarchy throws light on how communication systems in *formal organisations* function, and helps to explain how relations of power are structured and maintained.

Many studies of organisational communication argue that 'the dominant factor in managerial relations ... is the existence of a power structure' (Rosemary Stewart, 'The Reality of Organisations', 1993, p. 95). Such structures govern the possible range of interaction, between all the employees of a company. The power structure is often not quite the same as the official organisational hierarchy, because it also includes groups and individuals who have achieved influence through informal means. Informal systems of *communication* always exist alongside formal structures.

high contrast lighting: in films, a form of lighting in which intermediate tones are missing, producing strong contrast between light and dark areas; used in film noir and other atmospheric genres like the thriller.

high definition television: see *HDTV*.

high fidelity: (also hi-fi) the faithful reproduction of sound within the complete range of human hearing. Used to distinguish products on the market which allow a full appreciation of recorded sound.

high resolution: a good quality graphics display on a computer, created by the use of a large number of pixels (the basic image-forming units) within the picture image.

hoaxes: the practice of placing false information with news organisations, for financial or other reasons. Hoaxes have been perpetrated on a number of organisations, including the 'Sunday Times' which published documents it had been told were Hitler's diaries.

Hollywood: once the centre of the US *studio system,* Hollywood remains an important centre of film production, though it now tends to commission independent companies and no longer maintains the same type of studio facilities.

Hollywood is noted for its use of what has been called 'classic narrative realism', a system which uses certain established film conventions to present narratives. In the past, Hollywood was noted for its skill in the production of particular genres. The musical, for example, was a particularly American form, beginning with 'The Broadway Melody' of 1929 (though music was used in the first sound film, 'The Jazz Singer' of 1926). Dance within the musical allowed the development of famous partnerships like Fred Astaire and Ginger Rogers, who first appeared in 1933 in 'Flying Down to Rio'.

Another notable feature of Hollywood was its *star* system, which ensured that public attention was drawn to a number of films which otherwise had little to commend them. The legacy of the star system is the star actor, who continues to command huge fees, though recently undercut by the use of *digital* stand-ins.

holography: the production of three-dimensional images which can then be viewed from different angles. Holographs are created using a laser beam. The beam is split, one part being directed to the object and then to photographic film, the other directly to the film. This creates an interference pattern which, when projected by a laser, produces the 3-D image.

Home Box Office: see *HBO.*

Home Service: from 1939 to 1967, the name of what is now BBC Radio Four.

house style: the style of copy, and therefore the whole character of writing, which is sustained across editions of the same magazine or journal or indeed across the whole output of a particular publisher.

human communication is meaningful *exchange* between human subjects which causes some change (intellectual, emotional, physical) in the participants. The problems which theories of human communication encounter are first, whether such exchange must always be face to face, second (growing from the first question) whether it qualifies as true communication if it is mediated by electronic means, third to what degree it requires the participants to use symbolic content and fourth, whether it must be *intentional* in all cases (see *intention).*

The first problem requires careful thought about proximity. If one person sends another a letter, and it reaches its destination and is then read and understood, all the conditions have been fulfilled except that no exchange has occurred. A written or other form of reply means a successful act of exchange has taken place. Immediate proximity is therefore not required.

In the second case, some forms of communication mediated by electronic means, remain examples of 'primary exchange'; a telephone conversation is one instance. Similarly, if an individual sends a message on a videotape to a friend, and it is seen by the recipient, then there is little difference between this and the example of the letter mentioned above. However, where an industry produces a film for general consumption by an audience, the communicative act is an example of 'secondary exchange'; the audience can make no direct 'reply' to the content of the film, but the message itself becomes (if the film-maker is lucky) diffused through culture in general.

The third issue, about the use of symbolic content, is answered by the fact that some forms of communication use 'informal systems' rather than established symbolic forms like written language. These systems, which some think act more directly on individuals than do symbols, are sometimes thought to include intonation and gesture.

human interest story: a newspaper story which focusses on an individual or individuals, and uses an emotional perspective in the hope of manufacturing empathy in a readership. Richard Keeble, clearly disapproving of this type of item, describes the human interest story as 'focusing on success, failures, tragedies, emotional/sexual histories of people [which] eliminates or marginalises more abstract and deeper cultural, economic, political, class-based factors'.

Hunt Committee: a committee set up in 1982 to examine the future of cable systems in Britain. The report, produced in six months, put little emphasis on regulation, favoured the creation of a number of cable channels, and encouraged the use of funding from advertising. Pay-per-view television was regarded as a threat to important sporting events, while cable services directed only at affluent suburban areas, were also disallowed.

hybridization: a theory that cultural forms are spread on a global basis, with the result that they interact with local cultures to produce a hybrid form.

hype: a word which gained currency at the end of the 1960s, as a noun meaning an exaggerated degree of publicity, and as a verb meaning the process of promoting any commodity beyond its intrinsic qualities, as in 'hype up'. The entertainment industry is known for the way that it builds up its commodities, from products to individual performers.

hyper-reality: a state of existence which typifies advanced societies, in which reproduction and *simulacra* seem more real than genuine objects. The sign refers, not directly to reality, but to other signs, so that human knowledge is no longer of the real, but of signs and their 'excessive' and overwhelming presence.

Baudrillard, among others, called this condition 'hyper-reality'. He identified three historical phases of simulation: the period which produces counterfeits, where the difference between original and copy is clear; the era of production, where the difference between labour and the object produced is obvious; and the modern era, where objects are perfectly reproduced, to the extent that the code is more important than the object. The social becomes 'absorbed', and it becomes 'impossible to ... prove the real... all hold-ups, hijacks and the like are now as it were simulations ... inscribed in advance in the decoding and orchestration rituals of the media' ('Simulations', 1983, p. 41–2).

hypersensitize: the process of increasing the emulsion speed of film, using chemicals, light or vapours.

hypodermic model: the term 'hypodermic' means something (usually a drug of some kind), which is introduced beneath the skin. A model is a either a theory about how a particular communication process works, or else a diagram expressing the same concept. The 'hypodermic model', is the notion that media messages are 'injected' into audiences, with direct effects upon the groups which receive the 'drug', but it was never proposed in exactly this form. That is to say, the writers associated with a view of the media as intrusive and powerful in its influences, did not use the term. 'Hypodermic' theory has been attributed to their perspective by other writers.

For example, Eldridge et al., writing in 'The Mass Media and Power in Modern Britain' (1997), claim that the *Frankfurt* school (p. 126) 'promoted a hypodermic model of media effects whereby media messages were directly absorbed into the hearts and minds of the people'. In the case of the Frankfurt group, it is worth noting that its members did witness the growth of a totalitarian state which used a combination of direct coercion, public rallies, and media forms like radio and film to promote obedience. In such a society, a theory of strong forms of mediated influence does not seem out of place.

In the postwar period, laboratory experiments carried out by Bandura, Ross and Ross in 1963 did search for direct effects, and seemed to take a lead from behaviourist principles; since that date, a number of public arguments have focussed on the degree to which direct effects can be created. The National Viewers' and Listeners' Association, a pressure group which once exerted some influence on British broadcasters, appeared to believe in the 'hypodermic' principle. Opposition has come from long-standing critics of such approaches, such as Martin Barker (see his work on 'video nasties', comics, and consult the book 'Ill Effects', 1996).

hypothesis: in media and communication research, a hypothesis is an idea or supposition to be investigated or tested. If, for instance, a researcher wants to investigate the representation of age in mainstream film, he or she might start with an idea about the way that age is portrayed, before in-depth study has taken place. This initial idea, which might have prompted the whole investigation, could be 'representations of age in mainstream film are limited to a number of restricted roles'. Hypotheses are useful if the investigator has a strong feeling about a particular topic, and wishes to investigate the soundness of that perception.

icon: in ordinary usage, an icon (from the Greek 'eikon') is an image, usually associated with paintings or statues of religious significance. On occasion, those film stars whose images have achieved widespread circulation, are referred to as movie 'icons'.

In *semiology*, however, an icon is one of three classes of *sign*. It is distinguished from the two other types (*index* and *symbol*) by the idea that it bears some close resemblance, either through its appearance or character, to the thing or 'object' it represents. So, for example, an icon could be a photograph, painting, map – or even a passage of music which imitates natural sounds.

The concept of the icon emerged from a system proposed by the American mathematician and philosopher Charles Sanders *Peirce* (1839–1914). The full impact of Peirce's work, however, has yet to be felt. Peirce placed all types of sign in a larger framework, made up of the sign (or 'representamen'), the object to which it refers (living things, ideas, actions and discourses), and the 'interpretant' (the effect produced on the human subject, which could be the creation of a more developed sign, or an equivalent to the original sign). Paul Cobley, in 'The Communication Theory Reader' (1996), argues that Peirce's work on semiology (or 'semiotics' in his case) must be seen in the context of his extensive work on phenomena in general.

iconography is the study of images, or sometimes the illustration of a book; in either case, not to be confused with *semiology*, the study of signs and their function.

iconoscope: a camera tube, developed by V.K. Zworykin in 1923, which uses a high-velocity electron beam.

idea: a mental conception about something, or a *representation* produced in the mind.

idealism is the doctrine that reality is a mental phenomenon, based on ideas. The more extreme form of idealism is the notion that matter exists only in the form of ideas in the mind.

ident: a shortened form of 'identity', it is used in the TV industry to refer to the image or logo used to identify specific programmes or channels, such as the symbols used on 'Top of the Pops' or the four circles identified with Channel Four.

identification is the idea that members of an audience (film, television, theatre and so on), strongly associate their own feelings or predicament with that of certain characters in the *narrative* being followed. The notion of identification is used in the debate about the supposedly negative effects of television and other media forms. *Social identification*, on the other hand, is a theory of how individuals establish their own *identity* through positive attachment to a variety of social groups.

identity: the concept of identity embraces the notion of an 'identical' state, where one thing is entirely the same as another. When used to refer to people, however, identity is the sense of self which each individual possesses. The contradiction between similarity and difference provides the ground upon which human identity is constructed. It is often said that each human subject is unique, yet at the same time a person's individuality is only evident where it is placed within the context of a wider group or community.

When identity is explained as a 'sense of self', the same challenge is encountered. If self is individuality, individuality in turn usually means the possession of a distinct set of attributes which mark out one person from another. However, as Williams notes in 'Keywords', 1976, p. 161, 'individual' originally meant 'indivisible' (unable to be divided) which suggested 'a necessary connection' between people. Williams argued that this definition seems paradoxical because the modern sense of 'individual' emphasises 'a distinction from others'.

identity (social construction): the social construction of identity (as opposed to the biological formation of an individual), occurs as the human subject forms relationships. Hogg and Abrams in 'Social Identifications' (1988), draw attention to the active construction of identity by individuals, emphasising the value they place on membership of certain groups. The positive sense of self-worth gained from such attachment is they argue (p. 7), 'very different from merely being designated as falling into one social category or another.'

Oakes, Haslam and Turner (in 'Stereotyping and Social Reality', 1994) investigate the way that group character is created through the interaction of individual and group identity, while Harre and Gillett, writing in 'The Discursive Mind', argue that, in order to have a sense of self, a human subject must also have a sense of place or 'location'. This is a sense of place in space and in time, together with an awareness of social location (constructed by age, ethnicity, class and so on). Finally, the individual must also be conscious of his or her status as a moral actor. *Postmodern* theories of identity, in contrast, advance the argument that identities have become fragmented, detached from established communities and established modes of life.

idiolect: a word for the personal form of dialect used by an individual (from the Greek 'idios' meaning 'own').

ideological belief: a belief which is shaped by an *ideology*. Not all beliefs can be described as 'ideological'. To qualify as an ideology, a belief must be more than a single idea. For example, the conviction that blood sports are wrong does not constitute an ideology, because it refers only to one aspect of lived experience. In fact, some writers believe that a number of more developed social concepts, like 'environmentalism', do not qualify as free-standing ideological formations. Slavoj Zizek, for example, writing in 'Mapping Ideology' (1994), believes that environmentalism may be conservative, socialist, liberal-capitalist, feminist and so on, depending on how the causes of environmental degradation are explained.

To be ideological, a belief must also have a significant impact on a society, which suggests that it should be recognised by substantial numbers of people as a distinct doctrine. Some beliefs, such as traditional conservatism, or authoritarian socialism, may have declined in strength, but are still identifiable as part of the legacy of organised ideas, and continue to appear in public debate. Finally, to be ideological, a belief must be related in some way to the use of power in society.

ideological state apparatus: (or ISA) a term used by *Althusser* in 1969 to describe those agencies and systems (such as state education) established party politics, the family and the media, which help shape public consciousness, ensuring that 'subordinate' groups accept the established social order.

Departing from the emphasis placed on the economic 'base' of society, Althusser decided that the political and ideological 'levels' of the social order had what he called 'relative autonomy'. In this model, the economy is still regarded as the major force in society, but it cannot reproduce all the conditions required for the smooth running of the system. For example, education is required both to train the workforce, and to get individuals to accept their role as workers (as opposed to managers or decision makers).

The social structure (what Althusser called the 'reproduction of the relations of production') is only partly maintained through ISAs. Besides ideological forms concerned with socialisation, the ruling class has the option of using the 'repressive state apparatuses' (the army, police and so on), which represent the threat of force.

It is clear that the various types of ideological apparatus are different in a number of respects. The family and the legal system, for example, have widely diverging aims and operate in different ways. The question of how 'authority' uses an ISA like the *media*, is a complex issue. The strength of an ideological apparatus is exactly its 'relative autonomy'.

ideology is the general framework of all those ideas and beliefs which offer a coherent, but incomplete, critique of 'things as they are'. Ideology in general is created by the modern preoccupation with the condition of society, and is characteristic of a world in which major structural changes require explanation.

An ideology (the singular case) is a specific example of organised belief, which is recognised both for its individuality, and for its importance in setting out an agenda for the public interpretation of acts, events, objects and social practices.

For example, socialism offers an explanation for the character of modern society, and a particular remedy for its ills. Feminism produces another view of social reality. Conservatism provides a yet different perspective. All three approaches make criticisms of the material conditions of life as they are experienced by members of a society. Each makes reference to recognisable aspects of our world, and each relies on offering some plausible explanations of social phenomena. An ideology must 'make sense' to large numbers of people, even if they do not accept all its precepts.

Ideology exists wherever *signs, discourses*, objects and representations, are used in an attempt to explain material reality. It is an 'incomplete' version of lived experience for three reasons: first, because society itself is made up of contradictions and controversies, secondly because it must work at an abstract level of description, and thirdly because the contest to establish meaning and influence leads to an emphasis on those features which might support a specific case, with the consequent neglect of other aspects of reality.

ideology (history): at the end of the eighteenth century, 'ideology' was used to describe the study of ideas in general. However, it soon came to mean a certain type of strongly held belief. In the nineteenth century, most descriptions of ideology treated it as a negative or undesirable conviction, held by individuals who were either fanatical or dangerous.

Karl Marx (1818–1883) used the term to indicate a form of belief which distorted the real conditions of life in a class society, and was used by the ruling class to maintain its dominant position in the social order. The traditional Marxist explanation of ideology is 'forms of consciousness' which determine the outlook of human beings. There is a difference, according to Marx, between the interests of people and the 'form in which these interests are experienced.' This approach to ideology concentrates on a split between ideas which influence people, and their 'true' interests (though these are always difficult to locate and describe).

The use of ideology continues to be split between a 'neutral' concept, describing the 'world-view' of a particular group or social class, and the 'negative' use, in which systems of belief are employed to deceive people. Jorge Larrain, in 'The Concept of Ideology' (1989), notes that there are significant failings in both positions.

In the first version (p. 118) when 'every point of view has an ideological character ... [ideology] ends up with very little meaning and loses its critical capability'. In the second case, 'ideology is confined to the conscious lies and illusions of political parties and groups', which Larrain feels ignores the fact that ideology also exists in the social structure itself.

idiot board: a term used in film and television to denote a cue card; the board carries the words due to be spoken by a performer.

illocutionary acts: an illocutionary act is that type of utterance which suggests some kind of real function within the context of public speech. Examples of illocutionary acts include issuing commands, asking questions, and making requests; the term therefore implies that the participants understand the 'rules' of the whole speech event. Illocution is a purposeful form of speech which essentially comments on phenomena. In 'The Communication Theory Reader' (1996), Paul Cobley uses a simple example to demonstrate the difference between a locution (a speech act which describes something) and an illocution (an utterance which performs an act). He notes that (p. 18) 'a traditional advertisement may describe a product (locution), whilst simultaneously exhorting the reader of the advertisement to buy the product (illocution).'

image: an image is a representation in visual form (photograph, painting, etc.) or alternatively a mental 'picture' of some part of human experience. The word has also come to mean a general impression (of a person, event, or object) which can be manufactured and then 'managed' (a politician's image is a useful example).

imagined communities: Benedict Anderson's term for the sense of national identity which is held by different groups of people. Dictionary definitions of nation usually emphasise the existence of a large community of people, of mainly common descent, history, culture, language, and so on, usually inhabiting a particular territory and under one government. Anderson however (in 'Imagined Communities', (1983)), describes the nation as 'an imagined community ... it is imagined because the members of even the smallest nation will never know most of their fellow-members, meet them, or even hear of them, yet in the minds of each lives the image of their communion'. He notes that, regardless of inequality, 'the nation is always conceived as a deep, horizontal comradeship'.

IMAX: an extremely large wide-screen film process, in which the 65 mm film stock is run horizontally through the camera. When printed, the film is transferred onto 70 mm stock for projection. IMAX is an integrated system, in which camera, projector and the huge screen (which can be from 45 to 70 feet high) are all designed to produce a spectacular cinematic experience.

The image itself occupies 60–120 degrees of the lateral, and 40–80 degrees of the vertical fields of human vision. By the mid-1990s, there were some ninety IMAX cinemas worldwide, including one established in Bradford's National Museum of Photography, Film and Television, in 1983. The type of subject selected for IMAX has varied, but all have been used to show off its visual impact; ballooning, mountaineering, space exploration, and the internal workings of the human body, were representative of the content shot for the early short features. A high proportion fell into the 'natural history' genre, while 'Blue Planet' of 1990 (shot from one of the space shuttles), graphically illustrated the Earth's ecological problems. A film called 'Fires of Kuwait', shot during the struggle to put out the burning oilfields after the Gulf War, was notable for the intensity of its images and for what some called its lack of political balance.

The problem of finding suitable subject matter is not unusual when the chief aim is to establish pioneering technology. The drawbacks of the IMAX system, and its successor, the *OMNIMAX*, lie in the conflict between the aesthetic qualities traditionally demanded by film-goers, and the danger that audiences will be overwhelmed by the scale of sound and image.

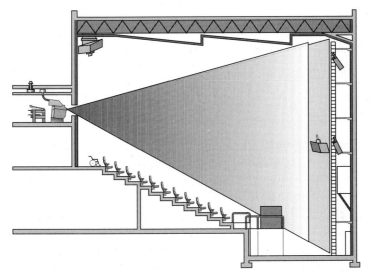

IMAX

immediacy: one of the 'news values' which supposedly motivate news organisations, immediacy is the idea that a story should be reported as soon as it 'breaks'.

immersion: a term which refers to the individual's absorption into the world of *virtual reality*, where their senses receive information which relates to the virtual and not the real world. With the use of realistic sound and increasingly convincing three-dimensional graphics, the power of immersion increases.

impartiality: the notion that broadcasters should be equitable in their treatment of established political parties and, by implication, that the most appropriate form of professional conduct is an even-handed approach to the representation of controversial events.

Philip Schlesinger's 1978 study of news, 'Putting Reality Together', was based on a study of the values and discourses found in the BBC's newsrooms. Schlesinger found that balance and objectivity were concepts which provided a framework for journalists' professional practice. Schlesinger argues that reliance on this idea reinforces the existing social order.

implicature: in conversation, implicature is a form of meaning which is conveyed through indirect or implicit methods. The linguist and philosopher Paul Grice (1975), noted how ordinary speech events often contain implied meanings. He argued that there is a 'co-operative principle' at work in conversation. This includes the following fundamental assumptions:

- that speakers will be truthful (the maxim of quality)
- that the participants in a conversation should provide the right quantity of information required during interaction
- that the information provided should be relevant
- that speakers will be clear in what they say to one another.

When a speech exchange appears not to fulfil these rules or 'maxims', we will probably assume that co-operation has taken place at some deeper level. For example, if one person asks another 'Shall we go out?', and is answered by the statement 'It's midnight', such a response may appear to be irrelevant. In fact, the statement could be entirely justified, if there is a good reason why midnight is a bad time to leave the house. Some critics have argued that some forms of speech depend, not on a co-operative but on an 'adversarial' principle. Others note that the main principle of co-operation can be reduced to the maxim 'be relevant'.

impression management: a term used by Erving Goffman in his book 'The Presentation of Self in Everyday Life' (1959). Impression management is a technique which withholds negative information about the self, and of highlights those positive characteristics which might make a favourable impact on others. Social roles therefore take on the aspect of public performances, so that individuals display a variety of skills in the drama that is social interaction.

imprint: a term which refers to a publisher's credit line on a book's title page and, by extension, the 'titles' or books which the company produces under one or more names. A publisher using several imprints is an example of *branding*.

impulse system: an American term for an interactive cable television system that allows a viewer to choose programmes by pressing buttons on a control panel.

in-camera editing is the shooting of material in the order in which it is to be viewed. In reality, few films are made this way, but in-camera editing makes the task of editing easier because the material is already in the correct sequence.

incorporation: a theory that 'oppositional' ideas can be incorporated into the capitalist system, and thus neutralised.

independent station: an America term for a television station which is either independent of the major networks, or which carries only a small proportion of network material (usually less than ten hours of network programmes per week).

Independent Television Commission (ITC): the successor to the Independent Broadcasting Authority, the ITC was set up by the 1990 Broadcasting Act and formally succeeded the IBA on January 1 1992. Responsible for the licensing and regulation of all commercial television in Britain, including that provided by cable and satellite, the ITC was to exercise 'a lighter touch' than the IBA. The ITC's first significant job was the selection of companies for the commercial franchises which were awarded in January 1993.

index: an index is a type of *sign* which relates to the thing it represents or indicates, through some direct or causal link. For example, the smell of cooking could be an index of food, just as the sight of swirling leaves is an index of high winds.

Index on Censorship: a bimonthly publication dedicated to analysing censorship of information by governments and other official bodies. Index on Censorship is produced by a non-profit-making organisation called Writers and Scholars International Ltd. In the November/December edition of 1994, which dealt with freedom of speech after the collapse of communism, the editor wrote 'memories are short, and getting shorter, in the world of the communications revolution ... a burning issue is the question of how nations, each with their own language, culture and set of national loyalties and priorities, manage to relate to one another'.

indexical sounds: natural sound is usually thought to be indexical (see Andrew Crissell, 'Understanding Radio'), because it is linked to real events in the world. Music, on the other hand, can be symbolic in the sense that it creates a more diffuse and emotional effect.

indexical terms: these are terms of reference (such as 'I', 'you', 'here' and 'tomorrow') which indicate the 'content or social force of an utterance' (Harré and Gillett, 'The Discursive Mind', 1994). They also indicate the speaker's place or 'location' as an actor in time and space. The meanings generated by indexical terms depend upon the context in which they are used. Referring to context, Harré and Gillett use the statement 'I can feel a draught'. The indexical 'I' in this case indicates the physical location of the speaker, but the statement only carries weight if the speaker is regarded as reliable. Thus, the 'social force' of a statement can also vary according to its relationship to the social location of the speaker.

indigenous sound: any sound which is not dubbed on to a soundtrack, but which comes naturally from the object being filmed or recorded.

indirect questionnaire: a form of research which contains 'disguised' questions. For example, if an investigation intends to discover a viewer's attitude to violence on television, and does not want to ask a 'leading question', an indirect question might be asked. In this case, the researcher may ask the respondent to talk in general terms about his/her experience of watching a genre known to contain representations of violence (thriller, police, western, etc.), so that the individual's attitude to such material can be assessed.

industry: an industry is a branch of trade or manufacture. The television industry, for example, is the system of production which employs groups of people to create television content. In addition, the concept of industry is often associated with mechanical or technological production. As a term, industry retains its earlier association with the idea of hard work or sustained effort.

inflection: the modulation of the human voice as it gives emphasis to certain parts of speech (used in Price to describe the ideological emphasis given to certain mediated messages). Grammatically it is the change in a word (usually its ending) to indicate variations in meaning (thus 'go', 'goes', 'going' show inflection).

infomercial: a slang term indicating a form of advertising prevalent in the USA, which concentrates on producing information about a particular product.

informal context: in political meetings, formal speeches may not be as effective for the transmission of ideological attitudes as informal contexts (such as conversations which follow official business). Michael Billig ('Ideology and Opinions', 1991) studied the activities of two branches of the Young Conservatives, and found a clear division between socialising and the necessary but 'dull' political activity required at election times. Billig offers a theory of the discursive formation of belief (p. 97): ' ...it is ... a matter of picking up Conservative habits in a Conservative environment. Slowly, common turns of speech, and thereby common turns of thought, are adopted, and the member drifts into Conservatism without having made a conscious political choice.' Such influences work within informal contexts.

informal meanings: meaning is often created through methods which are not particularly systematic or rule-bound. This includes gesture, dance, mime, music, visual and three-dimensional art, and especially intonation. All appear to create specific meaning in certain contexts.

information overload is the condition that exists when an individual or a group is presented with more data than can be processed; it is also sometimes applied to to a society as a whole.

information processing: the idea that a primary function of the human subject is a cognitive one - i.e. that incoming information is classified and sorted for use. The model of the human being as a processor of data has been criticised for suggesting a passive model of understanding. A turn has been made instead towards active models of cognition, in which the human subject does not simply process information, but concerns itself with 'explanation seeking' (see for example J.M. Moravcsik, 'Thought and Language', 1992).

information society: an economy which is driven by the acquisition and use of information, and which has a high proportion of its workforce dedicated to information processing rather than the production of goods. The term is usually used positively, to indicate a society which has achieved a high degree of technological advancement, but can also mean a society which has become dependent on the endless circulation of data.

information technology (or IT) is a term which is still current but which no longer expresses the excitement it once generated; information technology is the use of computers and telecommunications to process, store and disseminate a wide variety of information. More than this, IT became for a period a central concept (similar to the later 'buzzword' *digital*) in a technological *discourse* which some commentators believed disguised the true significance of global communications policy. Robins and Webster, for example, insisted that IT training and education 'tells us nothing about the emergence of a new international division of labour shaped by increasingly centralised corporate concerns' ('Information Technology: Social Issues', 1987, p. 154).

infra-red film: film capable of recording light rays in the shorter part of the infrared spectrum (700–1300), and which is invisible to the human eye.

in-house: those production facilities which are available within a company or an organisation; alternatively, material (a film, video, or other production) which is made by a company and then used as part of an internal training programme.

ink jet printer: see *jet printer*.

innateness: the idea human organism is 'programmed to speak.' Noam *Chomsky* believed that the 'striking uniformity' of the grammars found throughout the world, and the fact that it was unlikely that humans would ever be able to acquire all the complexities of speech from experience, were evidence of (Aspects of the Theory of Syntax, 1965); 'the general character of one's capacity to acquire knowledge.'

inoculation effect: the idea that a potential customer for a product may be forewarned and, as a result, become less susceptible to advertising and other forms of persuasive message.

input: in computing, information that is fed into a computer.

insert: in film and video work, an insert is the post-production addition of a shot to a particular scene. The principle of 'insert *editing*' is that new visual or auditory material is placed on an existing control track.

Institute of Journalists: one of the two trade unions which journalists may join (the other is the *National Union of Journalists*).

institution this is an established form of social organisation involved in some form of public activity, and which has therefore a recognisable public character. The BBC for example, is not just a television and radio facility located in a set of buildings; it exists within a set of public relationships. An institution is therefore formed by the relations of regulation, production, distribution and consumption which exist between official government bodies, industries, audiences and the artefacts and texts which form the currency of exchange. Manuel Alvarado, in 'Learning the Media', gives a list of seven 'institutional determinants', which shape the media institution: finance, production practices, technology, legislation, circulation, audience construction and audience use. Denis McQuail, writing in 'Mass Communication Theory', provides a description of the typical media institution:

- it is concerned with the production and distribution of 'knowledge' in the form of information, artefacts, and ideas
- it provides channels of communication which allow groups of people to communicate
- it operates in the public sphere and produces messages which have some public significance
- participation in the media is largely voluntary
- it is linked to the market and the industry through its dependence on technology and finance

- it has no formal power of its own, but is linked to state power, through legal mechanisms and 'legitimating ideas'. (See *legitimation*.)

instrumental communication: the use of *communication* in order to achieve or obtain something. In every deliberate act of communication, the person or persons involved in creating the 'message' will have some aim in mind. This may be intended to benefit the communicator, or may be an attempt to achieve wider social benefits. Forms of the instrumental mode include *'affective'* and 'informative' communication.

integrated circuit: a circuit made up of inter-connected semiconductors, placed on a silicon chip.

integration is the incorporation of ideas and/or behaviours into the social system; alternatively, the integration of radical groups into mainstream political life.

Intelsat: established in 1964, Intelsat stands for the International Telecommunications Satellite Organisation. It operates a worldwide satellite system, and has members from some seventy countries.

intensity is a term used to describe the concentrated attention that some news stories receive. Also refers to the strength of a light source as it relates to the amount of illumination shed on the subject.

intention: deliberate purpose, held in advance of a *communication* act or formed/re-formed in the course of exchange. One of the questions faced in studies of communication, is whether or not it must be intentional in all cases.

Can communication be said to take place if a person does not intend to communicate? Clearly, if a person X appears to communicate something without intending to (for example, casting a look at another person, Y), it may be that Y will think they are in receipt of some kind of information, but Y cannot be sure what the involuntary act really means. Is the look reproach, affection, the desire to silence the recipient? There is no definite meaning, and therefore no real exchange is possible until more information has been obtained. Burgoon and his co-authors (see 'Human Communication', 1994, p. 21) call an event which carries no intention but is interpreted as an attempt to communicate, a case of 'ascribed communication'. An attempt to communicate which goes unrecognised as such is 'attempted communication', while only a deliberate act of communication and a deliberate recognition and reply, is considered to be a true case of communication. Where no intention and no perception of intention takes place, Burgoon *et al.* call this 'behaviour'.

Coulthard ('An Introduction to Discourse Analysis', 1985) writes (p. 20) 'there is no real need to concern oneself with the speaker's intention because interaction proceeds according to the listener's interpretation of the force of an utterance'.

interaction: the action and reaction between individuals which becomes an exchange. Interaction between human subjects is achieved through the use of language and its supporting systems, such as *body language* and *intonation*. Analysis of human interaction takes various forms. One tradition, popular in many American colleges, is largely behavioural in spirit and has a strongly 'therapeutic' purpose (see for example Patton and Giffin's 'Interpersonal Communication in Action', 1981). It does not examine real speech events. Another approach has grown from the 'symbolic *interactionism*' of the American sociologist George Herbert Mead (1863–1931), which emphasised the active and creative aspects of human behaviour.

Interaction is also used to refer to the 'new' multi-media forms which allow greater manipulation of computer programmes. True interaction remains a property of human communication, but the term has achieved currency in the computing industry. Computer interaction has achieved greater success with computer games than in the educational uses first proposed by software manufacturers.

interactionism: or '*symbolic interactionism*' (so called because language is a symbolic form), emerged from work done by George Herbert Mead (1863–1931), a US philosopher and sociologist. Mead placed language at the centre of *human communication*, believing that it allows individuals to become aware of their own individuality. The use of symbols means that human beings are freed from the limits of personal and immediate experience.

Mead and his pupil Herbert Blumer, saw *interaction* (in Blumer's words) as 'the collective and concerted actions of individuals seeking to meet their life situations'. Thus, symbolic interactionism studies the human perspective on events, valuing 'the active, creative components of human behaviour'. Anthony Giddens, ('Sociology', p. 718) notes that this is different from those approaches which stress 'the constraining nature of social influences on our actions'. According to symbolic interactionism, communication enables individuals to gain an objective view of their own personality and social role. In sending messages, the individual is engaged in an act of social reinforcement.

interactive technology: technology which presents information in a form that mimics a dialogue with the user. An operator can modify or terminate a programme and receive responses from the system for the purposes of guidance.

interactive television: a television system that is capable of providing a form of electronic 'interaction', using a computer and a modem. The prime examples are the 'home shopping' services available in the USA. Another use of such technology is the 'instant referendum' or opinion poll, carried out as the audience at home watches a programme with a political content.

interactivity: the facility which some branches of technology offer users; consequently users' experience of 'interaction' with software, through the modification of data or the alteration of the flow of a program.

Interception of Communications Act: an Act passed in 1985 which makes the 'intentional interception' of electronic communication an offence punishable by a maximum of two years in prison and a £2000 fine. Government interception of communication is exempt, provided a warrant is obtained beforehand. The state thus continues to collect information obtained through phone-tapping and electronic surveillance, with little legal restraint on its activities.

interface: the meeting point of a computer and an external entity, such as an operator or a piece of software.

interior monologue: in film, the use of an aside or a direct address to camera, made by a character on-screen and intended to be heard by the film's audience.

interleaving: in CD-I, a technique for inserting one part of a program into another, so that delays in processing can be overcome by switching to the clear program.

internal processes: arising from the idea that '*intrapersonal communication* is an invalid category and should be replaced with the term 'internal processes'. The theory of the intrapersonal depends on accepting the idea of a 'dual' self, in which the 'core' self and the self which supposedly reflects on this core, are able to communicate.

Arguing that self-awareness is not the same as communicating with oneself, because communication requires an exchange of meaning between distinct individuals, Price ('Communication Studies', Ch. 2) notes that the weakness of the 'split' self theory 'is shown by the fact that the 'core' self never answers the 'reflective' self'.

internal symbolisation: a psychological theory of *representation*, which states that individuals 'internalise' symbols which stand for real experiences. 'Internal symbolisation' proposes the existence of a mental 'fund' of images and symbols. According to this theory, people use these symbols when they wish to refer to real phenomena.

International Broadcasting Society: founded in 1985, this organisation was established in Scandinavia. Its purpose is to promote broadcasting co-operation between more and less industrially developed nations.

International Broadcasting Trust: a British educational trust formed in 1982, with the intention of raising the profile of less developed nations, and the relationship between such countries and Britain. The Trust produces programmes designed to educate the population, and is composed of about sixty member organisations, including voluntary bodies and official groups.

Internet: the network of linked computer systems which provides users with access to information, images, sounds and so on. The Internet developed from the ARPANet, a military project used to exchange research information, which was set up in 1969. By the mid-1990s, the Internet had over 30 million users, and was growing at the rate of some one million per month. Steve Rimmer, in 'Planet Internet' (1995), claims that 'the Internet is something of a leaderless planet ... the Internet backbone is really a sort of dedicated telephone system for computers'. Computers connected to the Internet can put items onto the system, without encountering censorship. 'Newsgroups', dealing with a variety of subjects, allow users to leave messages and respond to the queries and replies of others. Electronic mail or 'e-mail' provides a fast service for messages from anywhere on the net, though e-mail is not a particularly private method of communication.

Lack of censorship encourages both freedom of expression and the production of explicit material, some of which has prompted newspaper campaigns against pornography on the Internet. Some commentators fear that attempts to police the system are actually directed against its democratic (perhaps anarchic) structure, rather than ultimately against the more offensive and puerile content which some users produce.

interpellation: interpellation is the social process through which individual human subjects have their place (or *social location*) confirmed by the 'symbolic order' (language in its various forms). The term was used by Louis *Althusser* (1918–1990) to express the idea that individuals cannot exist outside what he saw as the all-encompassing power of *ideology*.

Althusser shows how interpellation works in practice, by using the example of an individual who is 'hailed' by a police officer; the subject is challenged by the shout 'Hey you!' The individual who is thus addressed, recognises that he/she is 'called to order' and therefore effectively admits recognition of his/her *subjection* to authority.

This is a useful insight into the power of language, though there is no guarantee that this model of response will always apply in a similar situation. Interpellation could be described as a specialised mode of *address*, which attempts to reinforce a relationship based on inequality of power.

interpersonal communication: a form of *communication* which occurs when two people are engaged in some form of exchange. Some commentators believe that true interpersonal communication can only occur when the participants are in close physical proximity. Others think that one-to-one interaction mediated by some form of electronic link, also meets the criteria of the interpersonal. Interpersonal communication includes the following elements:

- mutual recognition of the participants
- reciprocal exchange using established codes
- awareness of physical and social context
- use of both personal and social roles
- some change of state, whether physical, intellectual, or emotional.

interpretant: according to *Peirce*, the interpretant is a phenomenon produced by a *sign*; it is usually, but not always, a mental concept. The original sign produces an equivalent or even a more 'developed' sign in the mind of an individual. Therefore, we could say that a sign leads to an interpretant, which leads in turn to a new sign. However, not all interpretants simply lead to another set of signs.

There are three types of interpretant. The 'immediate' interpretant, is that which carries a whole range of potential meanings; it is the sum total of the effect that the sign might be expected to produce. The second type is 'dynamic', a direct effect actually produced by the sign on a real individual. The third form of interpretant is called 'final', in which Peirce moves towards the possibility of action. This last stage is that which is achieved if a sign is allowed to work out its full potential.

interpretation: the process of discovering meanings in texts, events, objects, artefacts and so on. Interpretation will depend partly on subjective factors like experience, belief, and so on.

intersatellite link: the transmission and reception of signals between satellites.

intersubjectivity: a term used by Fiske in 'Key Concepts in Communication' (1994), to describe the range of individual responses produced by cultural artefacts (photographs, films, etc.). These responses are subjective but are shared by other individuals from the same culture, who respond to the same connotations. Therefore, such responses are 'intersubjective'.

Fiske maintains, however, that some individual responses will not be shared (p. 157); 'my subjective experience of sentimentality may be unique to me, but the connotation of the photograph will be shared by other members of my culture'. It is not clear why the experience of sentimentality should remain beyond the reach of intersubjectivity.

intertextuality: the relationship suggested by texts which share recognisably similar content, form, or style. Intertextuality is sometimes produced deliberately, in order to create references which an audience will recognise. A film, for example, may contain a sequence in which the central character escapes from jail. In an attempt to capture the same style, an advertisement may well reproduce a similar scene, this time perhaps with the product as the 'magical agent' which helps free the prisoner. In turn, a news report might carry a story about a prison break out which has been foiled (it is not unusual for such events to be compared, during the news items themselves, to fictional narratives dealing with the same subject). What is the effect of the connections made by an audience, between these three cases? Are they likely to treat the different texts as carrying different messages, or will some aspects of each piece colour the way the others are seen?

intertitles: printed titles used in the body of a film; such titles occupy the space a number of shots would have taken, rather than appearing as an additional element somewhere in the frame. Intertitles were used in early cinema, but also crop up in certain modern contexts. The popular US comedy 'Frasier' uses them.

interviews: a research method which tries to obtain primary data through structured or unstructured interaction between a researcher and an individual or individuals relevant to the study being undertaken. Interviews are used in a variety of settings and contexts. They may be conducted on a one-to-one basis in laboratory conditions, as group interviews in a 'neutral' setting, under informal conditions in the subjects' homes, or in any number of combinations. The purpose of the interview may be open or concealed, but it is usually organised in one of three ways:

- structured, where the order and wording of questions have been pre-determined and each respondent is asked identical questions in the same order
- focused, in which the questions concentrate on specific issues but the interviewer is permitted to phrase the question in whatever way he/she thinks fit
- unstructured or 'discovery' interviews, in which the researcher engages in conversation with the subject and then pursues interesting points as they occur.

Interviews have been used extensively in many media and communication research projects, often combined with *ethnographic* studies based on close observation of the subjects concerned. Shaun Moores ('Satellite Television and Everyday Life', 1996) believes that (p. 31) 'it is possible – even on the basis of our one-off conversational interviews conducted in domestic settings – to identify key patterns of meaning and power in families or households, and to open up a series of issues concerning the interpretations and experiences of media consumers'.

intonation: the modulation of the voice. Intonation is used to provide clues to the meanings that a speaker wishes his/her listeners to appreciate. There is a difference, for example, between the intonation used when someone is sincere in offering another person praise, and that employed when their actual intention is to be sarcastic.

intrapersonal processing: although some commentators, notably G.H. Mead in 1934, identify a concept known as '*intrapersonal communication*' (that which occurs within and with the self), other writers cast doubt on the communicative status of internal self-reflection. The activities which take place within the individual (*cognition, perception, memory, emotional* responses and so on), are never exclusively 'internal'; each emerges from interaction with the natural and social environments. The notion of intrapersonal communication depends on the theory of a 'split self', in which there is a difference between the 'knowing' reflective self and the self that is known.

Gilbert Ryle, in 'The Concept of Mind' (1973), accepts that the mind has the ability to look back on events and thoughts, but argues that this 'self-checking' is part of the usual mental process and not something which happens outside it. In support of this argument, Ryle identifies those mental states such as panic which, while in progress, do not allow any form of retrospective thought. Harre and Gillett, in 'The Discursive Mind' (1994), also object to the notion of 'an inner entity'. They prefer the idea that the mind is composed of the *discourses* that people encounter in their daily existence (see *location*).

Features of intrapersonal processing include the following:

- perception
- values, attitudes and beliefs
- cognitive and reflective thought processes
- emotional responses
- subjectivity and self-concept
- the creation and interpretation of meaning.

invitation and acceptance: one of the three structures, identified by William Labov in 1970, which occur during conversation. Each participant in a conversation uses forms of words which invite a response from others, while acceptance is the process of taking up such invitations.

ISA: see *ideological state apparatus.*

ISBN: International Standard Book Number, which should appear on all published books.

issues: those areas of contention or debate which arise throughout a social system. In media and communication studies certain issues remain permanently on the agenda, shared perhaps with other academic fields. Public debate, sometimes orchestrated by the media, raises many of the same questions, though often in a different form.

Examples of issues which are common to academic and public interest, include violence in the media, censorship, bias in the press, and the question of monopoly ownership.

IT: see *information technology*

ITC: see *Independent Television Commision.*

ITT: International Telephone and Telegraph Company.

J

jargon: 'specialised' forms of speech, designed either to meet some particular technical challenge (sociological terminology, or the description of new technologies, for example), or to signify the condition of belonging to a particular group (occupational, sub-cultural, leisure and so on). (See also *argot, slang.*)

Jensen: Klaus Bruhn Jensen, a communication theorist working in Copenhagen who produced 'The Social Semiotics of Mass Communication' in 1995, representing a turn to the pragmatism of C.S. *Peirce.* Jensen argues against the rather abstract *semiology* of *Saussure,* and for an approach which sees 'representation of the world through signs as merely one form of social action' (p. 11). His attitude to *postmodernism* may be summarised in his argument that 'no social structure of some complexity could exist without procedures for ending language games ... and initiating collective action'.

jet printer: a printer that sprays ink from jet nozzles onto the paper, to produce high quality documents. Ink droplets are guided to either the paper or a gutter, where they can be recycled for later use.

journal: any publication which appears on a periodical basis. The word comes from 'diurnal', occupying one day (and so is also used as an alternative for 'diary').

journalism: an occupation devoted to writing for newspapers, magazines, television, radio and other outlets. Journalism is an activity conducted in the public sphere, but which is governed by widely divergent models of conduct.

In news journalism the major split is between concepts of 'social responsibility' and the pursuit of the sensational. Although serious journalism is associated with broadsheet newspapers and 'flagship' television news bulletins, and low standards of journalism are automatically ascribed to the tabloid press, the reality is more complex. There is a clear difference between a populist approach and sub-standard journalism. Also, a number of practices are shared between different outlets; the main evening news on both BBC and ITN, for example, uses the 'headline' approach, emphasising significant items before full reports are given.

None of this is to deny the existence of irresponsible journalism. Popular and even 'sensational' material is one thing, lies and distortion quite another. The reputation of 'The Sun' in the 1970 and 80s is often cited as a case in point. Linda Malvern, in 1986, thought that 'The Sun' was to poison the world of Fleet Street journalism ... to compete in the circulation war, other popular papers changed their image' ('The End of the Street', p. 56). Despite some examples of successful humour, the paper was attacked for its attitude to black people, the gay community, women, and anything vaguely left of centre. 'The Sun' was, however, always known as a 'subs' paper', not a 'journalist's paper'; that is to say, the paper was written by sub-editors who reshaped journalist's work to suit a specific *house style.*

The usual description of journalistic activity, is expressed through the idea of news gathering. This suggests that news simply happens, so that journalists have only to collect material from their sources and put it into some kind of order. For example, many reporters talk about 'finding' stories. A different approach argues that all news is based on selection. The media writer Greg Philo (see Roger Fowler's book, 'Language in the News') believes that: 'news is not "found" or even "gathered" so much as made. It is a creation of a journalistic process.'

Some writers, starting with G.H. Mead in 1926 and going on to include John Langer in 1992, complain about the way that journalism produces 'stories' rather than 'information', arguing that the search for the facts always takes second place in the hunt for a good story. It is worth remembering that the *narrative* form is an essential method for the representation of human experience, so it is hardly surprising that information should be presented in this way.

News journalists rely on various sources for their information. A source is an individual *contact*, or a professional body which provides the journalist with statements, facts, or opinions. News sources may include news agencies, professional organisations, politicians, other media such as the press, and single issue groups such as environmental organisations. Richard Keeble, writing in 'The Newspapers Handbook', notes that 'media research suggests journalists use a remarkably limited range of sources'.

journo: a slang term for a journalist.

jump-cut: a cut which occurs within a scene, though the definition also includes very sudden cuts between scenes; when used with disregard to temporal continuity, jump-cuts disrupt the conventional practice of continuity editing. Narrative realism uses jump-cuts to remove 'dead time' from a scene, but disguises the fact by interweaving other minor shots. Some avant-garde directors, however, make the jump-cut a purposeful device, sometimes in order to alienate an audience. The American series 'Homicide: life on the street' used jump-cuts to keep the attention of the viewer, and to keep pace of the narrative moving at speed.

justification is the process of typesetting or otherwise arranging type so that all lines are of the same length and lie inside the same boundary or margin.

juxtaposition is the use of contrasting shots in order to produce a *narrative* structure which works through a process of comparison.

K

key light: the principal source of light on a film set, the key light is set above the action at about 45 degrees from the subject. In high key lighting, most of the light for a scene is provided by the key, but in low key lighting, much less illumination is supplied by this source, and more by other lights.

keyword: a word which provides the essential clue to meaning in a sentence, essay title, speech, and so on. A keyword is an operational word.

kinesics: the study of *communication* through *gesture* and *body language*, in the belief that certain movements will reveal mental attitudes or emotions. While some body language does indeed seem to provide strong clues to a person's attitude, attempts to found the study on a formal basis have not succeeded. Keith Thomas ('A Cultural History of Gesture'), believes that (p. 4) 'gestures tend to be polysemous [see *polysemy*] and their meaning can be determined only by the context'.

kinetoscope: a type of projector invented in 1887 by Thomas Edison and William Dickson. It was shaped like a cabinet and was designed for one viewer at at time. About twelve metres of film was joined in a loop and ran through a series of spools; the celluloid passed over an electric light. The viewer observed the moving pictures (a blacksmith at work, wrestlers performing, humorous stories, etc.) through a magnifying glass placed at the top of the machine. Edison and Dickson opened 'kinetoscope parlours' (rather like amusement arcades) in the early 1890s. Spectators paid to see the contents of six machines, which were switched on by attendants. However, Edison soon dispensed with the services of many such employees by using slot machines to accept the payment. For a while, the two inventors resisted the growth of public film shows (popularised by the *Lumières)* but soon realised the increased commercial advantage of large-scale performances. The kinetoscope had, however, pioneered the use of 35 mm film stock, which is still the standard size of film.

knock down is an American expression meaning to reduce the length of a news story.

Kristeva, Julia: a feminist theorist (b. 1941) whose research began with the study of *language* and *subjectivity*. Familiar with the work of Roland Barthes (she attended his lectures as a student), Kristeva spent the late 1960s interpreting the work of Michael Bakhtin. Unimpressed by formal approaches to language, she began work on the concept of 'semanalysis' which focuses on the materiality of sound and rhythm in speech. Poetic language in particular seemed to represent the unconscious dimension of human experience; Kristeva saw it as a disruptive force within traditional linguistics (and therefore very much a positive influence). Children's *aquisition* of language prompted further research, while the non-linguistic forms used by infants (cries, singing etc.), suggested to Kristeva links to the approach used in avant garde poetry. She opposed the idea of a fixed human subject, developing instead a theory of a 'subject in process'. Turning to the psychoanalytical methods of Lacan, Kristeva published works on a range of subjects, such as love, depression and melancholy. All her work, however, is centrally concerned with the human subject.

Kuleshov effect: Kuleshov was a Soviet film-director who produced an important effect through the *juxtaposition* or *montage* of shots. Producing narratives in a workshop after the Russian revolution, Kuleshov (whose pupils included Pudovkin and Eisenstein) took three identical shots of the actor Moszhukin and intercut each with shots of a plate of soup, a little girl, and a woman lying in a coffin. According to Pudovkin, the experiment succeeded in showing how juxtaposition can create meaning. Audiences appeared to find in Moszhukin the expression, respectively, of hunger, affection, and sadness. Kuleshov, unable to get enough film-stock to support his group's projects, often had to work with films made by others, and created narratives by making montages from different sources.

The Kuleshov experiment

L

language: that knowledge held by native speakers which, combined with the use of expressive faculties, enables them to communicate in spoken and written forms. All natural languages have three components, studied under these headings: phonology (the sound system of language), *syntax* (the rules of sentence formation), and *semantics* (the system of meanings).

Language is studied for a variety of purposes. One of the basic distinctions made by linguists is between the underlying structure of language and everyday speech. *Saussure* and *Chomsky* provided two notable examples. Saussure distinguished between langue (system) and parole (individual speech acts). Chomsky divided competence (knowledge of language) from performance (use of language in concrete situations). The functions of language include the following:

- referential, statements (true or false) which refer to things in the world
- ideational, the communication of ideas
- regulatory, statements which set conditions for the performance of acts
- aesthetic, showing consciousness of the form and quality of utterance itself, connected to poetry
- emotive, language use which is directly connected to emotional response to events
- phatic, ritualised exchanges used to facilitate communication and reinforce social norms
- metalinguistic, where language is used to reflect on its own structures and meanings.

language (power): the study of the capacity or *power* of language (what it can and cannot do). The study of power in language is not solely concerned with the utterances made by powerful individuals, or the 'types' of language which are considered to have powerful effects ('the language of power'). The study of power and language should really be concerned with how the structures and use of linguistic expression allow various individuals, groups and classes to organise social existence. Foucault noted that 'the prohibitions' surrounding language revealed 'its links with desire and power' (see Crowley, 'The Politics of Discourse', p. 1).

language/thought debate: this debate concerns a number of issues: which of the two phenomena is the 'dominant partner' in the human individual; how people actually process language; and how adequately language represents thought. Some linguists argue that thought is dependent upon, or caused by language; see for example the theory of *linguistic relativity*. Others believe that language is dependent upon the level of cognitive development achieved by an individual; this means that, without an advanced capability for rational thought, language will not develop.

Those who see language as dominant or primary argue that it sets limits on what it is possible to think. Edward Sapir, a linguistic relativist, thought that a community's 'language habits' predispose individuals to make certain choices of interpretation.

Fiedler and Semin (in 'Language, Interaction and Social Cognition', p. 79), insist that, 'many psychological phenomena which are usually conceived as cognitive, motivational or emotional processes ... are permanently installed in language as an autonomous system above and beyond the individual.' Yet another point of view is found in the work of Vygotsky who argued that speech and practical activity were two entirely separate modes of behaviour, coming together at about the age of two years to produce language.

Taking a broadly Chomskyan position, Stephen Pinker ('The Language Instinct') breaks away from what can be a frustrating dispute, by arguing that the 'representations underlying thinking' and 'the sentences in a language' are simply not the same. He believes that mental processes are different to language (p. 81); 'people do not think in English or Chinese or Apache; they think in a language of thought.'

This 'language of thought' is called 'mentalese'. (For further but quite advanced reading see J.M. Moravcsik 'Thought and Language', 1990).

langue: langue is *Saussure's* term for the system of rules (or 'differences') underlying speech. Saussure kept langue (language as a structure) separate from 'parole', the infinitely variable speech of individuals. Saussure wrote 'in separating language from speaking we are at the same time separating: 1) what is social from what is individual; and 2) what is essential from what is accessory and more or less accidental. Language is not a function of the speaker; it is a product that is passively assimilated by the individual'.(See 'The Object of Linguistics' in 'The Communication Theory Reader', ed. Cobley, 1996, p. 43)

John Sturrock explains (p. 8) that 'langue is the term Saussure gives to the 'system' or totality of language stored in the collective consciousness. If langue is structure, then parole is an event.'

laser: a light source that sends out concentrated synchronous, monochromatic light, and which has a number of uses in surgery, communication, micro-photography, and so on.

laser printer: a high speed printer that uses a laser beam to create lines of print or images. (See also *jet printer.*)

latent image: in photography and film, the undeveloped image, formed by exposure to light, which requires a chemical process to be seen.

layout: a diagram of the structure of a page which will eventually go to press. Newspaper layouts will contain headlines, masthead, position of illustrations, columns, and so on.

LCD: see *liquid crystal display*

lead story: in a news bulletin or on the front page of a newspaper, that item which is considered most important by an editor, proprietor, or news organisation.

leader: an *editorial* article in a newspaper that selects some aspect of the news and devotes itself to an analysis of the significance of the event. A leader is expected to represent the newspaper's view of certain debates, and to make a direct intervention in public debates.

leading article: see *leader.*

legitimation: this is the process through which governments and other dominant groups exercise the right to control the direction of society through the consent of the subordinate (see *hegemony*). However, consent from the population is based on a government's ability to deliver a social 'contract' which many political parties have traditionally promised to deliver; health services, financial benefits, education and so on. When governments find they cannot meet, or where they are unwilling to fund such commitments, popular disillusionment sets in and a 'legitimation crisis' occurs.

leitmotif: a musical phrase used in film whenever a certain person, situation, idea or sentiment is displayed on-screen. It is used to provoke interest in and awareness of the film world.

lens: an optical device made from glass or other material which uses refraction to force rays of light to converge or diverge, thus producing an image on a white surface or on light-sensitive film. In photography, the lens elements are mounted in a plastic or metal cylinder called the lens barrel. The focal length of a lens is the distance from the optical centre of the lens, to the point at which it throws an image into sharp focus.

letterpress: a relief printing process in which the raised letters or shapes are inked and then pressed onto paper.

levels of context: see *context (levels)*.

library footage: film clips taken from a television company's previous reports, or from commercial film libraries which specialise in stock images of certain sites and events; they are then used to illustrate some aspect of a programme or feature.

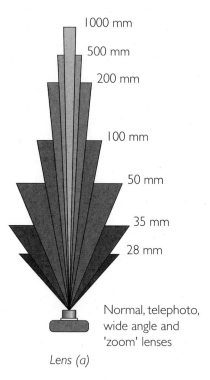

1000 mm
500 mm
200 mm
100 mm
50 mm
35 mm
28 mm

Normal, telephoto, wide angle and 'zoom' lenses

Lens (a)

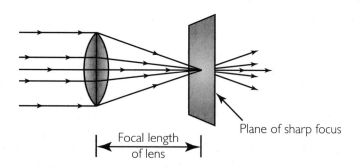

Focal length of lens

Plane of sharp focus

Lens (b)

lifestyle: an approach to marketing which places product choice in the context of a wider representation of consumer values. The use of psychological approaches to *branding* has entailed the determination of consumer identity; certain products come to stand for the habits and style choices of the customer, but go further to embody the values and social conduct of designated groups. Built upon a confused mixture of class-based representation and social identity theory, advertisers have made an intervention in life which circumvents the idea of necessary purchase and turns moral value into consumption.

lift: the use of information, or more usually finished text, 'stolen' from the pages of a newspaper, journal, etc., for use in a rival publication.

lighting: both a source of illumination for film production and one of the major codes used in the cinema. In early film, natural light was the only source, so some studios were constructed like large greenhouses. In 1893, Edison and Dickson built their first studio workshop for the creation of *kinetoscope* films. It was called the 'Black Maria' and included a roof that could be raised to let in sunlight. The whole building could revolve on a circular track, to follow the course of the sun. In the early part of the twentieth century, artificial lighting began to be introduced, while dramatic lighting effects were achieved in both Dutch and German cinema. Susan Hayward believes that lighting for dramatic effect 'became quite generalised by 1915 for ... two reasons: the predominance of studio shooting ... and the advent of the *star* system' ('Key Concepts in Cinema Studies', 1996). Traditional studio lighting systems were made up of three components: *key-lighting* (directed at the main subject of each scene), fill-lighting (designed to light the whole frame), and back-lighting (used alone when certain effects were needed in horror movies or thrillers). (See page 132 for illustration.)

line drawing: a simple illustration made in one colour (usually consisting of black lines).

linguistic relativity: the idea that different languages provide different world-views. According to this approach, language forms predispose individuals to interpret the world in specific ways. The Sapir-Whorf hypothesis proposes the idea that grammars position their users (native speakers of English, German, Chinese, etc.) to understand similar events in quite different ways. (See *language/thought* debate).

linguistics: the study of language. Linguistics is divided into a number of different but related areas. These comprise:

- historical studies, which examine changes in the meaning of a language over time
- comparative linguistics, which studies similarity and difference in related languages (such as the Romance languages, French, Italian, Spanish)
- phonology, that part of language which concerns the system of sound used in language
- studies of grammar, often concentrating on sentence construction
- semantic study, often related to philosophical questions
- psycholinguistics, a field which explores the psychological processes at work in language use, and language (and second language) acquisition
- sociolinguistics, concerned with class, ethnicity, gender and other questions as they appear in language use.

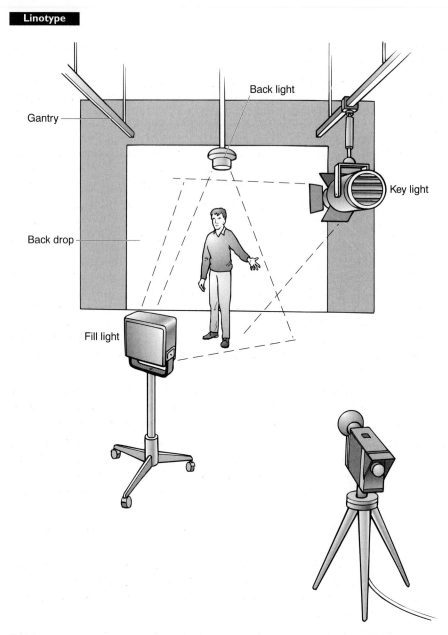

Back light

Gantry

Key light

Back drop

Fill light

Lighting

Linotype: a linecasting machine used in printing, first patented by Ottmar Mergenthaler in 1885. The Linotype machine arrived in Britain at the start of the twentieth century, and soon became popular because it integrated the two functions of type-casting and type assembly. By 1901 there were 8000 linotypes in operation, growing to 33,000 in 1916. Linotype is still used as a general term for any type of linecasting machine, although such technology is rapidly being replaced by computer based systems.

lip-sync: a film industry term for the *synchronisation* of actors' voices to their lip movements recorded on tape.

liquid crystal display (LCD): used in calculators, watches, some games, and many portable computers, LCD is a visual display made of two sheets of polarising material held together with a nematic liquid crystal. Images are produced when a low electric current is introduced; the liquid crystals align so that light cannot shine through.

literature: originally meaning polite forms of learning acquired through reading, literature is the body of imaginative and erudite writing which has been composed with a serious purpose, and which in turn is treated as a significant cultural form.

lithography: a method of printing invented by Alois Senefelder in Munich in about 1798. He discovered the system when he was experimenting with ways of making relief printing surfaces in stone. Lithography was the first printing process to use a flat and not a raised surface.

An image or design is applied to a flat 'litho' stone, using a grease-based marker or crayon. This type of limestone, once polished, draws in water. Therefore, a thin film of water is applied to the stone, so that the only area not to be affected is the design, which repels water because it is greasy. When ink is applied it stays on the greased area, while none spreads to the damp surface of the rest of the stone.Lithography was particularly important for the production of posters, and consequently for the growth of *advertising*.

live: a radio or television broadcast which is seen in real time, as events unfold, rather than one which has been taped or recorded. The tendency to include live reports in television news, in order to 'authenticate' reports, has grown in recent years.

lobbying: activities designed to affect the outcome of legislation or public opinion, sometimes organised by professional groups on behalf of unsavoury clients. Lobbying in America has become a major industry, while in Britain it became more controversial as a result of the activities of 'Ian Greer Associates', which were at the centre of the 'cash for questions' scandal in 1996/7.

local: media activity that takes place within a restricted area, such as the local reach of a free newspaper.

location: television and film productions will often use scenes shot on location, meaning any place besides a studio or the 'back lot' belonging to the film company. In many cases, a separate location department will look for suitable locations in which to shoot various scenes.

location (social): the theory advanced by Rom Harré and Grant Gillett, in a book called 'The Discursive Mind'. They argue that, in order to have a sense of *self*, a human subject must also have a sense of his/her place in space and in time. Next, the person must possesses an awareness of moral responsibility (his/her status as a moral actor). Equally, knowledge of the social place inhabited (constructed by age, ethnicity, class, etc.), is also necessary. The four 'locations' produce a system within which people live. (See *self* for more detail.)

log on: the first actions taken at the beginning of a computer session; the process of turning on and gaining access to the computer, using the required procedures, passwords, etc.

logical oppositions: sometimes referred to as *binary oppositions,* these are systems of opposites composed of two terms. The structuralist tradition associated with *Saussure* regards language as a system of differences; *signs* produce meaning in opposition to other signs. A logical opposition may be, to take one example, 'internal/external'. It is also an example of an 'antonym', a pair of words opposite in meaning. In addition, it is a specialised form of antonym called a 'complementary pair', because the concept 'internal' means 'not external' and the term 'external' indicates some state that is not internal. The same could be said of 'alive/dead', because 'not alive' is dead and 'not dead' is alive.

Some philosophers have found the binary or logical opposition a source of frustration. *Derrida,* for instance, sees 'oppositions' in philosophy as exclusive, neglecting complexity and the possibilities of difference. One of the aims of *deconstruction* was to show that philosophy is in a state of contradiction or paradox.

'Presence/absence' is one of the antonyms Derrida uses to express his dissatisfaction with this state of affairs. Derrida argued that the concept of presence can therefore be 'de-constructed', which would involve (see Jonathan Culler's 'Deconstruction' p. 95) 'the demonstration that for presence to function as it is said to, it must have the qualities that supposedly belong to its opposite, absence'. The idea here is that objects moving in time and space (the 'arrow's flight' is the example used) exist in a state of paradox, because at any given moment they are supposedly in motion and yet at the same time occupy a definite place.

Hartley ('Key Concepts', 1994, p. 30), notes that oppositions like 'land/sea' are mutually exclusive 'and yet together they form a complete system – the earth's surface'. He cites media representations to describe how an initial binary opposition, such as 'masculinity/femininity' can be followed by a whole series of other exclusive categories which are linked to it and thus read in its light; so that the first parts of both 'outdoors/indoors', and 'public/private' are assigned to 'masculinity' in each case, while the second parts are ascribed to 'femininity'. In this way, some form of ideological reinforcement of cultural norms is supposed to take place.

long shot: a shot taken at some distance from the subject filmed.

long take: a camera shot which is held for an extended period of time, uninterrupted by a cut. It is often used where a director wants to reveal the extent of a set, a landscape, or wishes to follow a particular character. The long take can also be used to focus on one aspect of a scene, thus creating an extended study of a significant object.

loop: a length of film or tape which has been joined end to end to create a continuously repeating picture or sound; used to help actors achieve synchronisation with the words spoken on screen.

low contrast: lighting which lacks sharp definitions of strong light and shadows; greys and intermediate shades predominate.

low-budget: any production which is hastily produced, shot according to a tight schedule, lacks established stars and lacks financial investment. Some low-budget films become significant successes. In America, a low-budget film is any feature-length production which costs less than about $500,000.

Lumière: in 1895 the Lumière brothers (Auguste and Louis) were among the first to make use of film for the purposes of public entertainment. Their films, lasting about a minute each, were shown in theatres, with perhaps as many as ten items on the programme.

Russian writer Maxim Gorky, after seeing a Lumière film in 1896, wrote that 'there appears on the screen a large grey picture, "A Street in Paris" ... as you gaze at it you see carriages, buildings, and people in various poses, all frozen into immobility ... but suddenly a strange flicker passes through the screen, and the picture stirs to life. Carriages coming from somewhere in the perspective of the picture are moving straight at you, into the darkness in which you sit ... and all this in strange silence, where no rumble of wheels is heard, no sound of footsteps, or of speech'.

Dai Vaughan, writing about reports of early performances ('Early Cinema', 1990 edited by Thomas Elsaesser), thinks that (p. 64–5) 'what most impressed the early audiences was what would now be considered the incidentals of scenes: smoke from a forge, steam from a locomotive, brick-dust from a demolished wall. The movements of photographed people were accepted without demur because they were perceived as performance ... but that the inanimate should participate in self-projection was astonishing'.

The Lumières sent out camera operators to the Far East, Europe, Russia and many other places. When these men reached a new district, they would film the locality and then incorporate this material into their public shows. Lumière camera operators were present at the coronation of Csar Nicholas II; when food was distributed to the populace after the event, a crush occurred during which 5000 people were killed. The film was seized by the Russian police to prevent the disaster being seen abroad.

Lumière films include 'La sortie des usines Lumière' ('Workers leaving the Lumière factory'), 'L'arrivée d'un train en gare de la Ciotat' ('Arrival of a train'), and 'L'arroseur arrosé', which is sometimes called the first 'filmed fiction', featuring a gardener who gets soaked because a boy stands on his hose, releasing the pressure once the gardener begins to look down the tube.

M

magazine format: an arrangement of film or (more usually) television content which resembles the internal organisation of a typical magazine; features, tips, 'articles' and other material is presented in clearly defined sections.

magic lantern: a device invented by Athanasius Kircher in the seventeenth century, used for projecting still images in the form of slides. A lamp would be placed inside a box. The box had a hole cut in one of its sides. A lens was placed over this aperture and each slide could be placed in turn behind the lens. In a darkened room, the image could be projected onto a screen.

Magnum: the Magnum Photographic Agency is an organisation run by photographers. The purpose of the agency is to control the use of its members' images. Traditionally, newspaper editors and proprietors exercised complete power over the use of photographic work, but Magnum set a precedent for independence.

The establishment of Magnum took many years, but its early history can be traced to a conversation on a Paris city bus in 1934. Quite by chance, two photographers met on a bus running between Montmartre and Montparnasse. Henri Cartier-Bresson was examining a Leica he had just had fitted with a new lens. A man opposite leaned forward and asked what kind of camera he had; the questioner was David Szymin, whose professional name was David Seymour. A few weeks after the first meeting, Seymour (known as 'Chim') introduced Cartier-Bresson to a young photographer called Endre Friedmann, a lively individual who became better known as Robert Capa.

It was not until April 1938, however, that the idea for the agency began to take shape, and it took until 1947 for the final agreement to be reached, at the Museum of Modern Art in New York. The founding members of Magnum were Capa, Seymour, Cartier-Bresson, George Rodger, Maria Eisner and William and Rita Vandivert. On May 22nd 1947, Magnum Photos Inc. was registered with the County of New York.

A number of the group made their reputation as war photographers. George Rodger was present at the liberation of Belsen in 1945. Capa was with the American landings on D-Day and was killed covering the French war in Indo-China. Seymour died some years later in another conflict. Cartier-Bresson (see *decisive moment*), having produced some of the most memorable images made in the twentieth century, eventually abandoned photography for painting. Contemporary members of Magnum include Sebastiao Salgado, who made a considerable impact in the early 1990s with his exhibition and book called 'Workers'. This was composed of portraits of labourers, taken throughout the world. Some of the most dramatic feature Brazilian and Cuban cane cutters. (For more information on the work of Magnum, see William Manchester's 'In Our Time: the World as Seen by Magnum Photographers', 1989).

mainstream cinema: a reference to both the dominant form of cinematic institution, and to the practices associated with that institution. The dominant system is associated with Hollywood, although the studios have to a large degree abandoned the 'industrial' approach (where films were turned out as though on a production line), in favour of a greater reliance on independent film-makers, who can be commissioned for specific projects. The Hollywood conception of film, however, has remained fairly consistent, and has spread its influence across the world.

The concept of mainstream practices can be illustrated by the established methods of film production, but also by the kind of *texts* that are made. The standard text is based on a clear *narrative* development, focusses on one or two central characters (who are 'psychological' characters in the sense that we see the action from their perspective), and obeys realist conventions. The continuity of the film is unbroken, and there are no or few devices which might reveal the fictional status of the narrative (jump-cuts, direct address to camera, inclusion of film equipment in shot, etc.).

manipulation: the idea that individuals and groups may be 'managed' by various forms of unfair influence, sometimes using the threat of coercion but more usually by making appeals to the values, attitudes and beliefs already held .

manufacture of consent: Noam *Chomsky's* term for the process of opinion-formation in western states. Public consent for state action is not based on free access to a range of opinion, because some points of view are allowed a privileged position, while others are suppressed. The decision-making process is monopolised by powerful bodies like government agencies and media corporations, which are linked to other centres of power. The whole range of institutions forms a concentrated power-bloc which is able to put forward ideas in a systematic manner, and on an extremely large scale (hence the notion that the production of opinion is 'manufactured'). When certain opinions are excluded from debate, public consent for the capitalist system exists in name only. Herman and Chomsky's 1988 book, 'Manufacturing Consent: the Political Economy of the Mass Media', concentrated in particular on press treatment of international news and on (p. 3) the 'size, ownership, and profit orientation of the mass media'. Herman and Chomsky's approach should be compared with Gramsci's notion of *hegemony*.

manuscript: an original piece of writing, *handwritten* or in print, which is produced on paper.

market position: the position occupied by a brand within a marketplace, including the price and especially the image of the product concerned.

market share: the ratio of an individual company's sales to the total sales recorded throughout a particular market. Market share can be measured by volume (the total number of units sold) or by value (the revenue created). In the case of the media, some sectors (such as advertising and the press) always worked in the open market. Broadcasting was more protected, until 1993 when the effects of the 1990 Broadcasting Act included increased competition for market share. Rod Allen, in 'Broadcasting Enters the Marketplace' (1994), argues (p. 29) that once a television monopoly has been broken, 'a commercial broadcasting company, owned by shareholders ... has to change its agenda and it has to deliver a bottom line and the programmes simply become ... the currency whereby the sales people buy the audiences which they sell on to advertisers'. In such a case, market share is of vital importance, because advertising investment will decline if audiences are not maintained or increased.

marketing: the concept of marketing is based on the idea of meeting customer needs, rather than simply advertising products which already exist. If marketing is not merely selling, it implies the need to carry out extensive research into consumer requirements. In addition, decisions must follow a clearly devised marketing plan, including an audit of the company's assets in this area, the production of clear goals for sales, market share and so on, and the creation of a strategy which will achieve objectives within a defined budget. The 'marketing mix' is the idea that the correct product, price, place and promotion all work to meet the customer's needs.

Opposition to marketing argues that it is never really designed to satisfy human requirements, and in effect sets out to create needs through campaigns which remain in essence no more than sophisticated versions of traditional advertising. This approach perceives some forms of qualitative market research as socially divisive and negative (see *segmentation*).

Marxism: a political philosophy which emphasises the importance of economic structures in determining the general character of a society; Marxists argue that, under capitalism, the ruling class controls industrial production, values other groups only for their labour power, and exercises ideological domination through the use of agencies like the education system. In the case of modern societies, the media is believed to reproduce the dominant order through its hierarchical structure (management directing cultural workers), its social character (a centralised force which transmits information), and its role in reproducing the ideology of the bourgeoisie.

Early or 'classical' Marxism held a fairly straightforward view of communication in a capitalist society. The media were seen as the servants of the ruling class, disseminating ideas designed to keep other classes in a position of subservience. In recent years, Marxist theory has appeared in many guises.

The 'political economy' model concentrates on the structures of ownership and control which operate within the media. Information is supposed to be valued according to the amount of profit it generates. 'Critical theory' is associated with the *Frankfurt School,* a group which studied the rise of fascism in Europe. 'Critical theory' proposed the idea that monopoly capitalism had produced a 'mass culture' which encouraged widespread acceptance of the system. Theories of *'hegemony'* also represented an attempt to explain the power of culture (Antonio Gramsci advanced a theory of society which examined the way in which subordinate groups consent to the rule of the powerful). The 'social-cultural' approach to media and communication, associated with British cultural studies, examined how subordinate groups are integrated into society through the consumption of texts. As a perspective, it opposed the idea that the dominant order is simply reproduced by economic power; audiences are seen as active participants in the creation of their own subjectivity.

Maslow's hierarchy: a theory of human needs put forward by Abraham Maslow in his book 'Motivation and Human Personality' (1954).

Maslow believed that unsatisfied needs motivated human behaviour. He organised his description of needs into a hierarchy, as follows:

- physiological needs, which include all the most basic requirements of life, such as food and water and anything affecting physical survival

- safety needs are those concerned with freedom from danger and fear
- social needs include companionship, belonging, and friendship
- esteem needs come from the desire to achieve self-esteem and to gain approval from others
- self-actualisation is the highest level of human need, which Maslow described as 'to become everything that one is capable of becoming'.

Although the hierarchy of needs might seem rather rigid, Maslow recognised that human behaviour is more complex than this suggests, and that certain basic needs might be neglected in the quest for fulfilment. This appears where 'ideals, high social standards [and] high values' are placed before the requirements of comfort and safety.

mass audience: a conception of audience which emphasises its large scale, basic anonymity, lack of cohesion (except at the point of reception), and its subordination to more powerful forces. Mass audience theory emerges from models of mass society. In this scenario, the great bulk of people in industrialised nations forms a subordinate class, subject to the direction and influence of an authoritarian state. Individual and group ties are weakened, so that state power is able to act directly upon social groups.

In mass society, the media supposedly provides inconsequential entertainment in order to ensure the general docility of the populace. State propaganda, carried by the media, is used to marshal and direct belief. The mass audience thesis paints a picture of, at the very least, an authoritarian social system. An alienated population achieves solidarity only when it is allowed to celebrate bogus national triumphs, or when it receives third-rate diversion from television, radio and film.

The notion of a mass audience was formulated during the growth of totalitarianism in 1930s Europe. The idea is now often dismissed as outdated (Hartley in 'Key Concepts' actually commands his readers not to adopt mass society theory!). There may indeed be aspects of mass society and mass audience approaches which are no longer very useful, especially as mass *effects* are not always as dramatic as they were once imagined. However it continues to be useful because it reminds us of the essentially authoritarian structure of *mass communication*. It also reminds us that concentrated forms of public address are often used in attempts to direct perception and understanding.

mass communication: mass communication is the large scale dissemination of symbolic content to heterogeneous and geographically-dispersed audiences. Scale refers to the actual or potential capacity to create a significant impact on large numbers of the public. The content (whether informative, persuasive or for the purposes of entertainment), takes the form of commodities in a marketplace, which have therefore an exchange value as well as 'a symbolic reference with a use value' (McQuail in 'Mass Communication Theory'). Mass communication is shaped by powerful corporate bodies, organisations which possess a public character but which are also driven by commercial motives.

In mass communication, standardised output is required because capitalist enterprises need products which, wherever purchased, attain the same level of quality and generate a consistent level of return on investment. Mass communication is characterised by:

- large scale of operation

- high levels of industrial activity
- formal, centralised organisation
- institutionalised values and practices
- the mediation of authority
- a 'standardised' product directed to a mass audience
- the possibility of simultaneous reception of messages by audiences.

mass culture: the existence of a general cultural context in industrial and 'post-industrial' societies, which is created by the mass production, circulation and consumption of artefacts, texts, lifestyles and discourses. For many commentators, mass culture (produced and circulated by the media and other agencies) is bound to be inferior to other more exalted forms of artistic and social endeavour. Although some writers concentrate on the negative aspects of mass culture (standardisation, repetition, banality) others praise its use by audiences and consumers (negotiation, adaptation, subversion). The point about studying mass culture, however, is to take it seriously, not to compare it unfavourably with other cultural forms (which it 'mediates' anyway) or to celebrate it uncritically. Julian Stallabrass attempts to locate mass culture in its global context ('Gargantua: manufactured mass culture', 1996, p. 11) 'First World culture is founded on an economy which denies the great majority of people the necessary means to live a decent existence ... such a system is not easy to maintain; lies, threats and continual violence are its mainstays'.

master: any original videotape, film, audiotape or other source which is used to produce copies.

master shot: an uninterrupted shot (often a relatively *long shot*), usually taken from a fixed position, which may be used for subsequent editing; close-ups, cut-aways and other shots may be added to the master shot.

masthead: the title of a newspaper, appearing on the front page of every edition above the text; examples are 'The Guardian', 'Daily Mirror' and so on.

materialism: just as the word 'material' refers to matter or physical substance, so materialism indicates an outlook which stresses the importance of physical reality. This belief can be expressed in a 'materialistic' view of life, which emphasises material comfort, wealth, and so on. Alternatively, materialism can express itself in a philosophical sense, referring to the conviction that the 'solid' physical aspects of existence have primary importance in determining the structures of life.

Marxist philosophy uses the term 'materialism' to refer to the idea that all societies are based ultimately upon material or economic foundations. Engels thought that 'the ultimate cause and the great moving power of all important historic events' lay 'in the economic development of society, in the changes in the modes of production and exchange, and in the consequent division of society into distinct classes'.

Although regarded as rather *determinist* most Marxist theories of society do not suggest that *culture* is capable of being reduced to economic processes. *Dialectical materialism* is a refinement of materialist theory which argues that matter itself is dynamic and therefore subject to change.

matte: a term used in film-making to describe one kind of special effect. If a director needs a shot which cannot easily be produced on location or in the studio, the alternative may be to create it in 'laboratory' conditions. Suppose that the shot required consists of a mansion on a hillside. A suitable building is found, but the background is wrong, containing other structures which are too modern. First, a shot is taken of the mansion. Then, a separate shot is taken of a rural hillside, to be used as background. Once this has been done, the first piece of film is projected onto a white card and an artist outlines the area to be 'matted' out (in this case, the background). This area is painted black, then photographed. The film of the black outline, together with the original shot of the building, are combined. The same process is repeated for the shot of the background, at the end of which the two matted images are printed in an optical printer. Contemporary special effects have relied increasingly on computer-generated images. (See also *blue screen*.)

MCU: an abbreviation for 'medium close-up', one of a number of classifications of shots used in film.

meaning: meaning is the object of communication acts; in other words, communicators usually attempt to convey and interpret recognised forms of significance. A number of philosophers have attempted to define meaning. *Derrida,* for example, distinguishes between the *phenomenological* tradition, in which 'all experience is the experience of meaning' and 'meaning as an object of logical or linguistic enunciation', the deliberate attempt to use language to convey sense (see Cobley's 'Communication Theory Reader', p. 219).

The Russian thinker V.N. Volosinov argued that meaning is part of a larger 'theme' which can only be found in the complete interaction which takes place between speakers. For *Saussure,* meaning is created by the interaction between signs. Paul Grice, in 'Studies in the Ways of Words', notes that some theories only provide statements about the standard or general meaning of a sign, while (p. 216) 'no provision is made for dealing with statements about what a particular speaker or writer means by a sign on a particular occasion'. This is a reference to the way that 'non-standard' meaning arises from intention and context. Meaning is emergent, depending on general/conventional meaning, speaker intention, the internal arrangement of elements (taken from a system such as language), the external context, and the participants concerned.

media: the term 'media' comes from the Latin for middle. Media therefore stand between different groups in society, but do not occupy (in terms of opinion and power) an exact place mid-way between *'dominant'* and 'subordinate' classes, if such a point could be found. The media, defined as those institutions and techniques used to disseminate symbolic content to audiences, include radio, the press, television, the music industry, film and in some accounts advertising.

The media are studied for a variety of reasons: to discover their role in the propagation of culture; to investigate their relationship to the state and *dominant* ideology; to examine their economic structures; to establish an insight into their working practices; to determine the *effects* they may produce on *audiences;* to work out the meanings of the *texts* they circulate. The 'new' media, represented by the integrated computer-based programme, lacks many of the characteristics of *mass communication* and appears to represent a less public mode of exchange.

media buyer: an individual who buys space in in an advertising medium, whether in television, film, radio or print form. The job involves negotiating the most favourable positioning and timing for the display of a client's message, and requires decisions about the size and frequency of advertisements. Media buying is usually one specialised function within the media department of an *advertising* agency.

media event: an event which has been staged specifically in order to attract the attention of the media. Press conferences, visits to public sites, certain types of demonstration, etc., may all be classified as media events. Many occasions are now, at least in some respects, 'stage-managed' in the knowledge that media coverage can be expected. In other cases, events might be 'enhanced' by the presence of media, or may even be remembered through their mediation. For an account of an early example of media 'construction' of an event, see Lang and Lang's research into McArthur's tour of US cities in 1951 (in John Corner's 'Television Form and Public Address', p. 54).

media imperialism: imperialism is the extension of an empire by military conquest; media or cultural imperialism is a variant of the principle of expansion, through the cultural artefacts (television programmes, films, etc.) produced by western nations. The idea is that a dominant western/capitalist culture is communicated to a developing nation, always with negative effects.

Liebes and Katz, in 'The Export of Meaning' 1993 (Introduction, viii), who offer a critical perspective on the theory, begin by describing cultural imperialism 'as a continuation of economic imperialism by other means' which 'implies that an outside power exploits a weaker power for its own gain'. Steven Chaffee of Stanford University, in Korenzy and Ting-Toomey's 'Mass Media Effects Across Cultures' (1992) characterises the media imperialism thesis in the following way: 'American media products, the argument runs, undermine the indigenous culture of a less developed society. In importing Western television signals ... a country is also importing Western value systems and encouraging its young people to envy and seek to join the alien culture they are viewing'.

Chaffee goes on to say that 'the media imperialism thesis has rarely been tested empirically ... it is very difficult to identify the conditions under which the process in question might operate'.

media imperialism (research): Liebes and Katz carried out a study in Israel, designed to test the idea that the world has become a 'global village' in which a dominant culture is shared by many different national groups. These authors point out that 'Israel, like the rest of the non-Western world, is not homogeneous at all, otherwise there would not be so much concern about its integration'. Their study is an important qualification of the concept of media imperialism, asking whether the different ethnic groups in Israel 'might ... 'use' even the alien culture delineated by programmes like 'Dallas' to explore and redefine their own identities and to compare themselves not just with Americans but with other Israelis'. Liebes and Katz move from the large-scale 'imperial' problem (the conflict between national cultures), to consider struggles 'between sub-cultures within a nation, and between the sexes within families'.

While audience studies suggest caution in accepting the idea that western culture completely dominates the populations of developing countries, there are still fears that existing communication channels are (in the words of the heads of non-aligned states, meeting in Algiers in 1973) 'the legacy of the colonial past'. The major news agencies are western, while surveys of news media in the mid-eighties found that coverage of international news was limited; United Press International (UPI) devoted 71% of its coverage to the USA, 9.6% to Europe, 5.9% to Asia, 3.2% to Latin America, 3% to the Middle East and 1.8% to Africa. Domination of news outlets may therefore continue to affect what some have called the 'import and export of meaning'.

media strategy: a plan of action produced by advertisers, designed to select appropriate media for the messages they wish to direct to the public. Knowledge of the relationship between audience sub-groups and media formats is central to the process. For example, a local newspaper may be more useful for ads aimed at a specific community, but would be of no use if national coverage is required. The cinema may be a more useful place to advertise products aimed at 15 to 24-year-olds than television, because it is a recognised attraction for this age group. The characteristics and thus the strengths and weaknesses of each media form also need to be understood. Television is a suitable medium if product use needs to be shown, while press advertisements can allow a longer period of study.

mediation: as a general term, mediation is the provision of a link between two parties (or different interest groups). This link, usually some public or private body, can help to interpret each side's point of view. In media studies, however, mediation is a process which not only acts as a link between authority and public, but also 'mediates' the messages produced for public consumption. That is to say, mediation acts on and alters messages, and is not merely a 'bridge' from the source to the receiver. For example, a politician may want a certain message to be received by the public, but a media organisation may bring its own agenda to bear on the issue. The other point, which emerges from what has just been said, is that mediation in the context of mass communication has to process messages from the powers that be, rather than handle 'traffic' from the other direction. However much a newspaper or other media form may disagree with and alter the impact of a message, it must still pay most of its attention to the source.

medium: a medium is an individual form of media such as television or radio, or with regard to communication in general, any agency which stands between different parties in an exchange.

megabyte: a byte is made up of several (usually eight) bits of data grouped together to form a digit, a character, or some other value; a megabyte is over a million bytes (1,048,576 bytes) or 1024 kilobytes.

melodrama: a type of film based on a theatrical tradition which amplified the emotional undercurrents found in domestic situations. Most melodramas are concerned with sensational but 'small-scale' events, showing an interest in the perspective of the female protagonist which has led a number of feminist authors to re-evaluate the status of films like 'Stella Dallas' of 1937 and 'Mildred Pierce' of 1945. A 'male' version of melodrama can be found in films like 'Rebel Without a Cause' (1955) and 'Home from the Hill' (1959).

memory: an individual's capacity for remembering the events of his/her life. Memory is important for the productive use of experience through learning. In computing, memory is the facility which stores data.

mental replicas: the idea that representation is a mental process, in which objects or symbols are recognised because they 'activate' an identical image or conception in the mind of the observer. This theory implies that each person must be able to store, recall and then 're-use' information. The actual links made between symbols and real things are probably less straightforward than this process suggests. Words, for example, do more than produce a replica of their form or pronunciation; they may also create a feeling or memory which is quite dissimilar to the original stimulus.

The established theory (see Johnson-Laird in 'Ways of Communicating', p. 4) proposes that communication requires '. . . the communicator to construct an internal representation of the external world, and then to carry out some symbolic behaviour that conveys the content of that representation.' This in turn usually depends on belief in a *cognitive* model of human communication.

However, the idea of a 'store' of mental experience which is supposed to assist communication does not explain the fact that people are able to create meaning in situations which lie outside their experience.

mentalese: the 'language of thought'. Some linguists use the concept 'mentalese' to argue that mental processes are different to language. Mentalese is not the same as any of the world's languages, but supposedly the source from which all languages grow. Stephen Pinker, in 'The Language Instinct' (p. 56) wonders if mentalese is ' ... a silent medium of the brain – a language of thought ... merely clothed in words whenever we need to communicate.'

message: that content which initiates, re-orientates and closes the communication process; a message expresses human intention, is shaped by a mediating form, is carried as a signal, and is subject to interpretation if and when it reaches its destination. A single message is determined by a variety of forces. It may be formed consciously but informed by subconscious ideas. It can be put into any number of modes of communication (writing, speech, pictures), each of which will affect its structure; it will also be interpreted according to the expectations and inclination of the recipient. A message is simply an intention until it is sent. The concept 'message' becomes therefore the product of interaction, even where its core meaning may be understood differently by various participants.

metalanguage: from the Greek 'meta' meaning after, metalanguage refers to a way of describing or interrogating language or discourse. Barthes called metalanguage 'a semiotics which treats of a semiotics', and described the way in which every new social science (each way of describing the world) would replace the one which came immediately before it. He wrote that 'each science ... would contain the seeds of its own death, in the shape of the language destined to speak it' (see 'Elements of Semiology', 1990). An example might be postmodernism, the point of which is reference to (and thus a metalanguage concerning) the interpretation and status of modernism.

metaphor: the application of a name or descriptive term to something (an object, event, or creature), which does not, in literal terms, fit the thing described. A metaphor breaks a semantic rule (a rule of meaning) by making a statement which cannot be the literal truth, but which forces an audience to make an imaginative connection between two aspects of experience. Grice (in 'Studies in the Ways of Words',

1991) wrote (p. 34) 'examples like 'You are the cream in my coffee' characteristically involve categorical falsity'. Fromkin and Rodman ('An Introduction to Language', 1993) note that metaphors do not have to be totally outlandish; they show that (p. 151) 'John is a snake in the grass' can be interpreted literally to refer to a pet snake on the lawn named John. Metaphorically, the sentence has nothing to do with a scaly, limbless reptile'. The basis of metaphor is the creative use of linguistic power.

metonym: a metonym is a substitute for something; one attribute or element 'stands in' for an entire phenomenon. So for example, the word 'crown' can be used as a metonym for 'kingship' or 'royalty'. In a similar way, the media use metonyms (often visual) to represent a larger concept. For example, a picture of a snowdrift may stand for the onset of bad weather. Some media theorists are concerned at the use of metonyms, especially during ideologically significant events, because they believe them to be an over-simplified method of representation, leading to distortion of the truth.

microfiche: a microfilm format which ranges in size from 3 by 5 inches, to 6 by 9 inches.

microfilm: a miniature film format on which large amounts of information (greatly reduced in size) can be stored.

middle market: a newspaper term describing titles which serve a middle-class, 'middle-brow' readership; such titles lie between the serious broadsheets and the more frivolous tabloids, and are usually taken to include the 'Mail' and 'Express'. Such newspapers are characterised by a social conservatism, tempered by occasional campaigns on issues of 'social justice'. The 'Mail', although firmly right of centre, addresses a largely female readership and therefore must reflect the aspirations of 'career feminism'.

mimesis: a term taken from Greek, meaning the process of imitation. Mimesis is used in film theory, to describe some of the techniques used in *realist* film-making.

mise-en-scene: 'mise' comes from the French 'mettre', to put; 'mise-en-scene' means what is placed in a scene, or more specifically how individual shots in a film are composed. The content of a shot may include setting, lighting, spatial relationships and so on. The term originally referred to the scenery and setting of a play, or the visible surroundings of an event.

mixer: a device used for mixing sound from two or more sources. Inputs are adjustable, so that the level of sound from source may be controlled and mixed to a single output.

mixing: the process of combining a number of sound sources in order to create a new soundtrack.

MLS: medium long shot, in which the camera is placed at a moderate distance from the subject, showing most of the subject in its immediate surroundings.

model: a model of a communication process is 'a consciously simplified description in graphic form of a piece of reality' (see p. 2 of McQuail and Windahl's 'Communication Models'). An idea about communication is expressed in a drawing or design, in order to make communication theory more accessible. Models are either 'structural' (representing fixed components) or 'functional' (which show the forces involved in an event). Simple models involve message, sender and receiver, and are known as 'transmission' models. These (such as the ones produced by Lasswell, and by Shannon and Weaver) are often criticised for showing only a one-way process. Later models therefore involve graphic representation of two-way interaction. More sophisticated models consider intention and context as well as exchange (see Price after McQuail, 1996).

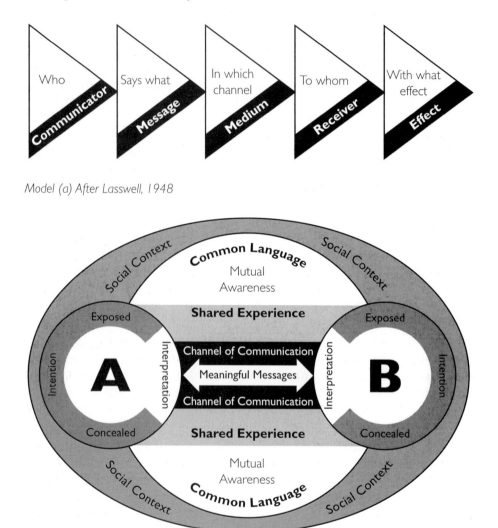

Model (a) After Lasswell, 1948

Model (b) After Price, 1996, from McQuail's description

modem: a device that converts digital pulses from a computer into a corresponding analogue signal for telephone transmission, and analogue signals from a telephone into digital codes for use in a computer. Modems are needed when telephone lines are used to link computers.

modernism: modernism refers to a number of social and cultural movements which celebrate the modern condition of life. The term was first noticed in the eighteenth century, when Samuel Johnson (in his 'Dictionary' of 1755), attributed the word's invention to Swift (see 'The Tale of a Tub', 1704). It was originally used to attack writers who appeared to corrupt traditional standards of written English with modern expressions. Eventually, by the end of the nineteenth century, 'modernism' was taken up as a cause by those who felt constrained by the cultural inheritance of the past.

Modernist movements exist within those 'advanced' industrial societies which seemed to drive technology forward. Some currents of modernism (such as futurism) welcomed the energy and power of the machine age, while others (dadaism for example) attacked the militarism which re-emerged in Europe after the First World War.

David Harvey calls modernism (see 'The Condition of Postmodernity') 'a troubled and fluctuating aesthetic response to conditions of modernity.' It was, in his opinion, 'more of a reaction to the new conditions of production ... and consumption (the rise of mass markets, advertising, mass fashion) than it was a pioneer in the production of such changes.'

modernity: the word 'modern' grew from the Latin 'modernus', which meant 'just now'. Modernity refers to the condition of life in contemporary society, the origins of which are thought to lie in the seventeenth century. The modern period shows marked differences to earlier types of human organisation and constitutes a break with 'traditional' social forms; however, this break can be over-dramatised, suggesting that contemporary life has almost nothing in common with previous human experience.

The development of technology and industrialisation is one aspect of modernity, but industrialisation cannot account for its entire character; industrial society was shaped by the social and economic system within which it developed – capitalism. In 'Modernity and Self-Identity' (1991), Anthony Giddens draws attention to three other dimensions of modern existence. He calls the first surveillance; the second is control of the means of violence; the third is the media.

Changes in belief and behaviour also occurred during the transition from traditional to modern societies. An emphasis on reason and progress, and an attachment to 'scientific' theories of social organisation, were all hallmarks of the 'enlightenment', as this period of intellectual and economic development is known. According to Graham Murdock (1993), modernity is 'a continual process of becoming', which includes:

- the rise of capitalism
- the development of the nation-state
- the ending of religious monopolies over thought and knowledge
- the emergence of 'a more fragmented and contested cultural field'.

modulation: the means by which a signal representing a sound is incorporated into a carrier wave, by modifying either the amplitude or the frequency of the carrier wave. FM stands for frequency modulation, and AM stands for amplitude modulation.

monitor: a Visual Display Unit (VDU) for computers, or a television set which is used for video rather than broadcast material.

monochrome: of one colour; in photography and television, the use of black and white film or the reproduction of a black and white picture.

monograph: a piece of writing or treatise devoted to one particular subject. 'Monograph' is used to refer to an article, paper, pamphlet or small book.

monopoly: exclusive control of a specific commodity or of a class of business or commerce. A monopoly can be conferred by government, as in the case of the BBC's incorporation on 1st January 1927. Alternatively, a monopoly can be built up through a series of private mergers or acquisitions.

Growth in commercial monopolies occurs as individual companies or groups take over other concerns; where this happens within the same industry, it is known as integration. Gaining control of different parts of a production process (such as production, exhibition and distribution in the cinema) is known as vertical integration. In practice, it is unusual for one organisation to control the whole of a specific market. This does not mean that attempts to establish monopolies do not take place. When for example, Rupert Murdoch negotiated the purchase of 'The Times' and 'The Sunday Times' in 1980–81, he provided assurances that 'The Times' would remain free from political interference. Despite this, Harold Evans, the editor on that newspaper, described 'an unnecessary and hazardous extension of monopoly power' ('Good Times, Bad Times', 1983, p. 490).

Murdoch and Golding (in an essay in 'Mass Communication and Society', 1977) note the underlying 'logic of cost ... consolidates the position of groups already established in the main mass media markets and excludes those groups who lack the capital base required for successful entry'. In the future, national regulation of powerful interests may ' become more difficult because of the multiplication of supply and the delocalisation of use in time and space' (McQuail, 'Mass Communication Theory', p. 24).

monotype printing: a *printing* system invented in 1889 by Tolbert Lanston. An operator used a keyboard to produce a code on a paper tape, which in turn fed into a unit which cast each individual letter and space in metal type.

montage: this concept comes from early Soviet cinema. Montage is the process of creating meaning through the juxtaposition of individual shots. In other words, the symbolic content of the shot becomes of central importance. One shot A, edited together with a second shot B, will produce a meaning C, which is not actually physically present in the film, but is produced in the minds of an audience. Montage also came to mean the use of rapid cutting from shot to shot, a style adopted by the makers of television commercials.

moral panic: the idea that 'a condition, episode, person, or group of persons' (Cohen, 1972) becomes defined as a threat to 'societal values and interests'. Moral panics are supposed to be creations of the media, which seize upon some state of affairs, or a particular incident, or the activities of a social group. Using their ability to publicise the subject chosen, the media first define it as part of a larger problem (linked to moral decline, growth of violence, etc.) and then place other events in the same category. The public becomes 'sensitised' to the situation and in time, the moral panic is further inflated as the media picks up on increased concern. Stan Cohen's 'Folk Devils and Moral Panics' argued that mods and rockers were practically created by the media, while Jock Young's 'The Drugtakers' took the view that marijuana users in Notting Hill became more deviant because of media condemnation and the subsequent use of increased policing. Belief in the concept 'moral panic' depends on accepting certain propositions about the media and society:

- that the event which initiates the panic requires amplification (i.e. that it might not really be as important as the media attention suggests)
- that the media really have the power to stir up significant public disquiet
- that, when it is achieved, such concern may actually be misplaced (and not, as in some cases, justified)
- that there is a link between media campaigns, public opinion, and some form of state repression.

morphemes: from the Greek for 'form', a morpheme is the most basic unit of meaning in language. A single word may be made up of one or more morphemes. The word 'quickly,' for example, is composed of two morphemes, 'quick' and 'ly'. Morphemes such as 'ly' can only ever make up part of larger words. The combination of morphemes into larger units may create new words.

morphology: in philosophy, the study of the form of words. Propp's 'Morphology of the Folk Tale' (1929), which came to the attention of Western critics in the 1950s, dealt with the narrative structures of Russian 'wonder tales' or 'folk tales'.

motif: a recurring image, theme or technique used in film, television or radio productions. A motif, used intelligently, can help to reinforce the structure of a *narrative*.

mouse: a hand-held device which, when moved across a flat surface, relays changes in its position to a computer. A mouse has many uses, including dragging files across the screen, highlighting text, selecting tools and opening folders.

MPAA: the Motion Picture Association of America; the MPAA code was a self-regulatory film code which pre-existed the imposition of national standards of film classification.

MS: a camera shot (medium or mid shot) placed at approximately halfway between a long shot and a close up.

Medium close up

Mid shot

Medium long shot

MTV: an abbreviation for 'Music television'. MTV was created in order to exploit low-cost programming provided by music videos. It began in August 1981 and attained an American audience of 1.5 million before becoming a global enterprise. Watson and Hill (p. 146) report that, by 1991, 'there were 201 million householders in 77 countries in 5 continents subscribing to the service'. The cultural impact of MTV has been the subject of a number of studies, including Corinna Sturmer's critique in 'Channels of Resistance', 1993.

mug shot: a jokingly disrespectful term for a newspaper photograph showing a person's head and shoulders only; it is a reference to the practice of taking or displaying pictures of a police suspect's face.

multiaccentuality: the idea that, although signs in a society are accessible to (may be 'read' by) all members of the same culture, conflict between the classes will result in quite different uses of signs; therefore, signs in a class society are multiaccentual, subject to various types of ideological emphasis, just as individual words can be pronounced or 'accentuated' in different ways.

multimedia: early descriptions of 'multimedia' referred to the process of combining more than one media form (e.g. slide projection, audio tape, video) in a simultaneous display. Contemporary definitions refer to the combination in one computer-based system of different elements (sound, video, CD-ROM, digital images) to form an integrated programme. The system can then be manipulated by the user to produce a variety of possible 'interactive' experiences.

For example, 'interactive' children's books have been produced which display a number of features. By using the mouse to move the cursor (the 'I' bar), an area of the screen may be selected. When this is done, information will appear on-screen, or various images will be activated, together with appropriate sounds or music. In some CD-ROM travelogues, a brief digitalised video image will be played, while a voiceover provides additional guidance. The user is able to decide which aspect of the presentation to run first, so that the entire experience is non-linear.

multiple exposure: a technique used in photography and the cinema, where a film is exposed repeatedly to different sources, with the result that multiple images are produced in the same frame or scene.

multi-track: a tape recorder capable of recording a number of audio tracks side-by-side on a tape; two, four, eight and more tracks are available on some recorders.

Mutoscope: a device produced in 1895 (the year of the first cinema performances) by the American Mutoscope Company. It consisted of a viewer, a series of photographs, and a hand-crank. When the crank was turned, the pictures were flipped through rapidly, producing the illusion of movement.

mystification: a process which is supposed to cover up the real relations of *power* in a society. When a phenomenon is 'mystified', its true nature is obscured and the individuals who use or observe the thing itself (an idea, a discourse, an object) are unable to recognise the deception.

The concept of mystification is not without its problems, however. In the first place, it has encouraged the growth of various theories which claim to 'de-mystify' events and texts. Since mystification is supposed to make the ideological appear 'natural', this suggests that there is some natural uncontested meaning which can be discovered if enough effort is invested. However meaning is constructed, it will be made up of a variety of value systems or discourses, and will not consist simply of a 'natural' centre covered by a thick layer of deception. Theories which try to show the 'real' nature of things, may end up constructing a new orthodoxy which characterises every message as a conspiracy.

myth: a society's way of expressing, in narrative or symbolic form, the significance it confers on its own cultural heritage. This stands in contrast to the view of myth as a fictitious narrative used by 'primitive' societies, or the idea that it is a story which is simply false. From a modern semiological perspective, myth is produced as a kind of forced resolution of conflicting interests, designed to benefit a ruling class. It is worth remembering that myths can only circulate if they seem genuinely useful to more than one group.

N

narcotization: a theory of effects which argues that the media produces apathy in its audiences. Narcotization is an American term taken from 'narcotics' (drugs) and was first used by Lazarsfeld and Merton in 1948. They wondered if 'increasing dosages of mass communications may be inadvertently transforming the energies of men from active participation into passive knowledge'. In this theory, it is the scale of communication rather than just the content, which has an impact on an audience, inducing a kind of social and political stupor.

narration: narration is the process of telling a story, using a number of devices to achieve that purpose (in film, *mise en scene, voiceovers,* and sound will all contribute). Writers like Branigan (1993) believe that cinematic devices work in a subtle manner, because they construct a narrative through implication. There is never a full exposition of the plot. (In fact, it would be impossible to construct something coherent within the available time if every development had to be shown as evidence!) Narration is concerned with how an event is presented, rather than with the content of that event. It works through a series of procedures, rationing the information an audience requires, generating curiosity, using the different levels of knowledge available to construct expectation, and so on. Narration is, according to Bordwell (1985), 'the organisation of a set of cues for the construction of a story'.

narrative: narrative can be explained in a number of ways: as the end-product of storytelling (a 'narrative'), the process of story-construction (made up of the plot and the devices used to deliver the plot), a mental activity that organises data into a pattern so that experience can be represented and explained and, according to Edward Branigan ('Narrative Comprehension and Film', 1993, p. 3) 'a way of organising spatial and temporal data into a cause–effect chain of events with a beginning, middle and end'.

Notice in Branigan's definition that two kinds of data, relating to space and time, are mentioned. It is also worth noting that the 'beginning, middle, and end' are not contained in individual scenes/passages from a text. They are created by the relationships between different elements, so that the first shot/sentence of a film/novel only acquires its status as 'the beginning' by comparison to other narrative elements. In some cases, of course, what we have taken to be the beginning turns out later to be a flash-back or flash-forward.

The essential part of a narrative is, therefore, that part which provides the most vital information, which allows the viewer/reader to construct meaning by moving forwards and backwards from that point. The beginning of a narrative sequence does not always provide this type of information. Narrative theorists include *Propp, Todorov,* and authors like Stephen Heath, who is less interested in looking for stable, logical structures, than in exploring systems of belief, modes of persuasion and values.

National Broadcasting Company (NBC): formed in 1926, it was the first of the major radio and television networks to emerge in the USA. It was for many years a subsidiary of the Radio Corporation of America, and is now controlled by General Electric. It has satellite interests in Latin America where it runs a Spanish language service.

National Cable Television Association (NCTA): a private body founded in the USA in 1952, serving the interests of cable television companies and opposed to government regulation of the cable industry.

National Council for the Training of Journalists: a UK training body for journalists. After the 1949 report of the Royal Commission on the Press, which drew attention to the need for better training for journalists, moves were made to improve provision for British trainees. In 1952, the National Council for the Training and Education of Junior Journalists was set up. This body, which became the NCTJ in 1955, was composed of representatives from the National Union of Journalists, the Newspaper Society, the Institute of Journalists, the Guild of British Newspaper Editors, and eventually the Newspaper Publishers Association and representatives of owners and managers from Scottish papers. The NCTJ offers a Certificate which requires candidates to achieve competence in shorthand at the rate of 100 words per minute.

National Film Archive: a division of the British Film Institute which acquires and preserves film and television material exhibited or broadcast in the UK. The archive contains over 80,000 titles, dating from 1895 to the present.

National Union of Journalists: the NUJ is a British trade union for journalists. It is organised in 'chapels' or branches. It has a 12-point code of conduct, covering issues such as ethics, the defence of press freedom, accuracy in reporting, avoidance of any intrusion into private grief, opposition to discrimination, and avoidance of commercial promotions. In recent years, it has been faced with the spread of personal contracts, growing unemployment and *casualisation* and declining power. Its 'equality style guide' was written to help journalists challenge sexist language in news reports. The NUJ has also collaborated with the Campaign for Press and Broadcasting Freedom in the 'people first' initiative, which tried to draw attention to the plight of the disabled. (see also *Institute of Journalists.*)

naturalism: a theatrical practice which was adopted in film and television. Naturalism shows people, objects and events in a realistic setting, using convincing dialogue and engaged in believable actions. The roots of a naturalistic approach may be found in the dramas of Ibsen and Antoine. Declamatory speeches and exaggerated gestures were avoided in such plays, and scenery and props had to be as faithful to the real as possible. Actors would 'become' their characters, rather than imitating their actions from the outside (a practice close to the 'method acting' of the 1950s). Antoine was responsible for the practice of treating the audience as part of an invisible 'fourth wall', which enabled them to assume the role of uninvolved spectators.

Naturalism made a fairly easy transition into the practices of film-making, since the camera could assume the position of the unseen audience, recording the realistic appearance and verbal exchanges of actors who, once again, behaved in an unforced and convincing manner. Naturalism has been criticised for its concentration on surface reality and the idea that, especially in television, it is used to make ideologically biased material appear uncontroversial. The theory is that, by providing a faithful imitation of life, certain ideas and beliefs may be introduced which also appear 'natural' (though whether these are accepted by audiences is a matter for debate).

NBC: see *National Broadcasting Company.*

negative: a negative is a developed section of film which displays the opposite tonal and colour values to the positive image that may be printed from it.

negotiated code: one of the categories used by Stuart Hall (1973) after Frank Parkin's (1972) explanation of audience response to ideological content in media messages. Although the broad thrust of the original message is largely accepted, it is modified where it impinges on the concrete experience and interests of the individual or group concerned. In later years Hall adopted the view that most interpretation was 'negotiated'.

negotiation: a process through which an individual or group alters the significance of a message; the message is usually received through a media source. The message itself is imagined as an ideologically-loaded attempt to present a 'dominant' *code* to an *audience*. (See also *active audience*.)

neologism: a word which has been invented (or adapted) to describe some new development in social reality (see for example *spin*).

neorealism: a style of film-making which emerged in Italy during the later years of the Second World War. It was a reaction to the sterility of fascist cinema under Mussolini, which had obeyed the regime's insistence that only a positive image of Italian life be portrayed. As a result, vacuous melodramas called 'white telephone movies' were produced. Neo-realism treated more ordinary but vibrant themes, featuring working-class life and using an approach which used non-professional actors in real settings. In addition, many films were shot outside the studio, utilising hand-held cameras and natural light. Well known neo-realist films included Visconti's 'Ossessione' ('Obsession', 1942), Rossellini's 'Roma Citta Aperta' ('Rome Open City' 1945) and De Sica's 'Ladri di bicicletti' ('Bicycle Thieves', 1948).

network: in the USA, a body which exists within a local, regional or national context, providing a substantial amount of programme material for affiliated stations.

networks of communication: the idea that, in *formal organisations*, there are distinct types of *communication* structure, each suited to a particular type of task. Networks may be set up deliberately in order to cope with some aspect of work, but may emerge without formal sponsorship. The list of networks is as follows:

- The circle network, in which communication flows between pairs of individuals, allowing the production of a number of opinions, although each person communicates with only two others.

- The wheel network, where one individual has a dominant role, since he or she controls the flow of communication between all other points of contact. This system is supposed to be useful for the completion of routine tasks, but is clearly undemocratic.

- The multi-channel network, where a more democratic exchange takes place.

- The chain network, allowing for rapid communication with little interaction between members of the group. There is little free interchange between subordinate positions in the chain, reinforcing formal authority at the top.

- The Y-shaped network, where the person at the meeting point of the separate parts of the figure is able to receive information from the other individuals. The majority of participants are unable to check the accuracy of the information passed through the network.

new media is an umbrella term describing media forms which have abandoned traditional analogue systems in favour of digital technology, or which have provided the basis for the integration of previously separate forms. In addition, new media includes those long-established delivery systems which now serve the digital 'revolution', such as cable and satellite. In sum, new media are recognised through one or more of the following processes: miniaturisation, transmission, greater capacity in storage and retrieval, and changing patterns of control. They include multimedia (which tends to integration of text, image and sound), the Internet (which alters traditional patterns of data consumption), the personal computer (which has helped to change work and leisure patterns), and virtual reality (potentially the most radical departure from previous systems). None of these forms has yet acquired a mass character. Although taken up by existing media forms, new media also represent a challenge to established patterns of consumption and control. The extent to which such forms have escaped centralised control is mainly due to the difficulty corporate power has faced in assimilating the technology and making it profitable.

new social movement: an informal collective created in response to a particular manifestation of social injustice, which works outside established political institutions in order to achieve its aims. New social movements are 'new' because they appeared after the class-based politics of the first half of the twentieth century, and because they are manifestations of an active and enlightened response to social and moral issues. Feminism, anti-racism, the peace movement and environmentalism are all examples of beliefs which challenge the established social order. It is sometimes said that new social movements are less concerned with economic issues; Inglehart, in 'The Silent Revolution' (1977), characterised NSMs as the consequence of greater affluence. With the decline in affluence and the existence of a greater gap between rich and poor, new social movements have incorporated economic arguments into their agenda, giving rise to radical sub-groups like 'Reclaim the Streets' and direct-action environmental protesters.

One section of the media has taken a considerable interest in the re-configuration of social life; advertising has to take account of social trends in order to locate the position of consumers in a changing marketplace. Advertisers have therefore, since the growth of feminist and egalitarian trends in the 1960s, tried to reflect such ideas in their forms of public *address*. As a consequence, diluted versions of the original message achieve circulation in society in general.

new social self: a reference to a form of social and personal change brought about by the growth of consumer society in the early twentieth century. Roland Marchand ('Advertising the American Dream') describes the 1920s in particular as (p. 214) 'an age of shifting relationships,' in which (p. 215) '... individuals had to be prepared to transform themselves for new roles and new opportunities, thus making them peculiarly vulnerable to shifting definitions of themselves by others.'

Industrial society was responsible for the destruction of older forms of community, concentrating individuals in urban centres as labourers and consumers. The 'new social self' was characterised by individualism and a sense of isolation in the midst of a mass society.

Leiss *et al.* ('Social Communication in Advertising') believe that the advertiser paid increasing attention to the promotion of goods and services which were not part of the essential requirements of life. In other words, various types of social need were catered for and a number of social 'types' addressed.

new wave (nouvelle vague): a French film movement which appeared in the late 1950s. The term 'nouvelle vague' was first used by Giroud, the editor of 'L'Express', to refer to a younger generation of left-leaning activists. The label was then transferred to a new kind of film-making, featuring young actors and fresh approaches to the film aesthetic. New wave films were characterised by their modest budgets, use of non-professional actors, location shooting and techniques of distanciation, whereby the audience member is made aware both of his/her status as spectator, and the essentially artificial nature of the 'construct' that is cinema.

Although new wave has been associated with the 'Cahiers du cinéma' group (made up of a number of influential film critics, including Chabrol, Godard, Truffaut, Rohmer and Rivette), it was also represented by other first-time directors and by a number of established film-makers. The work of Agnes Varda was important in setting much of the style which other directors followed. She often juxtaposed two stories, one personal and the other more generally social. Susan Hayward ('Key Concepts in Cinema Studies') argues that new wave cinema falls into two distinct historical periods, 1958–62 and 1966–68. The latter period was more overtly political than the former. Films from the nouvelle vague include Verda's 'La pointe courte' (1954), Vadim's 'Et Dieu crea la femme' (1956), Truffaut's 'Les 400 coups' (1959), Godard's 'A bout de souffle' (1959), and Godard's 'La Chinoise' (1967).

New World Information and Communication Order: an idea promoted by UNESCO (the United Nations Educational, Scientific and Cultural Organisation) in the 1970s. NWICO was an attempt to oppose the domination of news production by western agencies, by encouraging greater contributions from developing countries. The new information order was attacked by some powerful forces in the West as a form of restriction on freedom of information, and both the USA and Britain withdrew their support from UNESCO in the mid-1980s.

news means new information about events. The production and circulation of news in industrial societies is highly centralised, and is mostly controlled by large corporate bodies. Production is based on an elaborate division of labour and governed by the need to maintain or increase audience share of the news market, even where the news organisation is constituted as a public body. Peter Bruck (in 'Democratic Communications', 1992) notes that, although much of the news media seems to embrace sensationalism, and seems therefore anti-bureaucratic, they are 'on closer examination ... an integral part of present-day social administration and control'. Bruck believes, however, that the news system is not entirely closed (p. 140); 'the dominant system does not reproduce itself in an uncontradictory or conflict-free fashion'. This means there are opportunities for democratic renewal in the practice of news production.

news agency: an organisation which collects, edits and distributes news to subscribing publications. News agencies are vital to the newspaper industry, which often does not have its own reporters in place when a story breaks. News agencies use staff reporters and then 'stringers' or part-timers who feed in reports from local areas. Sub-editing the information is a major operation which runs around the clock. Subscribers used to take agency copy through teleprinter machines, but this now more usually appears directly on computer monitors. Some agencies have extensive operations; Reuters for instance runs a series of regional news services to the Far East, western Europe, North America, and West Africa. Many agencies also provide photographs.

International news agencies include United Press International, Agence France Press, Reuters and Associated Press. Two London-based agencies, Reuters TV News and WTN, dominate the wholesale market for raw video news footage, which news organisations can then edit to their own requirements.

Some smaller agencies operate in areas somewhat neglected by the major groups. The Gemini news agency based in North London, for example, brought a fresh approach to agency practices. It was founded in 1967 in order to promote reporting about Commonwealth countries, using work by overseas journalists. Often, mainstream organisations leave such reporting to British writers. Gemini advocates a liberal form of development journalism, in which a challenge is mounted to the rather negative images of less-developed nations which often seem to appear in the British media.

News Corporation: a global conglomerate founded by Rupert Murdoch. Murdoch's career began in Australia in 1953, when at the age of 22 he inherited his father's media interests. The growth of the News Corporation empire has been based on acquisitions, takeovers and a high degree of risk-taking.

To date, News Corporation consists of News International (its British subsidiary), the US film company 20th Century Fox, Fox television, book publishing interests in Australia, Britain and America (HarperCollins in the UK), the 'New York Post' in America, 49.9 per cent of Vox satellite, 99 per cent of Star TV (a satellite which broadcasts throughout Asia), newspapers in Hungary, Fiji, Papua New Guinea and Hong Kong, 15 per cent of Australia's Channel 7, a controlling interest in the BSkyB satellite TV company (through *News International*), 'The Australian' and over 100 other newspaper titles in individual states.

Rupert Murdoch's tactics in Britain, where newspapers like 'The Sun' were brought downmarket in order to undercut the position of its rivals, did not work as well in other countries. A number of attempts to 'go under' his rivals in both Australia and the USA did not repeat the success gained in Britain.

The entire corporation continues to take risks in order to expand. It lost £45 million in UK newspaper sales in 1994, but received over £186 million profits through BSkyB. In May 1995, the American company MCI, the second largest long-distance telephone company in the USA, announced that it would invest $2 billion over two years in News Corporation. MCI's cable network would carry Fox television and film. In 1995, Murdoch announced a deal involving the exclusive sponsorship of rugby league in the UK.

News International: a subsidiary of *News Corporation* which includes four British national newspapers; 'The Times', 'The Sunday Times', 'The Sun', and 'The News of the World'. The power of the group was greatly assisted throughout the 1980s by its closeness to the Conservative party. In 1981, for example, Rupert Murdoch was allowed to purchase 'The Times' and 'The Sunday Times' without a referral to the Monopolies Commission. In line with its proprietors' beliefs, the political direction of 'The Sun' changed dramatically, from 1972 when it supported the miners during their strike against the Heath government, to 1979, when it was firmly behind Margaret Thatcher. In 1980, after Thatcher's first election victory, Larry Lamb, then editor of 'The Sun', was knighted for his services to journalism. Conflict at 'The Times' between Murdoch and Harold Evans (the man he had appointed as editor), and internal disputes between Evans and his own journalists, led eventually to Evans' replacement.

The move in 1986 to Wapping from the environs of *Fleet Street* proved a major turning-point in the fortunes of the print unions, which declined dramatically. News International's success in shedding thousands of jobs could not have been done without the use of anti-trade union laws introduced by the Conservative government, and a deal made between Murdoch and the electricians' union. The print unions were further undermined by the imposition of fines and the seizure of assets. Journalists like Hugo Young left the Sunday Times in 1986, arguing that it now 'gave little space to discussions of poverty, inequality, injustice or other moral issues' (see Eldridge et al. 'The Mass Media and Power in Modern Britain', 1997). One successful News International tactic has been to reduce the cover price of its newspapers, thus creating a price war which its rivals cannot win. By mid-1994, sales of 'The Times' went up by 42 per cent as a result of this tactic. News International presently controls some 37 per cent of the UK newspaper market.

In 1995 Murdoch, disillusioned by Conservative legislation which restricts cross-media ownership, invited Tony Blair to speak to News International executives in Australia. In 1997 both 'The Sun' and (by April 27th, in the last week of the election campaign) 'The News of the World,' came out in support of the Labour party (or, more accurately, in favour of Tony Blair's leadership).

news journalism: the usual description of journalistic activity, found in the term 'news gathering', suggests that news simply happens, so journalists have only to collect material from their sources and put it into some kind of order. For example, many reporters talk about 'finding' stories. A different approach argues that all news is based on selection. Greg Philo (in Roger Fowler's 'Language in the News') argues that: 'news is not 'found' or even 'gathered' so much as made. It is a creation of a journalistic process.'

Despite the creation of 'media events' like press conferences, photo-opportunities and the like, some events are undeniably real, and news organisation has little control over when and where they occur. It is able, however, to present events in a certain light. Journalists usually look for what is often called an 'angle'. This is the same as asking 'what kind of event is this, and what approach can we use to make it interesting?' (See *news values*).

news management: techniques used by state agencies and other related bodies, to control the free flow of information. News management techniques include *censorship* (at source or after the event), *disinformation* (the release of misleading data), the *lobbying* system in Britain, the use of *D-notices*, informal contact with media proprietors and editors, and so on.

news values: those criteria that an event must satisfy before journalists and editors decide it is 'newsworthy' (worth turning into a story). News values were described in 1965 by two academics called Galtung and Ruge, who examined the kind of stories that news organisations seemed to regard as important. Since the publication of their work, the list of news values has been revised and updated. Although many of those who work in television and the press would not necessarily agree that they share the ideas set out below, news values still provide a useful guide to the way that institutional constraints affect the creation of news. The list comprises:

- Threshold: the relative 'size' of an event. If an event is thought too insignificant, it will not be reported. The danger may be that smaller incidents which later prove to have great potential, are ignored.
- Simplicity: where an incident falls into an established category (scandal, disaster), has a readily appreciated meaning (is easily understood), or where at the very least, the range of possible meanings is limited, then it stands a good chance of being reported.
- Recency: this refers to how 'fresh' an event is thought to be. An important story which has just occurred will probably be given more prominence than an event from the previous day. Stories are often allowed to become 'dead' issues, unless some new development occurs.
- Relevance: relevance means that an item makes sense within the broad context of the 'home' culture, touching upon a nation's concerns and interests. However, because of the diversity of cultural experience, what may seem interesting to one group may not seem relevant to another.
- Continuity: once a story has achieved notice, any further development is likely to continue to be reported, so that the event will be presented in narrative form.
- Composition: most organisations will attempt to 'balance' the type of news they report. For example, if a great deal of 'negative' material has been presented, then editors may try to find items which create a more positive impression.
- Personalisation: events are presented as though they are the consequence of individual actions, rather than the result of deeper structural developments.
- Reference to elite countries and elite persons: a great deal of western journalism is focused on news concerning the developed nations, so that events in less-developed countries are sometimes ignored. 'Elite persons' refers to the individuals who lead governments, and the rich and famous who also attract a great deal of attention. A trivial action carried out by a *celebrity* may receive extensive coverage.

- Negativity: most 'hard' news stories seem to deal with misfortune; crashes, deaths, natural disasters and other negative material seem always to attract attention.

newsbooks: small pamphlets which appeared weekly, emerging first on the continent and appearing in England in the 1620s. Contemporary reports described them as 'diurnalls', 'mercuries', 'currants', 'corantos', as well as 'weekly pamphlets of news' and of course 'newsbooks'. Because it was illegal to print domestic news, newsbooks were confined to reporting foreign events. By the 1640s, however, under the pressure of political upheaval, a number of unlicensed newsbooks appeared in print. The conflict between politically opposed newsbooks helped to fuel the political strife between King and Parliament which culminated in the English Civil War. The first newsbook of a distinctly political nature appeared somewhere in London at the end of November 1641. The title page carried the heading 'The Heads of Severall Proceedings in this Present Parliament'. Newsbooks were cheaply printed, containing in many cases the purest invention, but in others carrying political discourse of the most urgent and important kind. Titles of newsbooks included; 'A Perfect Diurnall', 'The Kingdoms Weekly Post', 'The Moderate Intelligencer', 'Mercurius Britanicus' and 'The Man in the Moon'.

newscast: a radio or television broadcast devoted to news reports.

Newspaper Publishers Association: a body which represents the owners of national newspapers.

Newspaper Society: a group representing owners of provincial newspapers in England and Wales, and of suburban London weeklies. In the early 1990s, the Society organised a National Vocational Qualification (NVQ) based on workplace assessments. Three headings were drawn up by the Society to cover their requirements; writing, production journalism and press photography. Richard Keeble ('The Newspapers Handbook', p. 346) writes of this sort of training 'a reporter covering a diary event, for instance, will be required to display accurate fact-gathering skills, an appreciation of any legal and ethical issues and the ability to file copy to a deadline'.

newspapers: publications appearing usually on a daily or weekly basis, which carry news and other forms of material (entertainment, *reviews, cartoons, editorials, features, advertisements* and so on). The traditional form of newspaper organisation is characterised by the concentration of a number of different functions in one place. Management, editorial and production is usually located in the same building, to facilitate the the goal of working under pressure to fulfil deadlines. Distribution of newspapers is usually, however, in the hands of a separate organisation. Newspaper workers are organised as hierarchies, with strongly demarcated lines of authority and control. In many countries, there is a regional as well as a national press.

National daily titles in Britain include: 'The Mirror', 'The Guardian' (run by a trust), 'The Independent' (controlled by the Mirror group and European business interests), 'The Sun', 'The Times' (both part of *News International*), 'Financial Times' (run by the Pearson group), 'The Daily Mail' (run by Associated Newspapers), and 'The Daily Express' (part of the MAI and United News and Media group). Sunday titles with a national circulation are: 'Mail on Sunday', 'News of the World', 'Sunday Times' (both News International), 'The People' (Mirror Group), and 'Sunday Express'. (See also *press, news values, news journalism and news agencies*).

newsreel: films showing major news events, included in cinema programmes from the early years of the twentieth century to the 1950s, when the practice began to die out. Well-known newsreel companies included 'Pathé' and 'British Movietone News'. The most celebrated American newsreel, documentary in many respects, was 'The March of Time' series.

niche marketing: while *marketing* is the concept of meeting customer needs and creating brand loyalty, niche marketing is concerned to identify smaller, more lucrative markets. The problems with this form of marketing are its negative effects on economic equality (poorer consumers become of decreasing interest to certain manufacturers) and the danger that the character of cultural artefacts (films, television programmes, etc.) will be determined by the advertisers and corporate bodies which provide the bulk of media funding.

Nielsen: a trans-national company that deals in audience research, best known for its television ratings in the USA, but also involved in the measurement of cable services and other new technologies.

night for day: the shooting of film by night, with treatment (filters, post-production) to turn it into a daytime scene.

nitrate base: cellulose nitrate; a base used for film-stock until the 1950s, which was highly unstable. It was replaced by cellulose triacetate.

noddies: cutaways edited into a scene to show the reaction of an individual. For example, in a traditional interview, shot with one camera and two people, noddies may be used after the interview is finished to show reaction shots of the interviewer (nodding in agreement for example).

nominalism: a philosophy which emerged in the mediaeval era, founded on the belief that general terms or 'universals' (a concept like 'blueness') have no real existence. Instead, individual objects or 'particulars' (in this case, blue things), and the *paradigms* to which they belong, form the only reliable evidence of the existence of things.

nonlinear editing: the use of *digital* technology to edit video data. It encourages free movement through linear narratives.

non-verbal communication is *communication* which takes place without the use of speech. Non-verbal communication includes *body language,* physical orientation, distance between individuals, appearance and *gesture.* To a large degree, non-verbal communication is ambiguous; there is no direct correlation between a particular stimulus and the observable outcome. Judy Gahagen (see 'Non-Verbal Communication') notes that (p. 73): '... in speech and conversation we use non-verbal signals to help the listener to follow the content of what is being said ... language, fully occupied as it is with carrying the ideational content of the communication, could not carry all the information relating to the mechanics of social interaction as well, and it is non-verbal communication which is used for this purpose'.

normative theories: normative theories of media organisations are models of how the media ought to operate, or how they might be expected to operate under certain conditions. In 'Mass Communication Theory', Denis McQuail identifies six normative theories. These are:

- Authoritarian theory, characterised by a drive to make the media conform to the wishes of the established order, often through the use of censorship.
- Free press theory, in which media would operate without the need for a licence or permit, and would remain free from any form of censorship.
- Social responsibility theory, in which media would fulfil certain obligations to society, based on high standards of conduct (truthfulness, accuracy and so on), and would avoid encouraging anti-social behaviour; journalists should be accountable to society as well as their employers.
- Soviet media theory, a state collectivist view which emerged from the now-defunct Soviet Union; the perspective of this approach is based on the idea that media should serve the interests of those who claimed to speak for the working class, relying on regulation and censorship and using media outlets to educate and socialise the society as a whole.

- Development media theory, based upon the needs of poorer nations, and requiring 'third world' media to reinforce national programmes of development, even at the cost of freedom of expression.
- Democratic-participant theory, a challenge to other models of media organisation, and geared to the needs and aspirations of an active audience, which has the right to establish its own media based upon local and group-centred requirements.

norms: established modes of behaviour appropriate to public existence in general, and to certain situations in particular; norms work on the basis of shared values and beliefs. Individuals will acknowledge (even if they do not obey) universal as well as particular behavioural expectations. Universal expectations are the generally accepted range of actions and declarations which it is usual to produce in any situation. Particular expectations grow from the types of conduct thought suited to any event, and are drawn from the general field of social convention. Clashes between different customs or standards of behaviour are quite common, where two or more social groups meet in some public or private space.

Sometimes, particular forms of behaviour are deliberately adopted, in order to set out the difference between one set of values and another.

nouvelle vague: see *new wave.*

O

obit (obituary): a death notice which appears in newspapers.

object: an object is any material thing which is presented to the mind, especially anything which can be perceived directly through the senses. In *Peirce's* semiotics, an object is that thing to which a *sign* (or a 'representamen') refers, located in either the human mind or the external world. Peirce used a three-part system to explain signification. The first element is the sign/representamen (firstness), the second is the object (the reference, known as secondness), and the third is the interpretant (thirdness, the combined effect of the first two). The object is similar to *Saussure's* signified.

objectivity: in philosophy, the doctrine that knowledge of *objects* comes before (and is more dependable than) knowledge of the *self* or subject. In the social sciences, objectivity means the pursuit of a balanced, fair and rational perspective on events, especially where controversial issues are debated, or where research is carried out into the nature of an event.

Traditionally, cultural theorists have harboured deep suspicions about 'objective' approaches, on the grounds that they mask an *ideological* purpose. Stuart Hall, for example, called it an 'operational fiction' (1984), used by the news *media* to construct a viewpoint which supports the dominant *ideology*. In his opinion 'all edited or manipulated symbolic reality is impregnated with common-sense assumptions'. It is certainly true that references to objectivity can provide editors and media owners with a formal defence for supporting the *status quo*, but objectivity remains a guiding principle for many journalists, enabling them to defend integrity and independence. Westerstahl (1983) divided objectivity into 'factualness' and 'impartiality'. Factualness means a form of reporting dealing in statements which can be checked against other sources, and which are then presented without comment. Impartiality is an attitude adopted by reporters. Each of these two categories is further divided, factualness into 'truth' and 'relevance', and impartiality into 'balance' and 'neutrality'.

obligatory scene: a scene put into a television programme in the belief that audiences always expect certain types of material, irrespective of genre. This may include representations of sex or violence.

oeuvre: a French term for 'work' which is applied to the character or quality of a writer's/artist's entire output. Oeuvre is usually applied to the films of directors who are regarded as 'serious' artists. (See also *auteur*.)

off screen: events which are not part of a film's *diegesis,* such as sound which does not come from the on-screen narrative, reported events which nevertheless affect the action, and so on.

off the record: a media briefing which is given on the understanding that the source will not be revealed. In Britain, the lobby system (which began in 1884 see lobbying) is a device used by government to provide information which cannot be attributed to a named government spokesperson. Journalists gather at Parliament and are allowed access to officials. From the *media's* point of view, the advantage is a regular supply of information. The party in power benefits from being able to shape the news agenda while avoiding responsibility for what has been said.

Official Secrets Act: a UK Act dating from 1911 which prevents public access to information classified as secret. The use of censorship is often increased during national crises; the Act was reinforced in 1920 during the war against republicanism in Ireland (before the partition of North and South) and again at the outbreak of the Second World War in 1939. The Act has proved to be a major force in ensuring censorship of information on a number of civil issues. Individuals in a number of occupations have to sign the Act. The revision of the Act, in June 1990, dispensed with a clause which allowed the 'public interest' as a possible defence during prosecution.

off-line: devices that are not controlled by, or in communication with, a computer's central processing unit. 'Off-line' is sometimes used of people who are not connected to a computer network.

OIRT: stands for Organisation Internationale de Radio et Télévision, an eastern European broadcasting organisation affiliated with Intervision (an organisation set up to allow programme exchange).

OMNIMAX: the second-generation version of IMAX, the OMNIMAX screen exceeds the periphery of vision, while the filmstock is nine times the size of standard cinema film. Like the IMAX system, OMNIMAX uses 70 mm film which passes through the projector horizontally.

on-air: a broadcast or satellite station which is going out live; in other words, as a public transmission or a recording is taking place.

on spec: a description of journalistic writing produced without having been commissioned; the term is sometimes used of unsolicited material sent to newspapers by members of the public.

one hundred and eighty degree rule: a line which is supposed to divide a scene in two; the camera keeps strictly to one side of the line while filming continuous action such as a conversation between two people. In this way, it provides the audience with a consistent frame of reference, showing first one person looking out to the right of the frame, and then the other looking to the left. It is a film convention which, if broken, confuses the audience because it appears as though the character has moved out of position, whereas in reality it is the camera which has changed its angle of address. (See *crossing the line*).

one on one: a news interview where a single journalist confronts one interviewee (a politician, for example). This format can allow in-depth questioning, encouraging an interrogative approach, but has been used on occasion as an excuse for sychophancy.

onomatopoeia: the suggestive characteristic of a group of words which imitate the sound made by the phenomenon to which they refer. Examples could be sizzle, plop, buzz, miaow, etc. Onomatopoeic words are sometimes given as evidence against *Saussure's* belief in the arbitrary nature of language, because they have a real link with the things they signify. Saussure believed that the link between words and things is accidental and has no material basis.

open mike: a microphone that is left on during a broadcast, enabling listeners to hear remarks which are not intended for public consumption.

open texts: Umberto Eco distinguished between texts whose structures are open, allowing for audience interpretation, and texts which are closed, leaving little possibility for different readings. An open text may experiment with structure, narration, temporal sequencing and so on; it is *multiaccentual* and does not display an 'ideological' intention.

operationalization: in research work, concepts need to be 'operationalized'; this means that they must be put in a form which can be measured. Suppose for example that the subject under discussion is 'violence in the media'. The first step is to set out all the elements each variable contains. Violence is a variable because it can be split into different categories, such as violence against the person, vandalism, violence in the cinema, cartoon violence and so on. The media can also be differentiated, by type, by function, and by social role, for example. Once these factors have been identified, it is possible to form questions which address the issue, or to write a series of statements and ask respondents to mark the one which is closest to their belief.

opinion leader: in two-step flow theory, an opinion leader is an individual who is interested in and knowledgeable about some public communication issue, such as election addresses, violence on television, etc. Less well-informed members of the public supposedly rely on the opinion leader to help interpret messages and form opinions.

opinion poll: the canvassing of public response to social and political issues. It is carried out quite intensively during election campaigns, when individuals are asked about voting intentions, the quality of party leaders, and major issues which are thought of most importance to the electorate. The usual method of polling is the sample survey, where individuals are contacted by telephone. Opinion polls are usually carried out by commercial organisations (Harris, *Gallup*, ICM, for example) in conjunction with newspapers. Most of the questions used in polls are therefore fairly straightforward. Some academic researchers regard them as unreliable, because the questions are too simple, failing to consider the social context of issues and the underlying motivation of the respondents.

optical disc: a disc which has been imprinted with information (perhaps a series of shots from a film), in the form of a series of microscopic pits burned into its surface. These can be read by a laser acting as a stylus, and translated back into images. (See also *compact discs*.)

optical effects: a term used to describe special effects work done in an editing suite, such as wipes, fades, dissolves, etc.

Oracle: stands for Optical Reception of Announcements by Coded Line Electronics. Oracle was the independent television companies' teletext service, until replaced in 1993 by Teleview.

organisations: an organisation is a human collective which is created in order to pursue an explicit purpose or goal (see *formal organisations*). Among the features of an organisation are the following:

- it has a set of official or public objectives
- it allocates roles to individuals and sets up a division of labour
- it institutes methods of control over individuals and groups

- it sets up specialised departments or sections
- it develops formally structured relationships
- it manages resources.

Organisational communication will take place in order to meet the following needs or eventualities:

- the presence of 'non-programmed' activity, i.e. that type of event which is not planned for, or foreseen by the official system
- the initiation, establishment and supervision of programmes
- the provision of data to pursue a course of action
- the focussing of attention on problems
- the production of information about the results of activities within the organisation.

orientation: in studies of non-verbal communication, orientation means the physical attitude adopted and the distance maintained, by each individual during an interaction. It can also be used to describe the ideological perspective adopted by one person/group with regard to another, or the attitudes and beliefs which provide the background to an individual's response to an event or act.

other: the other is that which is outside, and different to, the self. It may be another person, a group or class of individuals, the opposite sex in general, or an imagined figure or category. G. H. Mead used the term to refer to the general notion of the 'not self', an awareness of which he thought to be vital in the creation of self. Jacques Lacan also used the idea when he said that the human subject is created through the tension between the opposite poles of 'I' and 'you'. In later work, Lacan called language itself 'the other'. The usefulness of the term lies in its radical potential for showing how identity is constructed through contrast, though many writers simply use the 'other' to legitimise endless discussion of the self.

out-point: the electronic point which marks the place where a scene in video or film is to be stopped. A new 'in-point' is then set to introduce the next frame.

outside broadcast (OB): a broadcast made from a location outside a studio, using equipment transported in vans, which also serve as control centres and editing suites. (See page 168 for illustration.)

out-take: a piece of film or a video taped sequence which has to be rejected for release or broadcast use, because of a noticeable error in delivery of lines, a mistake in continuity, mechanical breakdown, etc. (Out-takes provide employment for Denis Norden, Jeremy Beadle, and other performers.)

over-shoulder shot: a shot used to show two characters engaged in conversation. A medium close-up shows the back of one person's head and their right shoulder, with the speaker's face in the right-hand side of the frame. The shot which follows reverses the relationship between the participants. The original speaker now appears as the addressee, with the face of the other character featured in the left-hand side of the frame. (See page 169 for illustration.)

ownership: the possession of something; communication research draws attention to the social, political and cultural consequences of different forms of media ownership. Media outlets may be owned by private companies (often powerful

Outside broadcast

trans-nationals), controlled by public or state corporations, or in very rare cases managed by democratic or co-operative groups.

It is also important to consider what exactly it is possible to own. Typically, this will include anything from part of a core industry (newspaper production, for example), to multi-divisional ownership (of a publishing company, a radio station, a cable system, etc.). The aim of many companies is to achieve both vertical and horizontal integration. Vertical integration is the control of production, distribution and exhibition in one type of media, while horizontal integration is ownership of more than one outlet. Increasingly, corporate power attempts to extend itself across the globe. Successful media giants include Time Warner, Matsushita, Bertelsmann, *News Corporation,* and many others.

Companies with an international reach present national governments with a problem. The trans-national corporation may have begun its operations in one country, might still be recognised as a national asset, yet will often only be interested in the preferential treatment provided by governments, in the form of investment, legal protection and other advantages. Vincent Mosco ('The Political Economy of Communication', 1996) finds the attitude of national governments to 'their' companies rather curious (p. 180); 'US policy makers worry about the consequences of

Over-shoulder shot

having almost half of the Hollywood majors under foreign control, rather than asking what makes the rest American'. Bagdikian, writing in 1992, found that the growing concentration of media power included the increasing integration of the news and entertainment industries. Media industries have been instrumental in spreading the process of transnational ownership because they are often involved in spreading information about other products (advertising is a particular case in point). The background to modern media ownership includes the increase in broadcast channel capacity, the end of the state broadcasting model in the former 'socialist' countries, and the growth of mixed broadcasting systems as the rhetoric of public service is replaced by the values of the marketplace.

P

page break: the place in a text where type is carried over to the next page; an indentation or line in a computer programme which indicates the point where page breaks will appear in the printed version of any file.

page proof: a printed copy of a text complete with page breaks, and usually all features of layout, used for checking mistakes and print quality (see *proofreading*).

Pagemaker is a software package used for desktop publishing; it was introduced in 1985 by the Aldus Corporation.

pagination: the process of numbering the pages of a printed text in consecutive order, or the page numbers themselves.

pamphlet: a short booklet with a paper cover, usually of at least eight pages.

panning shot: a steady camera movement along a horizontal axis. Panning shots are used to scan across a scene, providing the viewer with information which a fixed shot would not reveal.

paparazzi: a term which describes the unscrupulous photographers who make a living from taking 'candid' pictures of celebrities and film stars.

paradigm: a paradigm is a set of symbolic elements which has the potential to convey meaning. The usual example given (see Fiske in O'Sullivan, 1994) is the alphabet, in which the paradigm of 26 letters provides the opportunity to select combinations from the symbols on offer.

Fiske (p. 216) argues that 'letters chosen from [the alphabet] may be combined to form written words'. These combinations or words are called syntagms. Syntagms are therefore 'a signifying whole' made from 'a combination of units'. This seems clear enough, but there are some problems which must be addressed.

At the beginning of his definition, Fiske states that a syntagm is created when a unit from one paradigm is combined with 'units from another paradigm'. If this is true, then a syntagm cannot be made up from just one source (one paradigm). This would suggest in turn that words are not true syntagms.

It may be the case, however, that the alphabet is not a straightforward example of a paradigm. Fiske writes that 'letters chosen from it [the alphabet] may be combined to form written words'. This implies that the free 'selection' of any letter is possible, whereas letter combination is already 'pre-set' by larger units of meaning (morphemes and words). In speech, knowledge of sound combinations (or phonemes) is used to produce meaning.

Another point to note is that the alphabet is composed of two different kinds of letter-form, consonants and vowels, which have quite different powers in language. This can lead to the conclusion that the alphabet is actually made from two paradigms, from which the syntagmic level (words) may be constructed.

paradigms (film): in film, individual shots are paradigmatic choices (Monaco, 'How to Read a Film', 1981, p. 132). Monaco writes; 'once a filmmaker has decided what to shoot, the two questions are how to shoot it ... and how to present the shot'.

The choice of how to shoot the subject is made from the paradigm, while the presentation (the final edited sequence) forms the syntagm.

Monaco's example of choice is a shot of a rose. He writes that 'the rose is filmed from a certain angle, the camera moves or does not move, the colour is bright or dull, the rose is fresh or fading, the thorns apparent or hidden, the background clear ... or vague ... the shot held for a long time or briefly, and so on'. The shot which is actually composed creates certain meanings in its audience. Monaco considers this to be a paradigmatic connotation. In other words, the actual shot is taken from a paradigm which includes all the other possible shots of the same sort. It suggests a certain kind of meaning to audience members because they are somehow aware ('not necessarily consciously') of all the other shots of a similar type which might have been selected! So, according to this idea, a blurred close-up of a rose may suggest a particular meaning because it is compared with 'its unrealised companions in the paradigm, or general model, of this type of shot' (Monaco, p. 131).

In fact, Monaco's various examples of shot construction, including angle, timing, movement, focus and so on, are all paradigms in their own right. This means that a single shot could actually be a syntagm (a complete message which unfolds over time). Monaco, however, reserves the term syntagm for a sequence of different shots.

The other problem is that it is difficult to see how 'unrealised' shots, which cannot be studied, can be regarded as elements in a paradigm. To be part of the paradigm, any possible shots must be similar enough to the existing one to be recognised as its companions, but different enough to be real alternatives. If they are too similar, they are no longer individual units, and if they are dissimilar they fall outside the paradigm. The only 'evidence' offered for the existence of alternative shots, is the presence of the actual shot itself (created from a range of technical and aesthetic choices, not from other 'ready made' shots).

paralanguage: 'para', meaning 'beyond' or 'to one side of' something, comes from an ancient Greek term. The nearest modern meaning is a kind of close imitation, though 'para' also carries suggestions of irregularity, as in 'paramilitary'. 'Paralanguage', therefore, is a form of communication which stands in for, or imitates, some of the features and capabilities of *language*. It usually refers to vocal communication which remains non-verbal. So, for example, paralanguage could include the following: *intonation,* volume, and stress, as well as the sounds made to indicate indecision, hesitation and so on ('ums and aahs' as they are known).

parallax: parallax is the apparent displacement (change in position) of a viewed object, which is actually caused by the angle of observation. In the cinema, parallax is used to create a sense of depth. This is apparent, for example, when a movie camera remains fixed on an object but changes the angle of its perspective.

parallel action in the cinema is a narrative device which indicates that two (or more) separate scenes are meant to be occurring at the same time. The effect is achieved by *cross-cutting* between the scenes.

parody: an imitation of an established form, usually with a comic intention. A parody usually imitates an established genre, or copies a particularly successful media text. The popular British television series 'Red Dwarf' parodied a number of science fiction conventions, while a series of car commercials mimicked the form and content of Ridley Scott's 1991 film 'Thelma and Louise'.

parole: one of two divisions Ferdinand de *Sausurre* made in the study of language; parole is made up of the infinitely variable speech events which are produced by individuals. Saussure did not regard parole as a useful starting point for the study of language. On the other hand, an investigation of *langue* (the abstract system of rules underlying speech), was regarded as the true object of linguistics.

participant observation: a method of data collection in which the researcher takes part in the activities of the group under study. At the beginning of the exercise, it must be decided whether the approach taken is to be overt or covert. In the former case, the subjects of the enquiry are aware that they are being studied, though the real intentions of the researcher may be hidden. In the case of covert research, the true purpose of the work (and therefore the real identity of the researcher), is kept secret. Participant observation has produced some useful *ethnographic* studies, such as Elliot Liebow's 1967 research on black American males in Washington D.C., but it is usually more suited to studies of behaviour than communication. Conversational analysis, for example, requires the detailed recording of speech. This is sometimes done openly and on other occasions in secret, but in either case the verbal participation of the researcher would destroy the whole exercise. David Morley, in 'Television, Audiences and Cultural Studies' (1992), argues that participant observation of television viewing is not much use without interviews which can provide (p. 181) 'access to the kind of language, the criteria of distinction and the types of categorisations' used by viewers to explain their experience of television. Ethnographic study in general, however, has grown in importance in the field of media and communication. Shaun Moores (see 'Interpreting Audiences'), advocates (p. 4) 'an ethnographic perspective of a certain kind – one which is committed to critically analysing culture as well as describing it'.

participant roles: the term 'participant' refers to someone who takes part in an event; 'role' means the part or function adopted in a particular situation. There are three basic roles in any speech event; that of addressor/speaker, addressee, and hearer/audience. In some cases, the addressor and speaker roles are split. The addressee is the person to whom the address is made, while the hearer/audience role is that which observes and evaluates the event.

party election broadcasts: during British local and general elections, broadcasts are made by political parties for radio and television. A party election broadcast (PEB) is allocated to any party which has put up more than 50 deposits for seats. Between elections, broadcasts are called party political broadcasts. The conditions governing broadcasts are overseen by a body called the Political Broadcast Committee.

pay TV is any television subscription service where the viewer pays for the material watched. In the USA, 'pay TV' often refers to the payment made for each individual programme. Morley ('Television, Audiences and Cultural Studies', 1992) believes that (p. 211) 'the selection of programmes (e.g. in the form of Pay-TV) will increasingly begin to look like the selection of goods'.

PC: see *personal computer*.

PCM: see *pulse code modulation.*

Peacock report: the 1989 report on public service broadcasting. The Peacock committee argued that broadcasting should 'move towards a sophisticated market system based on consumer sovereignty', a system which 'recognises that viewers and listeners are the best ultimate judges of their own interest'. The committee advocated a free-market approach. In their analysis of new market forces in broadcasting, Corner, Harvey and Lury (see 'Behind the Screens', 1994) make the comment that 'such a perspective was in line with dominant tendencies in the broader political culture of Britain at the time ... Mrs. Thatcher and her government were concerned to promote both a 'reconstructed' British economy and a 'reconstructed' national value system'.

peak time: in television, that period of viewing (usually from six until nine p.m.) when the largest audience is watching.

Peirce, C.S.: Charles Sanders Peirce (1839–1918) was an American logician and philosopher. Peirce founded 'pragmatics', an approach to the study of knowledge and meaning which argues that human consciousness is mediated by *signs.* In Peirce's words, 'every thought must be interpreted by another ... all thought is in signs' (in Jensen, 1995). Peirce believed that the process of meaning-creation was continuous, that each interpretant of a sign (each idea or effect produced in the mind of a human subject) produces another sign. The difference between this 'unlimited semiosis' and Derrida's theory of *'differance',* where meaning is always deferred or 'put off' because each sign produces another, is Peirce's belief that signs produce 'a predisposition to act' (see Jensen, 'The Social Semiotics of Mass Communication', p. 11). In other words, Peirce's philosophy is more concerned with social action. Instead of seeing reality as created by language, Peircean semiotics accepts that signs enable people to understand and manipulate the real, even though the nature of reality itself will always feature in scholarly debate.

Peirce's studies were not confined to the properties of signs; these were part of a larger system of thought, which set out three levels of phenomena to be found in the world. These are 'firstness' (the actual quality of things, including the colour of objects, the feelings associated with events, even the taste of various foods), secondness (the actual, 'brutal' facts we encounter), and thirdness (thoughts and the way that the mind interprets or characterises the factual level).

As his work progressed, Peirce became convinced that individual signs were composed of many complex elements, moving beyond the simpler *icon, index,* and *symbol* categories usually associated with his name. Overall, his major contribution to communication studies lies in the value he places on the process of interpretation, and his interest in signs as real phenomena.

perception: is the act of observing, using any of the human faculties (hearing, sight, taste, smell, and touch). In media and communication studies, perception can mean sensory perception (the apprehension of the external world) and the social observations which people make (the value and worth accorded to different events, things, situations and people). In 'Communication Studies' (1996), Price sets out the following questions for the study of perception and communication:

- What faculties do we use to perceive our environment?
- How reliable are these faculties?
- Are such faculties always actively deployed?
- How do we communicate our understanding of the world to others?
- What social or environmental constraints are placed on our communication?

performance: see *competence*.

performative statements are those which match the performance of an action. The linguist J.L. Austin disagreed with the idea that a statement can only be used to describe some state of affairs or to utter some fact. Austin used the example of the performative statement 'I name this ship,' where this is not just a description of what is being done, but also the actual performance of the act itself. Austin discussed other types of utterance, including constatives (utterances not intended to produce factual information) and ethical propositions (which are used to produce emotion or proscribe conduct).

Austin noted that the performative utterance must be delivered by the appropriate person. For example, Coulthard notes (in 'An Introduction to Discourse Analysis') that a blacksmith may know the marriage ceremony perfectly well, but will not have the power to make the words socially significant. In some forms of performative speech, the utterance made does not depend on the status of the person concerned; anyone is allowed to utter the statement. Austin gives the examples of 'I warn you' and 'I apologise', where the act of warning or apologising is actually performed in speech.

periodical: a publication issued at regular intervals, containing a number of articles written by a variety of authors. Magazines and journals count as periodicals, but *newspapers* do not.

periodicity: periodicity describes the timescale within which news organisations operate; some writers argue that only dramatic or urgent events fit the time-frame of most news outlets, so that other, more longterm developments are neglected. (See also *news values*.)

permissions: an agreement sought by an author or publisher, to use copyright material in a specific publication. Permissions vary in cost, from free to reasonably low outlays for transcripts, or very considerable sums for pictures by well-known photographers. The term also refers to the kind of agreement reached between film-makers and those who own suitable locations they wish to use.

persistence of vision: the human eye is capable of retaining an impression of an image for a fraction of a second. When film is projected at 24 frames a second, persistence of vision produces the impression of continuous movement.

persona: from the Latin, persona means the part or character 'acted' by an individual (the characters in a play are referred to as the *'dramatis personae'*). In Jungian psychology, the persona is the 'mask' or outward face presented to the world. Another way of understanding persona would be to describe it as the public character adopted when individuals are called upon to fulfil certain social roles.

personal computer (PC): in the earlier phase of computer marketing, a PC meant the smallest type of computer, designed for home or office use by one individual. The power and range of the PC has increased as its role has expanded.

perspective is the illusion of distance caused by the convergence of lines towards a certain point; perspective is used in drawing to create an impression of depth and to show the relative position of things. When used to describe a human quality, perspective means the way that the mind perceives the relationship between various things (as in 'keeping the issue in perspective').

persuasion: a definition of this concept is given by O'Keefe in his book 'Persuasion' (1990). He states (p. 17) that persuasion is 'a successful intentional effort at influencing another's mental state through communication in a circumstance in which the persuadee has some measure of freedom'. O'Keefe covers here all the essential features of persuasion: intention, context, communication, freedom of choice and success. As O'Keefe says, 'when we say that one person has persuaded another, we ordinarily identify a *successful* attempt to influence'.

phatic communication: this refers to those seemingly unimportant, conventional or ordinary exchanges like 'good morning' or 'how are you?', which serve to open channels of communication, establish interpersonal relations and reinforce social cohesion. The 'phatic' function was established as a category of communication by Malinowski (1884–1942).

phenomenologism: a philosophical approach which begins with the study of appearances, and argues that things have an essence which may be discovered through description. The appearances which form the basis for such an inquiry are phenomena, what Ayer ('A Dictionary of Philosophy') calls 'the objects of experience.'

phoneme: a phoneme is a unit of significant sound in any given language (from phonology, the sound patterns found in language). Phonemes are used to distinguish between the pronunciation of words which have similar structures. For instance, the words 'sight' and 'fight' are distinguished by the initial sounds, [s] and [f]. The sounds or 'forms' of the two words are otherwise identical.

phonetics: this is the study of linguistic sounds and how they are produced and understood. As Fromkin and Rodman say in 'An Introduction to Language' (1993, p. 176) 'knowing a language means knowing the meaning of the sounds which represent morphemes, words, phrases, and sentences'. Although language is made up of individual sounds, natural speech does not produce 'breaks' between words or other units of meaning. Yet native speakers are able to separate or 'segment' the continuous sounds they hear, turning them into recognisable concepts. Encounters with phonetics occur when the 'illogical' structure of English words is scrutinised, and a phonetic alphabet is proposed instead.

photo essay: a comprehensive study of a theme or event, using photographs and captions. Photo essays are carried in a number of outlets, but the high point of the form was reached in the 1930s and 40s in magazines like 'Picture Post'.

photocropping: the practice of cutting an area or areas from a photographic print or negative, in order to strengthen its composition and thus its visual impact. (See *cropping* for illustration.)

photograph: an image produced by the action of light on a light-sensitive surface, fixed by a chemical solution. 'Photo' comes from the Greek term for light. Photographs are produced as documents, textual illustration, news journalism, art, portraiture, landscape and in a number of other forms.

Photograph – Mounted police clashing with demonstrators, London, March 1990

photography: the practice of composition and image-making associated with the chemical action of light on sensitive film. Courses in photography are often divided into the *aesthetic* aspects of the subject ('history and appreciation', for example), and practical and methodological content.

Aesthetics, history and appreciation may include:

- the styles of photography in a historical context, including portraiture, documentary and photojournalism, pictorialism and naturalism, realism, abstraction and surrealism, and contemporary art photography
- the role of photography and its relationship to other visual media
- the aesthetic and informational aspects of photography
- critical observations of the role of photography in society
- the interpretation of photographic representation
- the cultural and aesthetic influences associated with particular styles.

Practical work and theory of photographic practice may encompass:

- study of major historical processes, additive screen processes, subtractive processes, substantive and non-substantive processes
- knowledge and understanding of equipment, concepts and procedures - types of cameras, types of lenses, methods of focussing, function and effects of aperture and shutter, supplementary lenses, colour, filters and special effects, and care of equipment
- light and light sources, including, properties of light, characteristics of light sources used in photography, effect of light on surfaces, reflectors, inverse square law, control of lighting for effects
- health and safety
- exposure, including choice of exposure in different situations, metering systems, reciprocity failure and control of exposure for effects
- sensitive materials, including composition of negatives and colour reversal, sensitivity of photographic materials, selection of materials for appropriate purposes, relationship between contrast, speed, and grain size, selection of photographic papers for contrast, image colour and surface texture
- processing, to include printing and finishing.

*Photography – the view from Nièpce's window at Gras, 1826 (see **heliography**)*

photojournalism: the practice of reporting news stories through the use of photographs or, in a narrower sense, the use of photographs to support print journalism. In the latter case, the news photo is supposed to act as a visual 'key' to the article it accompanies (it is usually seen in the *context* of the printed page). The picture may also have a *caption* and may appear under a *headline*. At its best, a good photograph helps to reveal aspects of a story which would otherwise remain hidden or obscure.

The job of the photojournalist is to produce an image which not only records an event, but also makes a strong visual impression on an audience. Henri Cartier-Bresson's notion of the *decisive moment* refers to the idea that there is always a brief period of time in any event, when the perfect picture may be captured. This concept is still quite influential in news photography. Unlike the photographs taken by private individuals ('snapshots') or the practice of art photography, successful photojournalism is able to make a considerable impact on a large audience. Photojournalism is also closely related to *documentary* photography. Documentary photography is concerned to produce a record of a particular situation, with the aim of providing evidence (a 'document') for a variety of purposes (campaigns, government projects, surveys and so on).

photojournalists are those who practise the trade of photojournalism. The moral as well as *aesthetic* choices faced by photojournalists provides the dramatic tension in a number of films which feature the photographer as hero/heroine (compare the feature film 'Under Fire' and the documentary 'Pictures from a Revolution', for contrasting portrayals of American photojournalists recording the Nicaraguan revolution).

War photography is one of the most dramatic manifestations of photojournalism. The work of the early war photographers like Roger Fenton and Matthew Brady was not true photojournalism, in the modern sense, because their work could not be printed in newspapers. Fenton was British, and took photographs of the Crimean War, while Brady was an American photographer who employed a number of assistants to make images of the American Civil War.

Famous photojournalists include the various generations of the *Magnum* group, and the photographers who covered the Vietnam war (Larry Burrows, Don McCullin, Philip Jones-Griffiths, Tim Page, Mark Jury, David Douglas Duncan, and so on).

photomontage: is the combination of two words: 'photography', the action of light on a chemically-prepared surface, and 'montage', a technique of cutting apart and recombining different images. Photomontage is therefore a technique for combining different photographic sources in order to create new images. It is, however, more than a technical process; it is a method which allows the 'realism' of the photographic image to be questioned. Some argue that the end result, a rather surreal juxtaposition which still retains the technical accuracy of the original elements, is more 'truthful' than straightforward photojournalism.

It was common practice in the nineteenth century to use combination printing to add human figures to a scenic photograph, and to combine different elements from pictures taken at different locations. Another reason for the use of this technique was the difficulty faced by many photographers; it was almost impossible to obtain sharp foreground detail and 'interesting' skies, because of the imbalance between the different intensities of light. Therefore, photographers would take two separate negatives, cover the areas they wished to improve, and print twice on the same piece of paper.

Photomontage – 'Britain reduced to a skeleton' by Peter Kennard

photomontagists: in the early years of the twentieth century, a number of radical artists founded a movement called 'dada', which was anti-art and very critical of the established political system. In Germany, the dada group claimed to have been the first to invent the term *photomontage.*

In May 1916, George Grosz and John Heartfield produced a picture by pasting a series of advertisements, labels, and other images together. Soon, this technique was used by the dada group to attack the establishment. It was during the rise of the Nazi party in Germany, in the 1920s and 1930s, that photomontage became a powerful weapon in the fight against fascism.

John Heartfield, who tried to tell the truth about his surroundings through the use of startling images, became the most famous of the early photomontage artists. Instead of trying to take a completely accurate picture of something, Heartfield took many images and combined them in ways which revealed the reality beneath the surface of events. Other celebrated montagists of this era were Raoul Housemann and Hannah Hoch, but they did not posses Heartfield's talent for political commentary. The political tradition was continued in the later part of the twentieth century, by photographers like Klaus Staeck, Cath Tate and Peter Kennard, who made a particular target of Conservative government and the military build-up of nuclear weaponry like cruise missiles. Kennard's 'The Haywain' of 1983, which showed Constable's painting with the addition of a cruise missile, was one in a long line of powerful images. Many of his montages of warheads and weaponry were mass-produced and carried on peace demonstrations. Cath Tate's images are less polished, showing the raw edge of life in the 'enterprise culture' of the 1980s.

photo-opportunity: an event designed specifically for media coverage. A photo-opportunity is used by politicians and celebrities to gain the media's attention, with the emphasis placed on uncritical visual coverage.

pie charts are diagrams for displaying quantitative data, so called because of their circular shape and the divisions drawn from the centre outwards. Pie charts are useful in showing proportions relative to the whole; for example, information on the percentage of people watching various types of programme over a specified time may be effectively displayed in a pie chart.

Pilkington Committee: the Pilkington Committee was set up in 1960 to consider the cultural effect of commercial television. Its report, made in 1962, declared that ITV 'operates to lower standards of enjoyment and understanding'. The committee also complained about a 'comprehensive carelessness about moral standards generally' which it felt characterised commercial programming. In 1964, the BBC was awarded the second channel (which became BBC 2), largely through the influence of the Pilkington report. Most of its recommendations, however, came to nothing. Watson and Hill, in 'A Dictionary of Communication and Media Studies', argue that (p. 171) 'Pilkington established a set of judgmental criteria, albeit elitist-cultural, which have formed a rallying point ever since for broadcasting reformers'.

pilot: an episode of a television programme made to test audience reaction. If it is successful, other episodes follow.

piracy: the notion of piracy has taken two distinct forms, one associated with dishonest reproduction of copyright material (such as 'pirate videos'), the other with the illegal activities of 'pirate radio' which, from the mid-1960s through to the present, challenged legitimate radio stations.

pixel: an abbreviation of the term 'picture element'. A computer screen is divided into rows and columns of tiny dots or 'cells', each of which is a pixel, the smallest unit on the screen that can be independently manipulated and stored.

pixillation is an animation technique which uses stop-motion photography to take individual shots of a model or other object. The object is moved between shots; when the film is finished, it is projected to give the impression of movement.

Pixillation is also used to photograph real actors, in order to create a sequence of startling movements.

play back: the facility on a tape machine for reviewing a recording; the process of playing a tape.

plug: a deliberate reference to a product or service, made during a supposedly non-commercial programme or feature. Talk shows and interviews are crammed with references to books, plays, songs and other material produced by or associated with the programme's guests.

pluralism: pluralism is a theory which argues that society is made up of many different groups, and that political and social power is fairly widely dispersed among these groups. Pluralists also believe that participatory democracy (a direct form of political culture) is impossible to achieve in very large societies, with the result that 'representative' democracies (made up of voters and organised political parties) provide a reasonable compromise between different factions.

Pluralism has faced extensive criticism for its failure to examine the imbalance of power in modern societies, and for concentrating instead upon the notion that various interest groups have equal chances to intervene on issues of public policy. In media studies, the concept of critical pluralism (which acknowledges that some interest groups have greater access to social power than others) has received some favourable coverage in media textbooks, despite (or because of) its reluctance to oppose corporate power.

point of view is the perspective from which events in a narrative are seen or retold. In a literary *narrative,* 'point of view' is associated with the narrator of a story; either the character or characters who recount the story, or the omniscient (all-knowing) narrator (usually the author or the author's *persona).* In television drama and the cinema, however, complications arise.

Monaco ('How to Read a Film') takes the example of the 1945 movie 'Lady in the lake', in which the hero is the narrator. In order to show the central character on screen, a series of reflections in mirrors and other surfaces had to be worked into various scenes. Monaco also recalls Hitchcock's 'Stage Fright' of 1950, which uses a first-person narrator who tells a lie; but, because the lie had to be seen from the narrator's point of view, the only way of demonstrating its existence was to show it on screen. This led to confusion because it seemed to be part of the established world of the film, and thus was thought to have equal status with other scenes which were taken at face value.

In all films, the viewer is 'positioned' in the fictional space of the narrative through the use of a number of devices. The *establishing shot,* for example, helps the viewer establish a 'point of view'.

In 'Narrative Comprehension and Film', Edward Branigan argues that point of view in the cinema is not simply determined by technical devices (such as camera set-ups) but by (p. 70) 'broader ... considerations which define knowledge ... including a narrative schema which defines characters who may have a sequence of views'.

polysemy: from the Greek for 'many' and 'sign', polysemy is any sign's potential for creating multiple meanings. This does not mean that the number of meanings is infinite. The degree of polysemy in a sign will be determined by:

- the history of the sign (the range of associations it has traditionally produced)
- its textual context or relationship to other signs (it may be one small scene in a film which has to be seen in the context of the whole narrative, or a photograph which is read in the light of a caption)
- its inter-textual context (its relationship with other uses of the same sign in either similar or dissimilar texts)
- the context of its interpretation (groups of 'readers' will judge the meaning of the sign in the light of their own experience)
- the value attached to its interpretation (not just what the sign stands for, but the 'moral' standing of the sign).

popular culture: if the term *culture* has come to mean the entire range of activities which take place within a society, rather than the *aesthetic* pursuits of a minority, then the idea of popular culture draws attention even more closely to those pursuits, leisure activities and texts which attract large scale participation and/or a *mass audience*. Examples of popular culture may be soap operas on television, live sporting events, and activities like shopping. Within cultural studies, arguments have taken place about the relative importance of different forms, but the most significant disagreement has taken place over the meaning of popular participation in culture. To what degree can the populace 'resist' dominant values through consumption? Is it a mistake to characterise market choices as subversive? These issues have caused a rift between those writers who celebrate consumer behaviour and others who are wary of the growth of commodification. (See also *active audience.*)

portension is a term coined by Wolfgang Iser to indicate the anticipation a reader feels during the course of a narrative; portension is contrasted with 'retention' (what is remembered from the reading). The tension between these two states produces in the reader a 'wandering viewpoint'. (See also *point of view.*)

postmodernism is an approach to contemporary theory and culture which argues that established ways of describing social existence ignore the fractured and contradictory nature of contemporary life.

Although there is some doubt about the worth of *postmodernity* as a description of the present social formation, there is no denying postmodernism's impact as a cultural movement. The main feature of the 'postmodern' critique of established philosophical thought is, in David Lyon's words, 'the forsaking of 'foundationalism', the view that science is built on a firm basis of observable facts' (see 'Postmodernity', p. 7). Besides this hostility to one of the central tenets of the Enlightenment, postmodernism also distrusts any 'universal' or 'totalising' discourse; in other words, it opposes any 'grand theory' which tries to offer a coherent explanation for the way that the social order functions.

One of the major reasons given for the onset of the 'postmodern' condition is the existence of *new media forms* and the *information society*. Postmodern thought identifies this development as a radical departure from older social systems. In a world of endless media messages, some postmodern thinkers believe that reference to the real world has been overwhelmed by the surface glamour of media forms. In this scenario, human subjectivity becomes 'objectified'. Such an idea seems to suggest that media *audiences* are unable to resist the *power* of the *mass media*.

Some writers draw attention to the positive aspects of postmodernism. Michel Foucault ('The Foucault Reader', 1984) praises the 'positive and multiple', preferring 'difference over uniformity, flows over unities, mobile arrangements over systems'. The postmodern challenge allows a creative response to problems of theory but fails, exactly because it is 'disunified, multiple and contradictory'(Kuan-Hsing Chen's words in 'Postmodernism', 1991), to provide serious resistance when strong attacks are made against democratic models of public communication. Rather than set the modern and the postmodern against one another, David Harvey sees postmodernism 'as a particular kind of crisis' within modernism.

postmodernity: postmodernity is the condition of life in a society where old certainties (like the idea of rationality and progress) are supposed no longer to apply. The prefix 'post' refers to an event, a thing, or a period of time, which follows something else. The word 'modern' means the present time, or the most recent development of something. Therefore, the 'postmodern' would seem to be a state or condition which comes after the modern period. If the modern is 'the most recent', then it is difficult to see how any other epoch could replace it. Joanna Hodge notes (see 'The Problems of Modernity') that terms are often used to refer to both critical movements and historical periods, and that confusion can arise when the two are pushed together.

post-production is the final stage of work required once a film (or other media product) has been shot/recorded. Post-production involves editing, dubbing, the addition of music, and the creation of the director's and/or producer's cut (a version of the film which provides an alternative to the studio's final release).

post-structuralism: this is the approach to theory which was formed in response to the rigorous and rather inflexible structuralist tradition. Post-structuralists oppose the highly formal explanations of texts found in *structuralism,* believing that texts are formed through the 'double articulation' of what is said (what is actually there in the text) and what is unsaid (what is implied by significant 'absences'). Post-structuralism is closely associated with the work of Jacques *Derrida.* His book 'Of Grammatology' was published in 1967, and advocated the idea that meaning is always scattered or dispersed along the 'chain' of linguistic signification. This means that any sign's relationship to reality is always deferred (or 'put off') because reality is always mediated by language. Structuralism seems to Derrida to be an attempt to 'finalise' meaning, while in his opinion no such fixed interpretation of texts is possible.

In 'Deconstruction and Criticism', Derrida argued that (p. 84): ' ... a 'text' ... is ... no longer a finished corpus of writing ... but a differential network, a fabric of traces referring endlessly to something other than itself ...' Some writers, such as the American philosopher John R. Searle, argue against Derrida's belief that meaning is unfixed and boundless, arguing that certain types of communication, like performatives, reveal that people agree upon meanings at certain times. This would suggest that there are certain contexts in which meaning is fixed.

post-synchronisation is the process of adding dialogue to a film after it has been shot. Actors read their lines into a microphone while viewing their own performances (shown repeatedly on a loop of film), making sure that their words match the recorded movements of their lips.

power: the term power means both the capacity to do something and the active use of that capacity. For instance, power can mean the 'power' of speech (the mechanisms which produce spoken language), as well as the ability to use that speech to influence others (the gift of eloquence). The two meanings of power are also sometimes expressed as the difference between 'power to' and 'power over.'

In 1947, the sociologist Max Weber produced a definition of power which combined the notion of capacity and use. He believed that power is the probability that one actor within a social relationship will be in a position to carry out his or her own will despite the resistance of other individuals. Stephen Lukes (1974) argued that power has three aspects or 'faces'. These are success in decision-making, the ability to manage an agenda, and the manipulation of others. Lukes defined the third kind of power as follows; 'A exercises power over B, when A affects B in a manner contrary to B's interests'. He also recognised that this type of power can occur when B is unaware that his/her interests are being undermined.

power (approaches to): most commentators acknowledge the fact that there are certain inequalities in its distribution. Price ('Communication Studies', 1996) identifies four basic divisions among the various approaches to the issue of power:

- authoritarian, which sees institutional or state power as wholly legitimate, and which believes that inequality is a desirable condition
- pluralist, which analyses the existence of power in the western 'democracies' and sees it as broadly legitimate
- functionalist, which takes the view that, legitimate or not, power has an important function to play in society
- leftist, which regards the existing social order as fundamentally unjust and built upon coercion.

Gramsci's concept of power was called *hegemony*, which he defined as 'intellectual and moral leadership'. Thus power could be seized by the working class only when it developed its own ability to build a convincing intellectual alternative. More recent studies of power have emphasised the 'fractured' nature of the ruling class (see the work of David Coates (1974), Nicos Poulantzas (1980), and David Tetzlaff (1991) for more details). Michel Foucault examined the nature of power and *discourse*, while Althusser used the term *interpellation* to describe an address with a *will to power* behind it. Nofsinger on the other hand, (see p. 1 of 'Everyday Conversation'), emphasises the 'immense power of everyday talk'. Types of power can be described in a variety of ways, including:

- personal or subjective power
- group power
- institutional power
- state power.

power (research): communication and media research into power is usually concerned with the study of deliberate attempts to influence or persuade an audience. This means that election broadcasts, advertisements, newspaper campaigns, organisational communication, public speeches and ordinary conversations are all studied in detail. The *effects* tradition is especially concerned to explore the possible consequences of a supposedly powerful mass media (see Martin Barker and Julian Petley's 'Ill Effects' of 1997, for a comprehensive study of this issue).

In 'The Mass Media and Power in Modern Britain' (1997), Eldridge, Kitzinger and Williams study the various models of power used in media research, and conclude that 'personal experience, political consciousness and socio-economic position can alter people's trust in, and reading of, specific press, television and radio reports' (p. 179). However, they also note that 'experience and identity are not created in a media-free space'. Put another way, this means that the media does have some role in the creation of meaning, and thus some power to create part of the social landscape.

power phrase: an American term for a *sound-bite*, a short and supposedly effective catch-phrase which a politician can use to make an effective intervention in any public issue.

PR: see *public relations.*

pragmatics is the study of everyday speech, its participants, uses and context. Pragmatics investigates the ways in which speakers make sense of one another's utterances, in the light of the ambiguities found in language and expression.

predictability: the degree to which a television programme or film, conforms to an established format or genre. An audience expects the news, for example, to follow a certain pattern; content will appear in a particular order, starting with home news, moving to international items, and finishing with a light-hearted tale about a cycling hedgehog. McQuail p. 210 ('Mass Communication Theory') notes that 'several researchers have been struck by the regularity of the news vehicle'. (Maybe they should keep out of the road.)

preferred reading: the idea that various signs or public messages are intended to be read in ways which support the dominant forces in society. For instance, a news photograph may be presented with captions or headlines which lead the viewer to 'read' the image in a particular light.

premiere: the first showing of a film, an event which often draws in a host of 'celebrities', photographers, and other vital personnel. Sometimes applied to the first television screening of a film made many years previously.

press: the public institution formed by the print media, which includes newspapers, journals and magazines. In recent years, the term has been used by some to include electronic media forms. The early history of the press was characterised by active struggles between government regulation (and repression) and various attempts to establish a free press; its later development is marked by less generalised state interference and the drive to achieve and retain mass markets. The social power of the newspaper press in particular, lies in its ability to disseminate ideas on a large scale.

Press Complaints Commission: after the Calcutt Committee's 1990 report on invasions of privacy by the British press, the Press Complaints Commission was set up to monitor the conduct of newspapers. The Commission, which began its work on 1 January 1991, was to oversee the implementation of a voluntary code of practice,

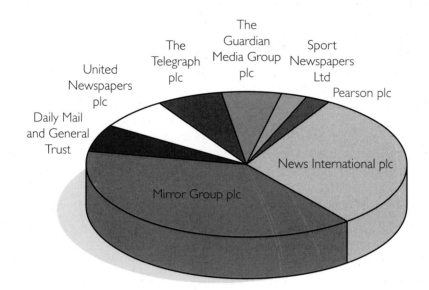

United
Newspapers
plc

The
Telegraph
plc

The
Guardian
Media Group
plc

Sport
Newspapers
Ltd

Pearson plc

Daily Mail
and General
Trust

News International plc

Mirror Group plc

Press – Newspaper ownership and percentage of sales in the UK (1994) from 'Investigating Mass Media' by Paul Trowler, 1996.

which warned against publishing 'inaccurate, misleading, or distorting material'. The threat was that, if the newspaper industry could not 'set its own house in order', government legislation would follow. By 1993, David Calcutt single-handedly produced a second report which attacked the PCC for ineffectiveness, arguing that it was overly controlled by newspaper owners.

press conference: a meeting held to announce a political event, to celebrate an occasion, to make public appeals, and so on. Politicians use news conferences in an attempt to set or influence a particular agenda.

press history: print made possible an educational revolution in Protestant countries in early modern Europe. The *newspaper* first appeared in the late 16th century, in the form of the *newsbook*. Early newsbooks were confined to reporting foreign events, because it was illegal to print domestic news. By the 1640s, a great many unlicensed newsbooks appeared. Joad Raymond, writing in his 1993 study 'Making the News', notes that 'the conflict between newsbooks fed the political conflict' between King and Parliament.

Restrictions on the press have taken various forms throughout its history. From the establishment's point of view, financial rather than legal control has often proved more successful in suppressing newspapers. In Britain, financial restriction took the form of 'stamp duty,' first imposed in 1712 and then bolstered in 1743.

Famous radical papers include the 'Black Dwarf' (founded in 1818), the 'Gorgon', the 'Political Register' (which became 'The Republican') and, from the second wave of radicalism in the 1830s, the renowned newspaper 'The Poor Man's Guardian'. By 1843, the laws against libel were moderated.

Attacks on the radical press became unnecessary, as bourgeois newspapers began to dominate the market. By 1854, 'The Times' had achieved a circulation of 40,000 copies per issue. The 'Daily Telegraph' appealed to a right-wing populism. The success of these publications paved the way for the later growth of mass circulation dailies like Lord Northcliffe's 1896 'Daily Mail'. In 1900, that title became the first newspaper to exceed a million readers.

The twentieth century saw the continued expansion of the British press, and clear political divisions between left-leaning papers like 'The Daily Herald' and the right-wing 'Daily Mail', which supported fascism at home and abroad throughout the 1930s. In the post-war period, a number of titles declined in strength. The traditional home of the British newspaper press was *Fleet Street* in London, but this changed in the mid-1980s, when a number of proprietors, led by Rupert Murdoch's *News International* group, left to establish new premises. Murdoch took his titles to Wapping in East London, in a successful attempt to break the influence of the print unions (see Linda Melvern's 'The End of the Street', 1986).

primary audience: the most important 'target market' for a product; that group which must be reached as a matter of priority. In many cases, a primary audience is discovered through research. At other times, a company may find that its product is taken up by a certain group, which then has to be considered in future product developments.

prime time: in the USA, a term used to refer to the peak television viewing period between 8 p.m. and 11 p.m. The attempt to capture the viewer's attention during this period is an important aim for all the competing networks.

print journalism: journalistic activity based on the gathering, selection and editing of news for magazines, journals and newspapers, as opposed to similar work in an electronic form.

printed circuit: an electronic circuit made of strips and patches of conductive material on an insulated board.

printing: the production of designs, books, newspapers, posters and other material by the application of ink to a raised, flat, or etched surface, which in turn transfers the ink to an absorbent material like paper, vellum, fabric and so on.

Although Gutenberg is usually credited with the invention of the printing press, the utilisation of metal type appeared in a number of different centres in and around the year 1450; the cities of Haarlem, Avignon, and Mainz all contributed to this phase of printing. Printing with metal type 'arose out of the sound theory that to make multiple copies of the same piece of written work you had to create a durable image of it in reverse' which could then be 'used repeatedly to transfer an inked impression ... onto paper' (F.W. Hodgson, 'Modern Newspaper Editing and Production', 1987).

From the earliest period, the basic principle was to make a series of 'master' letters which could be assembled into lines of type. At this point, a metal alloy cast of each line could be taken, which showed the words in reverse. The page took shape through the assembly of these lines. A mould of the page was then taken and transferred to the printing plate, which applied the image in reverse. 'Impression' or 'relief' printing is the term used to describe this form of production. The presses themselves were originally 'flatbed', and operated by manual force. In 1884, the invention of the Linotype machine dispensed with handcomposition; a keyboard operator could choose a line of type which was cast inside the machine by the injection of hot metal. Each line was then ejected into a tray.

From the early 1960s, a new method of printing began to emerge. This was the 'cold type' method pioneered in the USA. It is known as cold type because it avoided the use of hot metal to cast letters. Computers are used to compose individual stories, editorials, features and so forth. Copy (the term for written material) is sent electronically to an editor, who also works at a computer screen.

Once the newspaper has been completed, each page undergoes photo-typesetting; this process depends on the production of a photographic transparency of the page. From this, a smooth zinc or aluminium plate, coated with plastic, is made. This plate has a light sensitive surface. It is exposed to the photo transparency and then developed with a chemical solution. During printing, the plate picks up ink and transfers this to a rubber cylinder, which in turn makes direct contact with the paper.

New print technology, gradually introduced to the British press in the 1970s and 1980s, allowed the industry to dispense with thousands of jobs. Editorial staff cuts were introduced by Murdoch at News International, by Robert Maxwell at Mirror Group Newspapers, and by other proprietors. In Richard Keeble's opinion, these have 'decimated the industry' while 'printers' numbers have been reduced even more drastically' ('The Newspapers Handbook', 1994, p. 338). The high-water mark of trade union resistance in Britain was the Wapping dispute of 1985, after some 5000 print-workers were sacked by Rupert Murdoch.

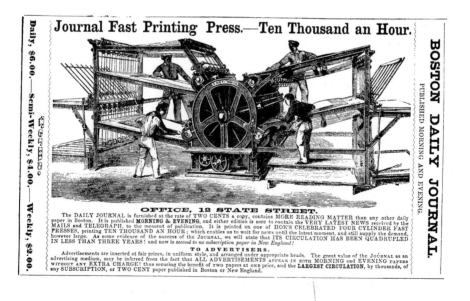

A 19th Century American printing press

problematic: a problematic is a question which a researcher uses to help focus the purpose and direction of his/her investigation. A hypothesis, on the other hand, is an idea or proposition which must be tested. In media or communication research, an inquiry may be pursued through the use of either a problematic or a hypothesis, which approach the same issue from a different perspective. If *identification* by children with television is the topic under investigation, a problematic might be 'to what degree do children identify with the chief protagonists of adventure series?'. A hypothesis, on the other hand, is used when the researcher has a definite opinion to test. In this case, it may state 'children consistently identify with the chief protagonists of adventure series'.

product awareness: the degree to which an audience shows familiarity with a commercial product.

product identification: the ability of an audience to identify a particular product, by referring to its appearance, logo, or other identifying feature.

product image: the 'character' of a product as it is constructed by those who market it; also used to indicate public perception of a brand's qualities.

product placement: the practice of displaying well-known brands in television programmes and films. The idea is to achieve a high profile for the product, and in many cases to attain a prestigious form of advertising which associates the brand with particular TV and movie stars. The manufacturer pays the production company considerable sums to 'place' its goods prominently in shot. Watson and Hill ('A Dictionary of Communication and Media Studies') note that (p. 182), 'as the worlds of big business and entertainment grow closer ... and as budgets for films and TV grow tighter, product placement threatens to become more assertive throughout the media'.

production: the development of an idea from its earliest form, to the point at which it becomes a finished product. Production involves a number of stages, during which the original aim of the exercise may alter. The term can apply to print, television, radio, multimedia and cinematic forms.

production department: any sub-division of a media organisation which actually makes a product or some part of a product.

production values: the degree of care taken with the preparation of a film's 'fictional environment'; the level of production values is readily observable. High production values indicate, for example, convincing attention to visual detail (props, costume, setting), careful preparation of narrative structure, and good quality of sound production. Quality in these areas does demand significant expense, but success cannot be guaranteed by money alone.

programmer: an individual who writes, designs and tests computer software. A programmer must analyse and encode a problem, establish input and output formats, create testing procedures, prepare documentation and ultimately supervise the running of the programme.

programming is the process of producing programmes for a computer. Programming requires the translation of the physical state of a problem into a language that a computer can understand.

project work: in A-level Communication Studies, the coursework paper which requires students to undertake a task which applies communication theory to a practical purpose. In order to begin work of this nature, students must pass through the following stages:

- identification of topic and audience for the subject chosen
- construction of a problematic, hypothesis or brief
- identification of information and research sources
- evaluation of different research methods
- execution of a feasibility test.

The project can take as long as six months to complete, and must be tested upon its target audience. At the end of the process, on oral presentation is made to a group of tutors and fellow-students. A thorough guide to project work appears in Chapter 6 of Price's 'Communication Studies' (1996).

promotion: the public advocacy of a cause, product, or person, often using the mass media.

proof: a printed sheet of a newspaper, leaflet, poster and other material (most especially a leaf from a book) which is run off so that it may be checked for authorial errors and printing mistakes.

proofreading: the process of searching for and then correcting errors and omissions which appear in printed material; consistency, punctuation, spelling, grammar, and typography are all checked.

propaganda: the modern definition of propaganda is the 'deliberate and systematic attempt' to shape perception, understanding and behaviour 'to achieve a response that furthers the desired interest of the propagandist' (see Jowett and O'Donnell, 'Propaganda and Persuasion', 1986). The term propaganda finds its origin in the Roman Catholic church, which set up a congregation of cardinals to spread its religious doctrines in foreign lands.

Successful propaganda depends on the method used to disseminate it, as well as on the scale and timing of the message. A common error is to suppose that propaganda is merely a series of lies; in fact, truthful material can be used in a propagandist way. At times, propaganda is obvious and open, as during election campaigns. On many other occasions, it is hidden, so that a number of common beliefs may in fact be based on material which has been fed into 'neutral' outlets.

Propp: Vladimir Propp was a Russian scholar who produced a book called 'Morphology of the Folk Tale' in 1928. In this work, he identified a number of situations, characters, and events which seemed to re-appear in the many Russian folk-tales he studied. Propp identified no fewer than thirty-two basic categories of action, which he called 'functions', and a smaller number of major events (preparation, complication, transference, struggle, return and recognition). He also drew attention to the existence of a set of basic character roles, such as hero, helper, and villain, which featured in the tales. Propp's system has been applied to film, revealing a great deal about the structure of the cinematic narrative. Propp's *structuralist* approach has to be seen in the light of *audience* research which emphasises the actual ways in which audiences make sense of texts.

prosthetics are artificial features made out of latex and similar material, which are used in films to change the appearance of actors. Widely used in horror films, prosthetics has become a specialist field.

prototypes: certain phenomena in any society are always regarded as belonging to a particular category, and are sometimes described as the 'originals' of the categories which are based on them. It is sometimes said that a prototype, rather than having an existence as an actual object, is a 'schematic representation' of what Taylor ('Linguistic categorisation', p. 58) calls the 'conceptual core' of a category.

The conceptual core would be the *idea* of the category based on an abstraction of all its agreed features. Price ('Communication Studies', 1996) suggests that prototypes may alter according to the context of use. In studies of news values, some authors have used the concept of prototypes to mean 'key events'.

proxemics: the study of the significance of physical distance during various forms of public interaction. Various attempts have been made to study proximity in the context of cultural differences, gender relations, power inequalities, and so on. The subject is an interesting but under-theorised element of communication study, often regarded as a peripheral part of the field. Erving Goffman's 'Gender Advertisements' (1976) includes an interesting study of proximity and power relations.

PSB: see *public service broadcasting*

psychographic profiling is a form of *marketing* which creates a set of consumer groupings supposedly based on the 'psychological' attributes of customers. The various attitudes, values, beliefs and 'lifestyle' choices of the population are sorted into a number of distinct categories which are used to predict consumption; this provides a 'profile' of certain types of person.

In the USA, a company called SRI International produced a 'Values and Lifestyle' classification system (eventually known as VALS2), which divided consumers into eight different groupings, called Actualizers, Fulfilleds, Achievers, Experiencers, Believers, Strivers, Makers and Strugglers. Arens and Bovee, writing in the fifth edition of 'Contemporary Advertising' (1994), give an example of how the VALS2 system works (p. 146); 'Conservative, blue-collar people with traditional values (the VALS2 Believer and Maker segments, which comprise 29 per cent of the US population) often choose country music [radio] stations. Higher-income men and women over 45 (the VALS2 Actualizer, Fulfilled, and Achiever categories) typically listen to news-and-talk radio'. This type of knowledge is useful to advertisers who wish to place their clients' products in a suitable market position. Psychographic approaches might at first sight appear 'more democratic' than the use of class-based divisions, but class has never in fact been completely abandoned; the two perspectives are simply combined. Profiling based on psychological attitude, is also used in the workplace, to identify those who might be selected for redundancy.

public access television: in America, a non-commercial cable television station, specially designated for public use. In Britain, a tradition of public use of a limited number of programme forms, such as the BBC's 'Open Space'.

public communication: communication which has a public or open character. Messages, ideas and discourses are made accessible to a wide audience and address, in turn, issues of public importance. John Corner, in 'Television Form and Public Address' (1995), reveals that his use of 'public address' carries (p. 1) 'two, related meanings; both an idea of television as a kind of public address system and an idea of it routinely addressing itself to matters of public concern and public value'. In modern societies, public communication depends greatly upon media forms, but is not necessarily initiated by the media.

public relations (PR): a form of promotion and/or image management, in which the public perception of a client (individual or corporate) is manipulated by various means. Public relations sometimes includes the provision of free goods and services, the use of staged events, and other methods, but successful PR most often works through media forms (especially press and television coverage).

public service broadcasting (PSB): a broadcasting system founded on the concept of service to a public within the framework of parliamentary democracy. PSB, as it is known, is usually distinguished from its commercial rivals whose first loyalty is to their shareholders and the profit motive.

public sphere: Jurgen Habermas' concept of an 'informed public arena' created by the growth in the 17th and 18th centuries of the press, public meeting places (like coffee-houses) and other forms which allowed public opinion to flourish. The relative freedom offered by this sphere of discourse declined, according to Habermas, when the press became commercialised and with the expansion of the state into areas such as the provision of welfare. At this point, in the words of William Outhwaite (see 'Habermas: a critical introduction', 1994, p. 9) 'public opinion ceases to be a source of critical judgment and checks' and becomes 'a social-psychological variable to be manipulated'.

Pulitzer Prize: awarded each year, this is an American award for outstanding journalism (with prizes also available in the fields of literature and music). The prize was created by the newspaper owner Joseph Pulitzer in 1947.

pulse code modulation (PCM): this is a technique for translating analogue information into digital form. The analogue signal is 'sampled' and the element obtained turned into a binary number. This number can then be transmitted as a set of electronic pulses. (See also *modem.*)

Q

quadrophonic: a system used for broadcasting four signals on FM radio, or a recording and playback system which uses four speakers, a separate signal being fed to each of the speakers.

qualitative research: this type of research is conducted through 'in-depth' investigation; its purpose is to discover more about the meanings attributed to events by individuals, rather than to record the number or quantity of events themselves. Pertti Alasuutari, in 'Researching Culture' (1995), describes qualitative analysis as 'reasoning and argumentation that is not based simply on statistical relations between 'variables' '.

There are four major methods available for use by qualitative researchers. Set out by David Silverman in 'Interpreting Qualitative Data' (1993), these are: observation, analysing texts and documents, interviews, and recording and transcribing. The study of personal documents (personal memoirs, letters, etc.) can be qualitative, since close analysis can reveal the attitudes and beliefs of individuals. Overall, qualitative methods provide insight into psychological as well as social phenomena.

quality means both the distinguishing characteristic of something and the degree of excellence which may be attained. The second use of the term has appeared in many debates about media content. Quality appeared in the form of a 'quality threshold' in the 1993 commercial television franchise bids. Television companies had to satisfy certain criteria, which included the provision of religious shows and children's programmes, but were not required to broadcast documentaries in 'prime-time' slots.

'In Britain', writes Geoff Mulgan 'the discourse of quality has traditionally been dominated by programme makers ... quality is seen in terms of production values defined by the community of producers' ('The Question of Quality', 1990). Quality remains a highly contested issue, since it is used by different public groups as part of a strategic vocabulary.

quality press: a term used to describe those newspapers which offer high standards in reporting and analysis, though sometimes loosely applied to the broadsheet press irrespective of its merits or the possible virtues of some tabloids.

quantitative research: a form of research suited to large scale enquiries, which uses surveys to provide information about broad social trends and simple preferences. Some sociologists believe that quantitative research is important because human behaviour cannot be measured and compared unless it is translated into numerical terms. The main method used in primary quantitative research is the social survey, which can be carried out using either *questionnaires* or structured interviews. Questionnaires are sets of written or printed questions which require answers to be inscribed in an ordered and rational manner. A structured interview is a set of questions which is read aloud to interviewees, so that the researcher can write down the answers. Quantitative data may be presented in a variety of forms:

- tables – the presentation of figures in columns and rows; the reader can see the evidence of survey results

- bar graphs – in which information can be seen at a glance, and the relative size or extent of each result is displayed
- line graphs – lines are presented on a grid to show features like change over time
- pie charts – useful for showing proportions relative to the whole.

QuarkXPress: a page layout program for the Apple Macintosh computer, produced by Quark Inc. It is used when high quality graphic design is required.

quarterly: a publication that is issued every three months in the year.

quarto: a page size produced by folding a particular sheet size twice to create four leaves, (i.e., eight pages); also, a book produced by folding sheets in this way.

question and answer: one of William Labov's (1970) three structures for conversation analysis. The other two are 'challenge and response', and 'invitation and acceptance'. The question and answer format may be found in a variety of situations, and will sometimes be used to disguise other forms of transaction. For example, 'Advances in Spoken Discourse Analysis'(1992, p. 111) prints this exchange: "Father: 'Is that your coat on the floor again?' Son: 'Yes' (goes on reading)." The father's utterance is a command/challenge disguised as a question. The son's answer displays recognition of the formal status of the remark, but does not acknowledge the true spirit of the exchange.

questionnaires: structured sets of questions designed to aid research by producing general information about the issue under study. When researchers design questionnaires, a number of basic preparations need to be made. These can be covered in the following questions:

- What will be the size of the sample?
- What questions will respondents be asked?
- Who will be addressed by the questions?
- How will the answers be recorded?
- What will be done with the results?

Marten Shipman ('The Limitations of Social Research', p. 80–87) lists the factors which can distort a response to a question. These are:

- the difficulty of the questions
- the danger of the question suggesting the answer
- the loss of face or prestige if certain questions are answered
- the way that the environment in which the questioning is done affects the answers
- the dangers of pre-coding answers (which can mean that responses are forced into categories decided in advance by the interviewer).

quotas: quotas are limits which are placed on the import of cultural artefacts from overseas (films, television programmes, etc.), in order to protect those products which are made within the home nation.

R

radio: radio was first developed as a means of point-to-point communication, rather than the broadcast system it eventually became. The first broadcast of music and speech was made in 1906 by the American R.A. Fissenden. Ten years later, the American Radio and Research Company began broadcasting concerts a few times each week. The Marconi company, licensed by the Post Office, began its first British broadcasts from Chelmsford in 1920, a year after the removal of a ban on the private use of radio, which had been in force since the outbreak of the First World War. However, it was not until 1922 that regular broadcasts were permitted. Marconi set up a London broadcasting station called '2LO.'

Again in 1922, the leading groups involved in broadcasting and the manufacture of equipment, were brought together in a consortium called the *British Broadcasting Company.*

Under its first general manager, John *Reith,* the BBC began to lay the foundations of a national network. By 1925, reception was available to 85 per cent of the population. The numbers of people using radio sets increased with great rapidity, from about three to four hundred thousand receivers in 1923, to some five million in 1924. It was not until the latter part of the Second World War, that the cost of wireless sets fell sufficiently to allow their purchase by the bulk of the working class.

A 'Home Service' was created in 1939 and by 1944 the BBC had begun to employ its own foreign correspondents. Andrew Crisell (in 'Understanding Radio', 1986) describes the BBC's radio broadcasts during the war (p. 25)' ... radio at last came into its own as a rapid news medium ... the BBC's 9 pm news bulletin commanded huge and avid audiences ...'

By 1946, the BBC had divided its radio network into the Home Service, the Light Programme, and the Third Programme, which Crisell calls 'an unashamedly 'high-brow' network devoted to the arts, serious discussion and experiment.' After the war, radio was challenged by television.

In 1967 Radio One was created but soon faced competition from commercial radio, established in 1973. By 1979, nineteen local radio stations had been created and by 1980, this had risen to 26. In 1994 nearly a hundred local and regional commercial stations were in operation.

random access memory: a type of computer memory which may be accessed without regard to the order in which information was stored. Systems which rely on sequential access require the operator to start at the beginning of a list of files and search through the sequence for a particular item.

ratings: a guide to the relative success of broadcast material, produced by estimating the numbers of people who listen to or watch a particular radio or television programme. A table of results is then produced. The publication of audience figures, expressed in numbers or percentage terms, is studied by programme-makers and advertisers. In the USA, a scale from 0 to 100 is used to indicate station rating; individual programmes may not survive a fall in ratings.

raw data: information about any aspect of social reality which has not been processed or studied, and which therefore has not been assigned any meaning.

reaction shot: in film and television, a cut or other movement to a character which shows their reaction to an on-screen event.

read only memory (ROM): computer memory which holds a permanent program, containing a group of frequently used instructions. In many computers the operating system is stored in read only memory. *Compact discs* (a form of read only memory) can be used for a number of purposes, but once programmed cannot be re-configured.

reader: in publishing, an individual who reads manuscripts, either to find out whether they might interest a publisher, or in the case of academic books, to provide a critical perspective on work as it progresses. The term 'reader' can also mean an individual member of an audience which consumes a print-based media product.

reader profile: a breakdown, by age, sex, occupation, etc., of the type of consumer or consumers who form the overall *readership* of a magazine, newspaper, or other journal in print form.

readership: the concept of readership implies the existence of a group which provides a publication's core support. In reality, readership is a more complex issue, since it is made up of an audience which changes in quantity and composition. Total readership can be calculated on sales, which includes subscriptions and direct purchases, but most newspapers are also in the habit of adding bulk or complimentary copies to their circulation figures. It is also useful to remember that many single purchases may be read by more than one individual.

real time: in the case of a television, film or radio production, we speak of 'real time' when the duration of the events on screen/on the air matches the length of time such events would take in real life.

realism: in philosophy, the belief that objects in the world have an existence independent of the theories or representations which are used to describe them. In studies of film and television, realism refers to a representational practice composed of different strands, from what John Corner (1991) calls 'straight imaging of the real' (in news and documentary) to 'imaginatively convincing' fiction (plays, feature films, dramas, etc.).

Even within the fiction category there are important divisions. Hollywood narrative realism, for example, uses codes (in shooting and editing) which have become 'naturalised' in use but are, when analysed closely, highly artificial. To take another example, *social realism* in film is concerned to present a faithful picture of working-class experience, but may well use established film technique. *Naturalism,* on the other hand, tries to bring the realist experience into all aspects of production. Many *new wave* approaches deliberately broke established conventions, using *jump cuts* and other techniques to remind the viewer of the artifice of film-making. One way of avoiding confusion is to split the concept of realism into realism of form and realism of content. In this way, productions which use different methods with different effects in mind, will not automatically be assumed to be realist.

rear projection: film production often requires scenes which cannot be shot on location; one well-established solution is to place actors in front of a translucent screen showing the background desired. The background is created by a projector which runs behind and is obscured by the screen. This projector is synchronised with the film camera which faces the action, thus ensuring that the two elements match and an (almost) convincing image is produced.

received pronunciation (RP) is a type of speech which, in terms of accent, inflection and emphasis, is supposed to represent 'standard' English, but which actually belongs to a middle-class discourse. The speech patterns of newsreaders are often described as belonging to received pronunciation.

receiver: in electronics, a device which converts electromagnetic waves sent out by a satellite or broadcast source, into sound or visual information. In human communication, a receiver is any individual who actually acquires a message, usually from a 'sender' who deliberately initiates an act of communication, but occasionally from a source which does not purposely intend to communicate. The term receiver is most often used in linear or 'transmission' models of communication, in which an unambiguous statement or signal travels along a well-defined route, despite various forms of interference. *Models* associated with this tradition include the Lasswell formula of 1948, and Shannon and Weaver's 1949 diagram. Transmission models are not necessarily unsophisticated, but they do suggest that the communication process stops abruptly once a message reaches its destination (see Price, 1996, p. 40 for a defence of Shannon and Weaver). They also place the receiver in a distinctly secondary position to that of the sender, a situation which is perhaps an accurate reflection of the relationship between traditional media and their public.

reception: the process of receiving, analysing and using media and other texts, which may be studied through audience research. Reception analysis has appeared in different forms, from approaches which attempt to typify audience response (the three 'positions', dominant, negotiated and oppositional, ascribed to the decoding process), to ethnomethodology, where the study focuses on the meanings that audiences ascribe to their own cultural consumption.

recognition: the ability of an audience to recall commercial messages. It may also be applied to the way that individuals and groups identify genre in media texts, as they notice *motifs,* events, characters and scenes which closely resemble material from other texts. (See also *resonance, intertextuality, genre.*)

reconfiguration: a term used in electronics to mean the re-arrangement of individual components which make up a single device. Its other application lies in the way that social systems are changed through political and economic intervention, such as alterations in patterns of taxation, employment, and welfare provision – in fact in any way which affects the relationship between social groups. Privatisation and deregulation are major weapons in right-wing programmes of social reconfiguration.

recuperation: the idea that resistance to any social or political injustice is capable of being incorporated at the ideological level, turning it into a less potent but still recognisable form. In a capitalist society, recuperation often takes place when an oppositional idea is made into part of a commodity. The idea may gain greater currency as a result of its entry into the market place, but can only appear in a distorted form. There are times, however, when a commodified message carries behind it the force of an entire section of corporate power; a good example is the entertainment industry, which has often promoted ideas which the state or other sections of private capital have found difficult to recuperate. Recuperation can work both ways; an oppositional tendency is sometimes able to capture an idea and change it into a critique of the system. Statements or attitudes which contain humour are often difficult to recuperate. It is doubtful if the nuclear industry will be able to overcome its representation in a popular commodity like 'The Simpsons', for example.

referent: the thing in the world to which a *sign* refers. Paul Cobley states that (see 'The Communication Theory Reader', 1996) the referent consists of both 'available things (the real chair ...) and unavailable things (e.g. Napoleon)', in which case there will be a long series of references between the object and all the signs which follow throughout history.

referentiality: the process of referring to things in the world.

reflex camera: a camera which contains a reflex mirror housed in the body of the instrument. The viewfinder can thus be used to directly compose a shot. (See also *single lens reflex.*)

regional press: those newspapers, journals and free sheets which are limited to a regional circulation; traditionally, the place where journalists wishing to graduate to the national dailies, begin their careers.

register: the appropriateness of an *address* to an *audience,* in terms of level of discourse and the tone of the event.

reinforcement: in media and communication theory, the idea that exposure to certain kinds of stimuli, such as *violence* on television, political messages produced by a biased press, or the encouragement of 'conspicuous' consumption in advertising, can strengthen existing behaviour patterns or beliefs in certain audiences.

In 1948, Lazarsfeld, Berelson and Gaudet made a study of newspapers which suggested that readers bought papers which reflected and thus reinforced opinions they already held. They used the concepts of selective perception and selective recall to explain how identical messages produced widely different responses in readers. In such a case, the prior dispositions of the audience led them to make various choices. Klapper (who published 'The Effects of Mass Communication' in 1960, based on work done in 1949) distinguished between three types of media *effect:* conversion, minor change and reinforcement. Blumer and McQuail, in 1970, argued that some television viewers did seek reinforcement, while others used political communication as a guide to possible courses of action. Work done in Glasgow University in 1991 resulted in a book called 'How Voters Change'. This suggested that interventions by the tabloid press during elections were able to influence the voting intentions of previously uncommitted voters.

Reith: the first Director General of the BBC, John Reith began his tenure of office in 1922 and resigned in 1937. During this period, Reith was credited with the promotion of elitist cultural values. Accused of 'cultural dictatorship' by the 'New Statesman' in 1933, Reith provided a bulwark against commercial values which lasted for many years. The term 'Reithian' is used as a description of the patrician values and beliefs associated with this period of broadcasting.

reportage: the practice of reporting events, especially where eye-witness accounts are used. (See 'The Faber Book of Reportage', edited by John Carey, 1987).

Reporters sans Frontieres: a group of journalists formed in 1987 to monitor freedom of the press; it publishes a yearly directory of material which details the actions of governments with regard to the press, and produces accounts of journalists who are persecuted or killed by repressive regimes.

representation: the process of producing meaning. A dictionary definition of the word 'represent' means 'to show a person or thing or scene' in 'a picture or play', and so on. This first sense, 'to show' something in a particular context, is very similar to the idea of 'presentation', where some kind of display or event is offered for the approval of an audience. The next definition offered by the Oxford dictionary is 'to describe or declare to be'. An example of this would be when someone 'represents' themselves as an expert on a subject like music.

Notice the difference between these two meanings. In the first case, a simple act of 'showing' has taken place. In the second case, there is more of the sense of a report, where there is no direct evidence as such to judge whether or not the statement is true.

The second meaning includes the idea of 'symbolizing' something. Suppose for example that someone wants to 'show' how a car engine works. He/she can of course make a physical demonstration if there is a vehicle to hand, but if not, the individual might produce a diagram which symbolises the various parts of the machinery, or could describe the function of the engine in words. In either case, the idea of representation is that something is 'represented' in a different symbolic form.

re-presentation: used when a writer wishes to make it clear that he/she is describing the 'showing' or presentation of an event, sometimes but not always in its original form.

research: the active and systematic investigation of phenomena, based on one of a number of traditions and governed by established forms of procedure. Modern approaches to research can be traced to the nineteenth century. The 'early' period (as identified by Jensen and Jankowski in 'A Handbook of Qualitative Methodologies', 1991), lasted from about 1890 to 1930 and tended to be qualitative. Later, a scientific paradigm, based on the 'objective' measurement of social phenomena, was applied to the social sciences. By the 1930s therefore, quantitative methodologies had increased in popularity at the expense of the qualitative approach. Quantitative sociology appeared to flourish between 1930 and 1960.

The current period, from about 1960 to the present, has seen extensive revisions of the 'scientific' approach. Blumer (1969) argued that people behave according to the *meanings* they attribute to their own experience of events and other material phenomena. This means that the sociologist must appreciate the perspective of the individual subject on the events or experiences under investigation, suggesting in turn that the relationship between researcher and subject will inevitably be reasonably close. Gouldner (1970), meanwhile, attacked the idea of 'grand theory.'

Developing a project/research brief must involve progression through the following initial stages:

- identification of a topic, together with a suitable audience or readership
- the construction of a problematic, hypothesis or brief
- identification of sources of information

- evaluation of available methods of research
- the execution of a feasibility test.

research department: a sub-section of a commercial organisation which investigates a variety of issues. In advertising, a research department will collect and analyse data on products, media outlets and consumers. In broadcast media, the term refers to a group which studies audience figures and programming.

research methods: the following is a comprehensive breakdown of research methods:

- direct observation; the unobtrusive observation of social interaction, a method used for the production of primary information
- *participant observation;* an attempt to participate in the activities of the group under scrutiny, another primary method
- structured *interviews* and questionnaires where basic primary data is collected from quite a large number of respondents
- unstructured *interviews,* in which the researcher allows the interview to proceed in the direction it takes
- *content analysis,* a form of textual study often based on categorisation and numbering, a type of secondary research
- *semiological* analysis, a form of secondary textual study, which proceeds on the grounds that there is a relationship between the appearance/structure of a text and the meanings it produces within a specific culture
- *narrative* analysis, where structures, transformations, character and the relationship between textual patterns of cause and effect over time are all investigated
- *discourse* analysis, which in the case of the study of conversation, is based on transcripts, while media texts are investigated for ideological content
- statistical analysis data, some of it 'raw', is analysed according to the principles of secondary enquiry
- study of *theory,* based on the search for useful perspectives on the social world or on textual material
- analysis of documents, data which is either already in the public domain or which is created specifically for the purposes of research.

resonance: the idea that certain types of media content make a particular impact on specific audiences. When something resonates, it echos, returns or reverberates with sound. In this case, a media message forms the signal which sets up resonance with an audience. The term was first used by George Gerbner to describe the response of viewers when their expectations are matched by what they see on television. For example, inner-city groups may find that violent imagery matches their perception of a society where violence is endemic.

reverse angle shot: sometimes called a 'counter shot', this is used during dialogue between characters. First one person is shown speaking, looking out of one side of the frame; then the next person is seen, looking out of the opposite side of the frame.(See also *over-shoulder shot.*)

rhetoric: from the Greek for the art of speaking, rhetoric was practised in ancient Athenian society, though it always had opponents who believed that eloquence should be allied with a moral purpose. Modern rhetoric is usually studied in a political context. Max Atkinson's investigation ('Our Masters' Voices', 1984), described 'the mass penetration of television and radio,' which has brought 'the sights and sounds of politicians directly into our living-rooms.' He pays particular attention to (xvi) 'actual oral performances,' available as a result of video recording (though he does not investigate the fact that such speeches are specifically geared to television; in other words, he neglects the idea that politicians prepare material which recognises in advance its own mediation).

Atkinson believes in the 'vulnerable' audience which is susceptible to 'the rhetoric of demagogues.' The evidence of this vulnerability is not entirely convincing, amounting to no more than the observation that (p. 6), ' ... large numbers of people ... react to public speaking in a more or less identical way.'

The basic rhetorical techniques employed in party political address include:

- the rule of three or the three-part list, where the speaker makes three points in a row, the third of which is supposed to secure applause (see *clap-trap.*)
- ridiculing an opponent's position, by constructing a flimsy version of his/her opinions (known as making 'paper tigers'), so that the politician's own policy can appear robust
- the use of contrast or juxtaposition, where two alternatives are presented to an audience, one of which is meant to be rejected in favour of the choice preferred by the speaker
- the inclusive 'we,' where the interests and opinions of speaker and audience are presented as though identical
- rhetorical questions, answers to which are supplied by the speaker
- assertion, the use of unsupported statements
- repetition, where a statement is repeated in the hope that it will eventually be accepted by an audience
- negative identification, in which a rival is identified as the cause of various misfortunes.

rhetorical psychology: a study of human motivation and opinion which examines public utterances of a discursive and argumentative nature. In 'Ideology and Opinions' (1991), Michael Billig examines the ideas and opinions expressed by 'ordinary' individuals, in the belief that: '... old insights about the rhetorical nature of argumentation can be used for exploring contemporary issues of ideology and opinion.' Billig's approach states that the holding of opinions is (p. 1) 'an essentially rhetorical and argumentative matter.'

right of reply: the idea that individuals have the right to respond to personal comments circulated by the media. In the USA the right of reply was once enshrined in Section 15 of the Fairness Doctrine. Channel 4 in Britain ran a programme called 'Right to Reply', which allowed viewers to criticise broadcasters, and gave broadcasters the right to defend themselves.

ritual: a ceremony or rite which marks some important communal event. In most rituals, the same elements may be noticed. First, the ritual will take place during some special time or occur on a particular date. Secondly, as already suggested, the event itself will be played out within a community. Thirdly, the participants will adopt one of a number of public roles. Fourthly, specific, rule-bound acts will be committed, including certain types of movement (dance, dumb-show, etc.) and speech-acts (the declamation of verse, the issuing of challenges, or the proclamation of some change of state or status). Fifthly, symbols of some sort will be used. At the end of the ritual, normal existence will be resumed. The anthropologist Bronislaw Malinowski argued that the use of ritual increases people's sense of control, diminishes anxiety and reinforces group unity.

road movie: a film which uses the open road and travel as metaphors for the human desire for freedom and adventure. In a road movie, the protagonists break free of social constraints, often initiated by some transgression or misunderstanding. In many films of this genre, the central characters are destroyed by the social forces they defy, often with a spectacular crash featuring as the denouement. Well-known examples include 'Easy Rider' (1969) and 'Thelma and Louise' (1991).

role: a mode of behaviour considered appropriate for a specific social context. Individuals acknowledge universal as well as particular behavioural expectations in every situation they meet. Goran Therborn ('The Ideology of Power and the Power of Ideology', 1980) sees role as the behaviour 'expected of individuals occupying a particular social position.'

Barnuld sees roles as negative, believing that ('Interpersonal Communication in Action', 1981,p. 43); '... it is when men interact in roles, speaking as they believe they should rather than as they feel, that communication is often corrupted.' Roles, despite some negative effects, assist human interaction, in that all parties know how to conduct themselves.

ROM: see *read only memory*

rostrum camera: a still or video camera mounted above a flat board which holds art work and/or titles for the introductions to programmes (see *Ken Morse*).

rotary press: a printing press that has two or more curved plastic plates mounted on a revolving cylinder. The plates either make direct contact with the paper, or transfer an impression indirectly (offset *printing*).

RP: see *received pronunciation*.

rule of thirds: a practice in film and video, where the eyeline of the human subject is placed in the top third of the frame, whatever the actual distance of the subject from the camera.

ruling alliance: the notion that, instead of a unified national ruling class holding sway over subordinate groups, the state is composed of an alliance of interests. This 'ruling alliance' may be in a dominant position but is subject to factionalism and discord, thus allowing oppositional tendencies opportunities to exploit its disorganisation. However, a ruling alliance is also more flexible, in that it is able to act when required, and to 'stand down' when the need for direct rule is less urgent. The groups it dominates are also fractured and suffer from disunity.

running time: the time taken for a tape, film or other material to run its complete course.

S

salience: 'salient' means something which is prominent or conspicuous; salience is the notion that an individual has certain interests, values, or experiences which make him or her predisposed to notice certain types of message, and less inclined to pay heed to others. Salience is also used to refer to the way that media outlets emphasise some types of news item over others, leading to repetition of individual stories, which then achieve prominence in the mind of the viewer.

sample: a sample is composed of a number of units, events, or individuals which have been selected from an entire field. In media and communication, samples are used in statistical/quantitative surveys, and also in some forms of *ethnographic* enquiry. Samples are used so that research can be conducted into issues like domestic use of television, attitudes to film violence, gender roles in advertising, and so on. If a group is selected in order to represent a wider 'population', then care must be taken over the construction of the sample (see *sampling*). If the sample has been properly constructed, the researcher should be able to reach conclusions about the wider group from which the sample is taken, if this is the aim of the study.

sampling: in media and communication research, the practice of selecting representative groups for study. Sampling may be carried out using a number of methods. 'Random' sampling takes place when the entire 'population' is given a number; the sample group is generated by picking out numbers at random, so that any one individual has the same statistical chance of being selected. Another method, 'quota' sampling (sometimes used in the social sciences but more often employed in market research) begins with a 'shopping list' of characteristics (sex, age, occupation, etc.) which the researcher then tries to collect (for example, thirty executives, thirty computer programmers, etc). 'Systematic' sampling is employed when individuals are listed on some form of record. Provided that the record itself is alphabetical and not arranged by gender or some other criterion, random numbers can be decided upon and applied to the list. If the sample is 200 out of 2000, this represents 1 in 10. A number between 1 and 10 is selected (say 4) and the corresponding individual on the list chosen. Then the 'sampling interval' (in this case, 10) is added to the number 4 to produce 14. The fourteenth name is selected. Next, 14 is added to 10, and the twenty-fourth person on the list is selected, and so on. 'Stratified' sampling is used when the population needs to be first divided into mutually exclusive groups, in which case the groups will be of different sizes. 'Theoretical' sampling, described by Strauss in 1987 ('Qualitative Analysis for Social Scientists') is based, not on applying conclusions from a smaller to a larger entity, but on relating the behaviour or opinions of one group to the that of the wider community. Pertti Alasuutari ('Researching Culture', 1995), advocates this method (p. 156); 'a narrow case-analysis is broadened ... through the search for contrary and parallel cases ... generalisation to the population level is not the only option'.

satellite: any electronic device in extraterrestrial space which transmits or relays a signal for the purposes of communication or intelligence gathering. The concept was first suggested in 1945 by writer and scientist Arthur C. Clarke, who argued that a communication satellite could be placed in a constant position above the earth. The first *geosynchronous* satellite was launched by the Intelsat agency in 1965. '*Early Bird*', as it was known, had the capacity for 240 voice telephony circuits, the equivalent of one television channel. However, the first communications satellite ('Telstar') appeared in 1962 when live television pictures were relayed between Maine in the USA, Cornwall and Brittany. Direct-broadcast satellite services arrived in Britain in 1989, when Rupert Murdoch's Sky network began transmission, ahead of British Satellite Broadcasting with which it eventually 'merged' to create 'British Sky Broadcasting'.

Saussure: Ferdinand de Saussure was born in Geneva in 1857, to a family renowned for its achievements in the field of science. The young Saussure, after a false start studying physics and chemistry, became a student of linguistics. At the age of twenty-one, he published a celebrated memoir on Indo-European languages. In 1881, Saussure began work as a lecturer in Paris, where he stayed until appointed professor of Sanskrit and Indo-European languages at the University of Geneva. His published output, however, dwindled as time went on, and his influence remained limited. The major work associated with his name (the 'Course in General Linguistics') was compiled after his death (in 1913) by colleagues and students, working from lecture notes and other material.

Saussure's importance lies in his departure from traditional approaches to the study of language, which were, in simple terms, either rationalist (language seen as entirely logical and a mirror of thought), or 'neogrammarian' (a nineteenth century tradition which studied the history of a language in order to determine its current status).

Saussure objected to the idea that these two traditions seemed to share, that language was a method of naming things, and that there was a material link between language and objects in the world. Instead, he believed the link between language and reference was entirely arbitrary. Saussure also advanced the cause of *structuralism*, pointing out that meaning is generated through the relationship between elements. According to Saussure, language should be understood as a system of *signs*, in which individual signs were composed of *signifier* and *signified*. Although Saussure insisted that language was a social, and not simply an individual phenomenon, his division of language into *langue* and *parole*, and his subsequent concentration on the former (the structure of language), led to a rather abstract or *idealist* approach to linguistics.

scandal sheet: a slang term for newspapers which concentrate on gossip, scandal and embarrassing episodes in public life. Such publications often pretend to condemn the moral depravity of certain types of conduct, while reporting them in close detail.

scanner: an optical device that is used to 'read' drawings, photographs and printed text, turning them into electronic representations that can be stored and reproduced in a computer. Desktop scanners usually cover 200 to 600 dots per inch, but can achieve considerably higher resolutions.

schedule: a list of programmes, together with the times at which they will be shown. In the case of film, the master plan of the production process.

scheduling is the organisation of television programmes over a week, so as to maximise their appeal to an audience. The process requires care because all channels are in competition with one another. A balance must be struck between keeping popular programmes in an established time-slot, and placing special material like 'premiered' films at peak viewing times. Weaker programmes are often placed between two popular items in the hope that the audience will watch all three programmes.

schemas: an outline or structure, or an arrangement of data already possessed by an individual which is then used to predict and classify new knowledge. Understanding is supposed to be achieved because schemas have a fixed value and a variable value; the variable value is understood through reference to the fixed value. Schemas are supposedly found in knowledge of grammar, in the way that people anticipate the structural aspects of stories, and so on. Some writers call schemas 'packets' of knowledge, while others compare them to scripts which represent commonly experienced, and thus easily interpreted events.

scopophilia: from the Greek 'skopos' a watcher, and 'philein' to love, comes scopophilia, a state of pleasure derived from observation. The term came to prominence in Laura Mulvey's 1975 essay 'Visual Pleasure and Narrative Cinema'. Mulvey was interested in the way that the cinema constructed the viewing-positions of its audience. From a feminist perspective, and using the language of psychology, Mulvey investigated gendered *spectatorship*. Her theory was that the pleasure derived from viewing was split in two; an active male part, and a passive female component. In this approach, both the male construction of the female image, and the male spectator's enjoyment of the female image on screen (through a controlling gaze exercised in the first instance by the central male character in the film), made the woman an object. The female viewer, by comparison, was alienated from the image. Man, according to this theory, becomes 'the bearer of the look', while woman is unable to exercise any control.

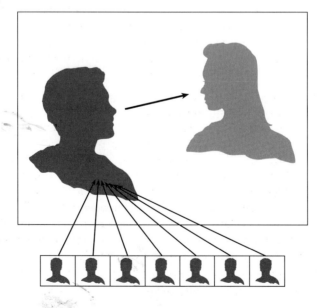

Scopophilia

Critics of Mulvey include the film theorists Lapsley and Westlake, who argued that cinema-goers do not respond to film purely in terms of gender and sexual orientation, but identify with 'fantasy scenarios' in which the central character may be either male or female. Mulvey, however, had argued that scopophilia was a condition in which the audience was separated from the action on screen, rather than brought closer through identification. E. Ann Kaplan, in 'Women and Film', notes that there have been many films in which male characters are subject to the female gaze, though she acknowledges that dominant female characters lose their (p. 29) 'traditionally feminine characteristics' once they seem to achieve power.

scrambler: a device used to encode or rearrange a video or audio signal, so that only authorised subscribers are able to receive the signal (using a decoder).

Screen theory: an approach to film, *spectatorship* and subjectivity associated with the journal 'Screen'. Throughout its history, the magazine has studied film using psychoanalytical theory, *semiology*, and *structuralist* approaches, though usually with a strong feminist perspective. 'Screen' drew attention to the power of cinema and applied itself also to television. It became an important resource for media studies, though it was sometimes criticised for valuing abstract speculation above audience research.

screenplay: used at times to describe a script for film or television, but most often the final script which most closely matches the on-screen production. In this case, the screenplay contains details of dialogue, each scene, camera set-ups, and so on.

secondary exchange: the idea that most media events do not involve a direct or primary exchange between sender and receiver. Instead, the media re-presents aspects of an audience's culture, which in turn are reinterpreted by different sub-groups. Exchange is thus secondary or more generally cultural in nature.

secondary research: in media and communication studies, as in the social sciences in general, secondary research is the investigation of sources already in existence (i.e. that data which is linked to, but not generated by, any specific enquiry). Secondary sources include official statistics, films, newspapers, television and radio programmes, written documents of a personal nature like diaries, and so on. Secondary research involves the study of data and the subsequent identification of material that is relevant to the problematic or hypothesis set at the beginning of the enquiry.

segmentation is the process of identifying specific social groups, 'lifestyle' choices or *sub-cultures* for commercial or political reasons. Segmentation is basically the division of the population into 'segments'. A range of organisations, from advertising agencies to political consultancies, have made attempts to classify the different 'types' of public individual, in order to reach their 'target market'. Once the subject has been identified and placed in a particular category, this information can be used for a variety of purposes. It can provide a consumer profile, furnish a rough guide to attitudes and beliefs (so that politicians know how to present their messages), or even help employers identify who may be selected for redundancy. Segmentation is not an entirely reliable tool, however. It is very difficult to categorise individuals with any degree of accuracy. Segmentation often depends on *psychographic* methods, which assume that questions about preference, attitude and personal 'vision' can be translated into a general estimate of character, ability and worth. (See overleaf for illustration.)

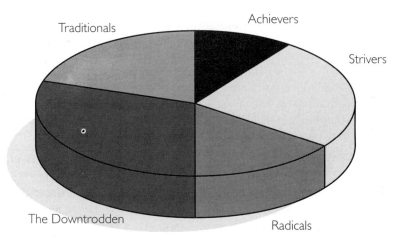

Traditionals

Achievers

Strivers

The Downtrodden

Radicals

Segmentation – Division of male consumers aged 25–40 by lifestyle

selective attention is human control of information through selection. Human beings perceive more than they can identify and report at a conscious level. A great deal of information may not be relevant, so the senses act to control the range of things it is possible to notice. This process is known as 'selective attention'. The idea of perception as an active process was described by R L. Gregory in 1966, who called it (see Gross 'Psychology', p. 224) 'a dynamic searching for the best interpretation of the available data.'

There are in fact two ways in which attention may be devoted to particular features in the environment. The first is where attention is drawn by a sudden change in surroundings. The second is where the individual concerned consciously directs their attention to a certain place. A 'selective attention' task (see Glass and Holyoak, 'Cognition', p. 52) is described as; '... one in which you are trying to pay attention to one input (the target) in the presence of other [stimuli].'

self: the individuality or essence of a person. One wing of psychology (see Murphy, 1947), calls the self 'the individual known to the individual.' A similar definition is found in R. B. Burns (1980), who describes the self as 'the set of attitudes a person holds towards himself'. These approaches suggest a difference between the knowing, reflective self and the self that is known.

Other writers attack idea of a split between conscious self and self as object, arguing that activities such as self-checking are part and parcel of the ordinary mental process. Gilbert Ryle, for example, in 'The Concept of Mind', uses the fact that some states of mind like panic (p. 159) 'cannot be cooly scrutinized' and that this lends weight to the idea that there is no such thing as the 'split self'.

In 'The Discursive Mind', Rom Harré and Grant Gillett object (p. 101) to the 'implication of reference to an inner entity.' They argue that, in order to have a sense of self, a human subject must also have a sense of place or location. There are four 'locations' in their system, as follows:

- a location in space

- a location in time
- a location as a responsible actor or agent
- a location as a subject, including age, ethnicity, gender, class and so on.

The self-concept, an idea which often appears in communication studies, is the 'cluster' of ideas held about the self, based on the descriptions individuals make of their own character, capability, limitations and so on. Self-concept encompasses all notions of self, including realistic and ideal selves, where the realistic self is an individual's perception of their 'true' qualities, and the ideal self is that which an individual strives to become. While some commentators, like Jorge Larrain (see 'Ideology and Cultural Identity', p. 147) refer to 'the unity and structure of the complete self' which 'reflects the unity and structure of the social processes in which the individual participates', *postmodernists* and a number of feminists argue that the 'completeness' of the individual has been called into question by the multiple identification that occurs in a fragmented society.

self-actualisation: first coined by Kurt Goldstein in 1939, self-actualisation is the highest stage of Abraham Maslow's *hierarchy of needs*. It is that condition of life which is reached when an individual fulfils their true potential.

Selsdon Committee: a 1935 report on the question of television broadcasting. The Selsdon Committee recommended that the *BBC* should be the body charged with the stewardship of television, and that the cost for its initial development be taken from the radio licence fee (which at that time was set at ten shillings).

semantic differential test: a method of measuring perception of the connotative meaning of concepts. The analyst first presents various concepts to a number of individuals, and asks them to describe these concepts on a series of differential scales, such as successful–unsuccessful, difficult–easy, serious–humorous, etc. The next stage is to identify the limited set of dimensions that define the 'semantic space' which gives meaning to the concept. In the original test of the propositions, carried out by Osgood and Suci in 1955, twenty concepts were described by 100 subjects. Three major factors were discovered: evaluation (good–bad, clean–dirty, etc.), potency (strong–weak, and so on), and activity (active–passive, fast–slow). Semantic differential tests are very useful for investigating connotative meaning.

semantics: the study of meaning in language. Native speakers retain knowledge of *morphemes,* word, sentence and other units of meaning as part of their understanding of language. The semantic properties of words produce a range of associations which help to create a complete picture of the sense of an utterance. Fromkin and Rodman, in 'An Introduction to Language' (1993), show how semantic properties work. They use this sentence: 'The assassin was stopped before he got to Mr. Thwacklehurst'. Here, the word 'assassin' reveals a number of pieces of vital information. It shows that the would-be assailant intended murder and that, by extension, Mr. Thwacklehurst is likely to be a prominent individual. Although semantic properties are not directly observable, they can be inferred from the errors made in speech. For example, an intended utterance like 'a stitch in time saves nine' which is actually delivered as 'a thread in time saves nine', reveals that 'stitch' is related to the act of sewing. If the actual utterance was 'a scar in time saves nine', then the association of 'stitch' with surgery would be demonstrated. The study of semantics includes investigation of the difference between reference and sense, investigation of the way that word and sentence meaning differs and study of the relationship between text and *context*.

semiology: from the Greek 'semeion' for *sign*, comes semiology, the study of signs and the meanings they produce in a society. Signs (physical objects with associated mental concepts), are used to describe experience and to represent events. As such, they are inherently social, being circulated and interpreted in a variety of situations and *contexts*. The two major traditions of semiological theorising can be distinguished as follows: the *structuralist* model, which emphasises the relationship between the sign and its place in the overall structure of language (it is structure which produces meaning); and the *pragmatist* approach (see *Peirce*) which understands 'semiosis' (Peirce's term) as a continuous process of meaning-creation which allows human beings to make interpretations and to carry out actions.

Semiology has always had a strong linguistic orientation, but it has been extended, notably by Roland Barthes, into other fields, particularly that of image analysis and popular culture. It has not been applied very often to those communication systems which create meaning primarily through sound or intonation, presumably because they are not as easy to describe in formal terms.

sensory perception: human awareness of external reality through the five senses. In order to function, human beings need to perceive an adequate range of physical elements. The five senses, sight, smell, touch, hearing and taste provide individuals with a composite understanding or perception of their environment. An understanding of the *communication* process should begin with questions about the extent and power of sensory perception:

- What faculties are used to perceive the environment?
- How reliable are such faculties?
- Are these faculties actively used, or do they act in a passive manner?
- How is communication between individuals carried out?
- What social or environmental constraints are placed on human communication?

serial: in film, radio and television, a set of instalments or programmes which contain the same characters, and which follow the same general narrative, so that storylines continue to develop across individual instalments ('The Archers' on Radio 4 is an example, or any television *soap opera*). In publishing, a serial is material which is issued in successive parts.

series: a series is a number of things, each of which bears some relationship to its predecessor; in the case of television or film, it means a number of individual programmes which share a common characteristic, but are different in other respects. For example, a series might deal with the same character in different situations, or could follow a similar theme, or most usually present a few central protagonists whose adventures 'start afresh' in each programme. A series is not bound to follow a narrative course laid down in any previous incarnation.

set-up: the positioning of cameras, sound-recording equipment and props for a particular scene or shot.

sfx: see *special effects.*

shooting schedule: the timing and order of scenes that must be shot to cover a day's work. Shots taken to fulfil this kind of schedule follow the demands of location and/or weather conditions, and do not pay attention to the sequential order of scenes in the finished production itself.

shooting script: the 'master' or director's script, containing all the details of camera position, lighting, etc. An actor's script, by way of contrast, would not require as much information.

short: a brief film, of between five and 30 minutes, which deals with a particular theme. In the Hollywood studios of the 1930s to 1950s, a short was a cartoon which ran between six and seven minutes. Channel 4 in Britain has commissioned a great many short features.

shot: an unedited piece of film featuring a single subject, event or scene. A shot is the basic unit of composition in the cinema.

shot/reverse shot: the established method of filming an exchange between two characters. The camera cuts between the two people, showing first one person A, addressing their companion B, then the second individual B looking at the original speaker A. (See also *over-shoulder shot.*)

sign: in Saussurean *semiology,* a sign is made up of two elements; a physical object (or representation) and its associated mental concept. The physical object is called the signifier and the concept the *signified.* A linguistic sign, for example, 'unites, not a thing and a name, but a concept and a sound image' (Saussure, 1974 edition). Language, in *Saussure's* view, is a system which structures relations between signs. Saussure did however, recognise the complexity inherent in linguistic signs, when he noted the difference between the phonetic and the semantic aspects of meaning.

In Saussurean linguistics, the connection between the sign and the thing for which it stands, is supposed to be 'arbitrary' (determined only by whim or accident). Throughout the history of linguistics, there has been sustained interest in the validity of signs; in the accuracy or otherwise of their reference to the world. As early as Plato's dialogue 'Cratylus', a character called Hermogenes says 'I ... cannot come to the conclusion that there is any correctness of names other than convention and agreement'. Socrates, in reply, argues that things, people, events and actions have an established, essential character, which is carefully reflected in the names they possess. The writer Gerard Genette accepted Plato's idea that names, in some fundamental but unexplained way, 'imitate' that to which they refer (see 'Mimologiques', 1976).

C. S. *Peirce* used the term 'sign' in a different way. The sign or 'representamen' as he called it is 'something that stands to somebody for something in some respect or capacity' (see Jensen's 'Social Semiotics of Mass Communication', 1995, p. 21). It 'addresses somebody ... creates in the mind of that person an equivalent sign, or a more developed sign'. The equivalent or more developed version of the original sign is called the 'interpretant'. The thing to which the sign refers (the real thing in the world) is the 'object'. Peirce saw the process of *signification* as continuous, with each interpretant of a sign (each effect produced in the mind of a human subject) leading on to the production of another sign.

Part of Peirce's system, was the division of types of sign into a three-part system (though this is only a small part of his work). An *icon* is a sign that relates to its object through some characteristic resemblance. An *index* is a sign that has a material link with the object. A *symbol* is a sign whose connection with the real is a matter of agreement or rule.

signal: in *transmission* models of *communication*, the physical form in which a message is conveyed. A message may be conveyed using speech; the signal in this case is composed of the sound waves which the human voice creates.

signifier/signified: in *Saussure's* system, this is the process which produces the sign. A signifier is a material thing which suggests a signified. The signified, in turn, is the concept called to mind by the signifier. This sounds fairly simple, but there are some points which need to be made. When semiologists argue that the signifier is the material substance that provides one part of a sign, it must be something human beings are able to perceive. In addition, it needs to be intelligible. In other words, the signifier must be noticed and understood.

So, when we are told that a vibration in the air, or a series of lines inscribed on a page, provide the material basis for the creation of meaning, we should remember that they only make sense as a spoken word and a written word respectively, when they appear in a recognised form (a certain series of sounds, a particular shape on the page).

Another point to note, is that a signifier is always supposed to make a reference to something besides itself. At the same time, signifiers are unavoidably also themselves (a word has a reference, but it also belongs to the general category 'word', a photograph may refer to something else, but it retains the status of a photograph).

Emile Benveniste, a renowned semiotician, believed that Saussure had omitted an essential part of the theory of meaning, a third element besides signifier/signified, which refers to the actual thing in the world. Although Saussure thought that the link between signifier and signified was arbitrary (meaning the connection between the sign and the thing for which it stands, is just a random or accidental event), Benveniste argued that the arbitrary relation was actually between the whole sign and the real thing in the world to which it referred. He noted, for example, that the pronunciation of a word and its meaning (signifier/signified) seem to be identical in the human mind.

signification: the production of meaning through the use of signs. Signification takes place in a variety of ways, through all channels of communication. Giddens (1984) places signification with two other structural dimensions which exist in society. These are domination and legitimation. The creation of meaning in modern society is therefore closely related to the use of power. One of the drawbacks of semiology as a study, is that the composition of signs has seemed more important than the effects they produce (their signification).

silences in text: the act of choice in narrative texts (what to include and what to exclude) sometimes leads to a situation where an obvious development in the plot is suppressed in favour of an outcome which suits the ideological purposes of an author/director. At such points, the 'forced' nature of the development or resolution leads to the uncomfortable sense that other, once-visible tendencies in the narrative, have been suppressed. At such points, 'silences' occur as that which should be represented in the story-world is cut out to achieve the 'official' outcome.

silly season: that period, usually during the summer months, when journalists perceive that since little of real value is happening, inconsequential stories must be carried. In some areas of the press, the silly season now lasts the entire year.

simulacra: images of things, but images which are deceptive, and essentially a mere pretence. Jean Baudrillard uses the idea in his essay 'Simulacra and Simulations'. He is convinced that life in modern times has become *'hyper-real'*, a state of existence in which people are bewildered by the appearances of things, a world in which media images refer not to reality, but only to other mediated events. 'Only signs without referents', Baudrillard argues, 'empty, senseless, absurd and elliptical signs, absorb us' ('Seduction', 1990, p. 74).

Baudrillard (see 'Simulacra and Simulations' p. 170), attempts to trace the 'phases of the image' in history, arguing that it has gone through four stages: '1) it is the reflection of a basic reality, 2) it masks and perverts a basic reality, 3) it masks the absence of a basic reality, 4) it bears no relation to any reality whatever; it is its own pure simulacram'. It is the last stage, that of the 'pure simulacram', which Baudrillard thinks modern society has reached. This idea is formed partly from his study of American culture, which in some urban centres forms a rough approximation to the 'postmodern condition'. As Stuart Sim writes in 'Beyond Aesthetics' (1992, p. 127) 'unlike Europe, nothing ever quite adds up to a pattern in America ... where signs appear to have no past'.

Another author, Christopher Norris, agrees that Baudrillard has noticed something significant about modern society (refer to 'What's Wrong with Postmodernism', p. 171). Norris argues that 'Baudrillard's diagnosis speaks directly to to a widespread sense that we are living in a world of pervasive unreality, a world where perceptions are increasingly shaped by mass-media imagery ...'

To take Baudrillard's perspective completely to heart, however, means that we must accept the following propositions; that the media has become the dominant force in society, and that images can 'float' free of reference to the real, without at some point having material consequences.

single lens reflex: a type of camera that allows a photographer to view through, and thus compose with, the camera lens. Single lens reflex cameras use a mirror prism system; a reflex mirror is housed in the camera body, and a prism and focusing screen are located in the viewfinder. The disadvantage of the SLR, besides a rather noisy shutter system, is the rather dim view obtained as the picture is being composed.(See overleaf for illustration.)

sitcom: a contraction of 'situation comedy'. A sitcom is a light-hearted programme based on a simple premise (a single parent in straitened circumstances, a group of friends who share an apartment, etc.), which provides the 'situation'. Sitcoms feature a cast of established characters who interact within a limited number of recognisable settings.

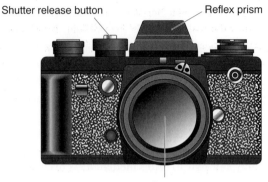

Shutter release button — Reflex prism

Lens

Single lens reflex camera

slang is a form of colloquial language; the members of certain occupations or classes appear to use slang either in response to the peculiarities of their work, or because a form of social solidarity is being sought. (See also *argot, jargon*.)

soap opera: supposedly called soap operas because many of the original programme sponsors were soap manufacturers. A soap opera is a serial which examines the lives of ordinary families, in a consistent setting. It uses the same cast members, and develops its own plots.

social context: the social framework which provides the background for action and interaction. Social context is found in the structure of an event and the associated conventions which surround it, in the range of 'references' made during a speech exchange, and in the discursive constraints recognised by participants (what it is possible and not possible to say).

social identification is a theory which states that human identity is created through the relationship between social groups and individuals; it goes further than this, however, arguing that an individual will actively choose groups for positive reasons, feeling some emotional attachment to them. Hogg and Abrams, who wrote a book called 'Social Identifications', argue that groups have 'a profound impact on individuals' identity.' The groups they identify include national, religious, political, ethnic, sex, tribal, and youth. Although it is not unusual to believe that social categories lead to differences in status, power and therefore attitudes and behaviour, these authors study how individuals express their own sense of belonging or 'identification'.

Other writers, like Oakes, Haslam and Turner (in 'Stereotyping and Social Reality') ask how group character is created through the interaction of individual and group identity. They conclude that the *identity* perspective emphasises the psychological reality of groups.

The idea that the individual feels a positive sense of self-worth from the attachment to the group is, as Hogg and Abrams point out (p. 7); 'very different from merely being designated as falling into one social category or another.' The 'psychological' group is one in which individual members have a high degree of awareness of other people in the group. Interactions develop to the point at which it is possible to identify set exchanges or patterns of communicative behaviour. A 'group boundary' is erected, while the group itself possesses clear goals and shared norms. It also encourages *affective* relationships (emotional attachments) between members.

The extent to which goals and values are actually held in common, depends on whether individuals:

- join a group willingly
- have full knowledge of the aims and objectives of the group
- sincerely accept the goals, values, and models of behaviour which the group appears to value.

social identity: a theory of *identity* which emphasises group aspects of belonging, and the reasons why individuals feel positive attachment to those groups actively chosen. The identity perspective perceives much group theory to be a disguised way of describing individual behaviour.

social landscaping: a term used of any public policies or private initiatives, which are concerned to change or re-design the way that social groups conduct themselves. Social landscaping includes processes like 'downsizing' in employment, changes in benefit payments, redistribution of wealth through schemes like the national lottery, and generally any measures designed to change the political, economic or social structure. (The term appears in Price, 1996).

social narratives: a term which draws attention to the way that *discourses* are often expressed in *narrative* form, and not just as statements about events. Social narratives offer broadly plausible ways of describing events in the world and are 'social' because they contribute to the ways in which meaning is reproduced. An example might be a discourse on 'media violence', which offers a coherent explanation of its function in society.

social process: the course of all the different relationships and operations which make up human society, including *socialisation, communication,* economic development, cultural formation, and so on.

social psychology is the study of the relationship between human identity/behaviour and the *social context* in which thoughts and actions are expressed. Social psychology explains human action by looking at the concrete social location of individuals and groups, rather than by searching for individual peculiarities in intellectual or emotional make-up.

social realism: in film, social realism is an attempt to provide an accurate portrayal of certain social conditions. It usually depicts ordinary middle or working class life, but often focusses on the lives of individuals who are caught in difficult economic circumstances. Susan Hayward ('Key Concepts in Cinema Studies') traces the origins of social realism to the *documentary* tradition associated with John Grierson, and identifies three movements which grew from this source: Italian 'neo-realism' of the 1940s, 'Free British Cinema' of the 1950s, and the French 'cinéma-vérité' group which appeared in the 1960s. (See also *realism.*)

social reality: that aspect of experience which is created through human activity, including economic, political and institutional structures, cultural production and discourse. A distinction can be made between social reality, which is the product of human society, and reality itself. Some writers believe that, although reality is usually perceived through our social constructions, there is still a world which cannot be reduced to language or *theory*, and which can be known and understood.

social responsibility theory: one of the normative theories of media conduct. Social responsibility theory emerges from US post-war dissatisfaction with the workings of the free market. Its main features are:

- the media has obligations to society
- high professional standards of truthfulness and honesty should be met by journalists
- the media should be self-regulating within the framework of the law
- media should be pluralist, reflecting the diversity of society and avoiding anything which might stir up dissension or discrimination
- public access should be provided to the media.

social subject: any individual inhabiting a social structure which:

- places him/her under the authority of formal government or power
- determines his/her position through a network of identifications and relationships with individuals and groups
- encourages the development of certain skills but discourages others
- allows the exercise of opinion and the use of argument within certain limits
- addresses him/her through a variety of texts and cultural forms.

The social subject, though 'positioned' by the power of address, is also one of many active social elements which re-form the terms of discourse through the collective use of common-sense. Notions about a host of issues, like appropriate sex-roles, loyalty, community, punishment, work, and other topics, provide the moral parameters within which subjectivity develops.

socialisation: socialisation is the process through which people (especially the young) acquire values and norms through a number of influences. These influences include upbringing, culture, language, education, social groups, economic circumstances, so on.

The media is one agency which helps to circulate meaning and thus has a role in the socialisation process. The exact nature of the media's role, however, is a matter of debate. Gerbner and Gross, writing from a US perspective in 1976, believed that 'television is the central arm of American society' and 'an agency of the established order'.

This model of society portrays the 'established order' (presumably the state) as exercising direct control of the media and its output. At times of crisis, it certainly seems that this kind of relationship can be brought about. However, Gerbner and Gross used the term 'enculturation' to describe a long-term process. Enculturation is the way that individuals are 'brought into' what has been called 'a consistent and near total symbolic environment which supplies norms for conduct and beliefs about a wide range of real-life situations' (McQuail and Windahl, 'Communication Models', 1993, p. 100). Thus, television becomes 'a world in itself' which envelops the viewer.

Objections to this approach start with the idea that the role of the media is over-emphasised, and go on to question the degree to which it is possible to separate media influence from other forms of culture. A number of writers have examined the the influence of 'global', rather than national systems of communication. Giddens, in 'Modernity and Self-Identity' (1991), believes the electronic media, with their greater reach into lives across the world, offer new definitions of culture and identity. Tony Spybey ('Globalisation and World Society', 1996) argues that (p. 114) 'global institutions are in the ultimate public domain and therefore subject to the widest possible range of counter-influences and counter-cultures'. In this sense, direct socialisation through the media appears to be an unlikely outcome.

society: society in general is the sum total of those relationships created by human beings; an individual society, however, is an aggregate of people existing within in a particular 'frame'. That frame can be a location in time, a physical space and/or an 'imagined' condition. Notice that society can exist without the intention of its participants, in the sense that relationships between individuals can be involuntary. An example of a (large scale) society is the nation-state, but the concept also includes the idea of sub-groups (like the class-specific notion of 'good society').

In addition, society can be seen as a powerful force which determines the relationships of those who exist within its boundaries; while the exact degree of influence is always in dispute, the idea of society as a framework which affects, yet is also changed by human relationships, is a useful way of thinking about its status.

Society has been seen variously as a structure (a network of institutions), as a 'recurrence' (a structure reproduced over time), as a contradiction (an uncomfortable compromise created by class conflict), as culture (produced by shared understandings and communication systems), and as process (composed of ever-changing social interactions).

sociogram: a method for recording group interaction, in which each participant is represented by a labelled circle, and lines are drawn between circles to indicate the 'direction' of speech acts.(See overleaf for illustration.)

sociolinguistics: the study of language use and class (or social position), and the relationships which may exist between the two. Sociolinguistics emerged as a sub-discipline in linguistics, responding to the idea that pure linguistic theory ought not to neglect questions of *social context*.

software: any computer programme which allows the computer itself (the 'hardware') to work.

sound: vibrations in the air or other medium which cause auditory perception. Sound can be analysed because it is meaningful, whereas noise is a random waveform which contains a mixture of any audible frequencies. Sound is one area of communication theory which is significantly under-theorised. This means not only that physical processes like transduction (the translation of vibrations in the ear into neural impulses) are rarely explained, but that issues which are central to communication theory, such as the contextual use of sound in film, are still relatively neglected. Other aspects of research into sound must include: auditory scene analysis (the study of how sounds from a single source are turned into 'perceptual units'), study of acoustic sequences like speech and music, the question of 'active' and 'passive' attention and auditory memory.

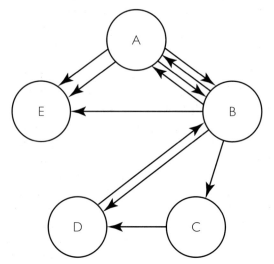

Sociogram of participation in a group context

sound-bite: a short statement or phrase used by a politician, designed to make an impact in the public arena. Although short, a sound-bite is carefully 'engineered', so that it can be used by news media. An example is 'tough on crime and tough on the causes of crime', used repeatedly by Tony Blair in the late 1990s. Political parties train their candidates to condense their speeches, so that the content is more likely to be reproduced in brief news bulletins. Hallin (1968) calculated that the time set aside for an American politician to respond to a question during television interviews, had fallen from 43 seconds in 1968, to nine seconds in 1988. This change in available air-time, and the proliferation of sound-bites in general, is usually blamed on the decline in political literacy, the influence of *spin* doctors, and the *news values* held by journalists. It is certainly the case that the political culture has changed, and that many of the brief statements used by politicians are worthless, but it seems unlikely that the public would accept a return to long-winded speeches uninterrupted by questions. Sound-bites are most objectionable when part of stage-managed events.

sound effect: a sound created for a film, radio or television production, to simulate a natural sound.

sound track: the sound (dialogue, sound effects, music) which accompanies a television programme or film. In a technical sense, the thin band which accompanies the full length of a film, and which supplies audio information. The audio track may contain single or multiple magnetic tracks, or what is known as 'variable density' optical tracks. The separate audio recording made on location or in the studio, is also known as a sound track.

spaghetti Western: a Western shot in Europe, with Spain or occasionally Italy standing in for the American West or the Mexican border. Sergio Leone made a number of Westerns, beginning in 1964 with 'A Fistful of Dollars', starring Clint Eastwood. Spaghetti Westerns were characterised by dubbed voices, brutal violence, gloating villains and near-silent heroes (partly explained by the removal of dialogue because Leone did not share a common language with his American star). These films were almost a parody of the entire genre, with rather melodramatic acting and rudimentary plot-lines. Many scenes are rather long and drawn out, though the best achieve an almost lyrical quality. Leone's 'Once Upon a Time in America', made in 1984 with a more substantial budget, reveals the same ponderous approach to film-making, though individual excerpts are impressive.

spectatorship is the condition or state associated with viewing; spectatorship is a special form of observation, created when individuals are brought together to witness an event, for example cinematic narrative. In the case of films they become specta-tors, interested in but removed from the action shown on the screen. Spectatorship has been theorised in a number of different ways, many of them derived from the psychological theories of Freud and Lacan. In one version, the male spectator believes that he controls the entire experience, but is in fact himself 'constructed' by the meanings of the text. In another, *voyeurism* lies at the centre of the event. Alternatively, the audience is confronted with an imaginary experience in which the absent (the realm of the imagination) is made present (through the signs displayed during the performance).

After Laura Mulvey's 1975 essay 'Visual Pleasure and Narrative Cinema', theories of spectatorship began to examine the 'gendered spectator', and to interrogate the dominant male perspective, arguing that the female form is sexualised and con-trolled by the male gaze. The female viewer is thus excluded from the symbolic order. This position was considerably modified by later commentators. Elizabeth Cowie, for example, argued that the female spectator could occupy a number of positions in relation to mainstream cinematic representation. All approaches, however, share an interest in analysing spectatorship as a condition linked to power and desire.

special effects (SFX): a variety of cinematic effects which create illusions on the screen. Special effects can be created using traditional methods of animation, com-puter graphics, glass painting, mattes and travelling mattes, multiple exposure, and so on. The whole of 'Toy Story' (1995) was created using computer simulation.

speech: the human faculty of verbal expression. Speech is produced by the passage of air through the larynx, which contains the vocal cords. These vibrate and produce pulses of air which set up a disturbance or noise. Variations in the speed of air pres-sure create a range of sound frequencies. This is then perceived as pitch, whereas the intensity of the variations represent volume. Speech is acoustic (or physical); the study of linguistic sounds is called phonetics.

speech act: the use of a genre of speech, a single utterance within a larger speech event, or the *performative* use of language which carries out an act in the process of speaking (e.g. 'You're fired').

speech community: a group of people who share the same linguistic code and, in the clearer cases, display a common attitude to the appropriate use of that code.

In such a situation, language is a bond which expresses the identity of the whole community.

speech event: an event which takes place in a particular context under certain conditions, revealing the use of established conventions of communication. The linguist Hymes described a speech event as a *genre* and a *speech act* as the performance of a genre. Some writers consider that speech events are examples of communication which require some type of formality, such as an after-dinner speech, a lesson, a sermon, etc.

Hymes thought a speech event the largest unit in which structure can be identified. A speech act, on the other hand, was the simplest form of utterance, and thus smaller and less easy to analyse.

spidergram: this is a diagram which resembles the body and legs of a spider. It may be used in the early stages of research or essay-writing, when a student wishes to write out all the related issues which grow from a particular subject or area of enquiry. So, for example, the centre of the 'body' (a circle) may contain the word 'genre'. The person drawing the diagram then marks, one by one, out a series of 'legs' (lines) which end in connected ideas, such as for example 'style', 'audience expectation', 'auteur' and so on. Each idea may then give rise to another related concept. The construction of a spidergram is spontaneous in that it allows for the random production of thoughts, and systematic in that it encourages the development of connections between various concepts.

spin: an interpretation given to an event, in an attempt to ensure that it is understood or 'read' in a particular way. It first appeared in the early 1980s, as a description of the practice of 'doctoring' certain political messages.

stamp duty: the first stamp duty, a tax charged on newspapers, was introduced in 1712. The purpose of this tax (in the words of Alan Marshall), was to 'keep the price of papers artificially high', so that the literate sections of the working class would be unable to follow the news (see 'Changing the Word', 1983). Throughout the eighteenth and nineteenth centuries, there was a constant struggle between government and the champions of a free press. Stamp duty was one attempt to restrict the spread of democratic ideas and thus limit the growth of political dissent.

It was however, possible to avoid the tax by exploiting inconsistencies in legislation. For example, longer newspapers could register as pamphlets, and thus achieve exemption. Unstamped newspapers were sold throughout the early part of the eighteenth century, although an Act of 1743 attempted to stop such titles. However, there were still about 35 local papers in existence in 1760, with nearly 90 others available in London.

The French Revolution of 1789 raised the stakes in the struggle between the state and all newspapers which were not merely government mouthpieces. The authorities characterised the radical press as the agent of a dangerous enemy. Duty was increased to two pence per copy, rising to three and a half pence in 1797, and four pence in 1815.

E.P. Thompson (in 'The Making of the English Working Class', 1968), argues that the working class became increasingly politicised, due to the influence of Methodism and the growth of industry. The growth of working class self-organisation helped increase the power of the radical political press.

Large circulations were achieved by the 'Black Dwarf', the 'Gorgon', and the 'Political Register' (later the 'Republican'). William Cobbett, the editor of the 'Political Register', avoided stamp duty by selling a paper devoted to opinion, rather than news as such. All publications, whatever their political stance, were becoming difficult to control.

Marshall, in 'Changing the Word' (p. 20), believes that stamp duty, 'by restricting circulation, and hence revenue and profits ... slowed down the introduction of expensive new machinery'. The result, in Marshall's opinion, was 'to allow the chronically underfinanced radical press to compete with the establishment press on the same terms'.

A second wave of radicalism, reflected in the rise of papers like 'The Poor Man's Guardian', was met with legal challenges which were, on the whole, ineffective. By 1843, the laws against libel were moderated. In 1855, stamp duty was abolished, followed in 1860 by the removal of the tax on paper. Marshall comments (p. 21) 'the abolition of the stamp duties opened the door to the new web-fed presses, and by the end of the 1860s newspaper production was becoming rapidly more capital intensive'.

star: an actor or actress who can command public attention and extensive remuneration whenever they appear on celluloid or in public. The Hollywood star system produced a number of bankable commodities. Stars in this era were part of the unit production system, and were contracted to work for a particular studio for as long as seven years. Stars represented an important investment. With the decline of the studio system, star players began to exert more control over their salaries, and in a number of cases went on to raise money for their own pet projects, which they could perhaps direct as well as appear in. (See also *studio system*.)

Steadicam: a system which enables a single camera operator to achieve steady shots. A cameraman named Garrett Brown, working with engineers from Cinema Products Inc., designed a harness which transfers the weight of the camera to the operator's hips. A spring-loaded arm damps the camera's movement, while a video monitor frees the operator from having to look through an eye-piece. The result is a shot which compares well with scenes taken from cameras mounted on a dolly or moved on a track. (See overleaf for illustration.)

stereophonic sound: this is audio information carried on a number of channels (from two to four), designed to produce the impression of a multi-layered 'sound environment'.

stereotype/stereotyping: a stereotype is the product of social construction, growing from group relations; an individual is assigned to a group and the supposed attributes of that group are applied to that individual. Allport (writing in 'The Nature of Prejudice', p. 20). indicated that 'the human mind must think with the aid of categories' and that once they have been formed, categories become 'the basis for normal pre-judgement'

The traditional approach to stereotyping, not only regards it as negative, but also embraces the idea that it is inaccurate or in some way flawed or inadequate. Fishman,

Steadicam

writing in 1956, believed stereotypes to be valid, to the extent that they reflected the actual interactions which take place between groups, (both those groups which were categorised, and those responsible for applying the stereotype.).

The established view of stereotyping, which sees it as an undesirable practice, could be explained as: the practice of making simplistic and usually negative social identifications of certain groups, in which the supposed attributes of the group are applied to all those identified (rightly or wrongly) as group members (from Price, 'Communication Studies', 1996).

There is no doubt that there is intent behind the use of stereotyping, but it is not necessarily malicious. Stereotyping is really about differentiating between one group and another; it is therefore contrastive and on occasion negative. The purpose of stereotyping would seem to be the need to create distinctions between the group to which one belongs and other groups; the intention behind this may be primarily to create identities for the *self*. Negative judgments about others may be a kind of 'side effect' rather than the primary objective of the process.

storyboard: a method for planning the sequences or individual shots required for film and television narratives; a series of illustrations is sketched out to show how the storyline will develop, including information on camera angles, sound effects, and so on.(See page 221 for illustration.)

strategic speech: speech which is directed to attaining a particular goal, and therefore uses certain strategies or devices to achieve the intended outcome, including persuasive styles, rhetoric, 'innocent' enquiry and so on.

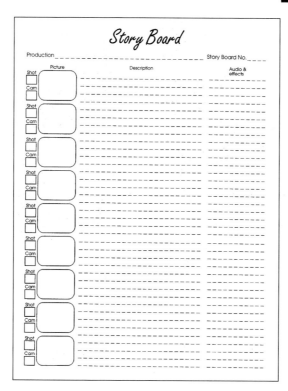

Storyboard

structuralism is an approach to textual analysis and social theory which emphasises the structures of the material under observation. In the field of linguistics Ferdinand de *Saussure* is the outstanding example of the structuralist approach. Structuralism searches for meaning in the structure of, and contrast between events, rather than in content as such. (See also *post-structuralism.*)

studio: any facility which contains equipment for recording radio, television and film programmes, or which allows designers to work on various projects.

studio system: an integrated system for making films, in which every aspect of the production, distribution and exhibition of a commodity is controlled by the studio. The studio system was one of the earliest examples of what has become 'the entertainment industry'.

The first studio system was created in France in 1910, where three companies (Gaumont, Pathé and Eclair) flourished. In 1912, the American Thomas H. Ince set up an early version of the Hollywood system. 1917 was something of a landmark, since this was the year Adolph Zukor acquired Paramount, a distribution company, and merged it with a production company he already possessed.

Zukor forced cinemas to make block bookings of his films, though there was some considerable resistance to this. 'Mass produced' films were the most economical to make, and were thus constructed according to a tried and tested 'formula'. Besides Paramount, other studios began to increase their strength; four were fully-integrated studios (Metro-Goldwyn-Mayer, RKO, Fox and Warner Brothers) and three others depended on the use of the other companies' movie houses for exhibition (Universal Pictures, Columbia and United Artists - the last of which was mainly involved in finance and distribution). In the late 1920s, most of the studios came under the control of banks and business groups, with the result that directors were hired for specific projects. Extensive resources were dedicated to advance publicity and the promotion of each studio's major *stars*.

The physical layout of the studios consisted of administrative offices, sound stages, accommodation for writers, and cinemas for preview work. In some cases, a producer would work with the same unit, consisting of a director and crew, on a number of films. The whole system was organised on an industrial basis, almost as a production line, with clear demarcation between different roles. Branston and Stafford ('The Media Student's Book', 1996), describe how the system worked (p. 241); 'integration meant that the studio had to provide its distribution arm and its cinema chain with a constant flow of A and B pictures, serials, newsreels and cartoons, fifty-two weeks a year'. The consequence of this was the production of specific types of film under a tight schedule, with certain studios specialising in one particular genre. The studio system as a whole lasted from 1930 to about 1949, when the US federal government forced the majors to sell their cinema chains. In the 1950s, independent producers took over some aspects of in-house production.

sub-culture: a collection of individuals whose notions of identity, shared interests, values, and behaviour, differentiate the group so formed from mainstream culture, and which may also bring it into conflict with dominant systems or other sub-cultures. A sub-culture may use social characteristics (ethnicity, class, etc.) to mark itself out, or might unite around a certain public style. The perception of such groups by other members of society may often be negative. Groups which are able to protect themselves from the negative effects of their difference are usually located in the upper echelons of society.

subjection/qualification: a theory of social control, proposed by Goran Therborn in 1980, which states that the 'manifold potentialities of human infants' are shaped by the social order in which they are born. Therborn, writing in 'The Ideology of Power and the Power of Ideology', believes that (p. 17) 'certain drives and capacities' are encouraged, while others are prohibited or disfavoured.

In normal *socialisation*, children undergo 'instruction', 'sanction' and 'affirmation', designed to bring them into line with the norms of the social group. Instruction is the use of direct orders (e.g. do this, do not do that), while sanction is the system of rules which governs the use of penalties or rewards; affirmation is encouragement of those actions thought to be morally desirable or beneficial.

Therborn's idea, however, is especially concerned with the power of the state. He thinks that limits are set to human potential by two factors; the way that life is understood, and the way it is organised. According to this theory, individuals are given roles which guarantee that the major relationships of power in the social order continue to exist. These roles are especially concerned with social class, but also include gender roles, which are essential for the maintenance of an unequal society.

This is where subjection and qualification enters the equation. Therborn argues that a contradiction often arises between the needs of a society to repress or control individuals ('subjection') and the requirement to train capable individuals who are can perform certain functions without supervision ('qualification'). Part of the reason that individuals turn against society, despite the fact that they may have benefited from its structures, is because '... new kinds of qualification may be required and provided, new skills that clash with the traditional forms of subjection.'

For example, as a society becomes more technologically advanced, it may be necessary to create a class of people capable of analysing and reproducing information. Such a group may begin to alter the traditional 'balance of power.'

Society may, alternatively, create new types of subjection which clash with established patterns of qualification. Price, in 'Communication Studies', notes that 'exercises in privatisation and cost-cutting may result in the disciplining of a workforce whose existing abilities or skills (qualification) do not alter'. Therborn writes (p. 17), that 'the effects of a contradiction between subjection and qualification are opposition and revolt or underperformance and withdrawal.'

subjectivity is the (sometimes unstable) social location created by and for human individuals. Subjectivity is created through a series of relationships, identifications, *discourses* and subjection to various forms of authority. The individual subject is a product of class, gender, age, ethnicity and so on, but the external references which compose these qualities (social groups, attitudes to gender-role and age, racial and national 'characteristics'), are themselves sometimes in a state of flux.

subordination is the condition of social inferiority based on the occupation of a lowly role.

subscription television is a system which requires its audiences to pay for the channel; the signal is sent out encoded and decoded at the point of reception.

subtext: the secondary readings which readers are supposed to discover in a *narrative;* it can also refer to the idea that there is a hidden intention in the text, a kind of ideological current which runs beneath the surface. Sometimes the subtext has been deliberately set out for readers to pick up.

subtitle: in film, a subtitle is a translation of the actors' words, which appears at the bottom of the screen; in book publishing, a subtitle is a secondary or subsidiary title which helps to explain the subject of the book.

superstructure: the framework of political and cultural existence which is erected on the economic base of a society; the superstructure is supposed to include the law, politics, and cultural institutions.

supplement: a separate section belonging to a newspaper, as in 'Sunday supplement'. Supplements sometimes appear in other forms, such as the updated sections of an encyclopaedia.

surrealism: an art movement which tried to represent the disordered states associated with dreams and the workings of the unconscious. Some film-makers were influenced by surrealism, producing work which explored fantasy and desire through the use of unusual imagery.

surveillance: 'surveillance' comes from the Latin 'vigilare', which means 'to watch'. This particular type of watching, however, is more concerned with supervision, an act of overseeing carried out by some form of authority. In modern societies, according to theorists like Foucault, 'sovereign power' is replaced by 'disciplinary power'. The first type of power is associated with the authority which is vested in a monarch or ruler. The second type, according to Foucault (see 'Discipline and Punish', 1977) is a form of authority which came to prominence in the late eighteenth century. Disciplinary power is identified by bureaucratic and technical control over the human subject, and can be linked to the growth of 'rational' systems of punishment like the use of specially designed prisons.

Foucault went on to illustrate his theories of surveillance by referring to Jeremy Bentham's design for a prison, known as the 'panopticon' (from the Greek for 'sight'). In the panopticon, each cell radiates outwards from a central observation post. The warders, looking out from behind Venetian blinds, are thus able to observe any cell without being noticed themselves. In Foucault's hands, the panopticon becomes a metaphor for modern society, in which a variety of bureaucratic organisations (health services, police forces, etc.) and public officials (psychiatrists, probation officers, and so on), carry out surveillance of the individual. The issue of surveillance has again been brought to public attention by the increased use of closed-circuit security cameras in public places, but surveillance presents a more general problem, as it includes the gathering of information on groups and individuals through electronic means (computer databases in particular).

symbol: one of three types of sign which were adapted from C.S. *Peirce's* work. A symbol is a sign which has 'some relation to the interpretant'.

symbolic content: any human intention which is expressed as a unit of meaning, drawn from a recognised code or form, such as language, binary code, music, etc. The meaning of 'go' is 'depart, leave, absent yourself', but the word itself, in standing for an instruction to leave, is an example of symbolic content.

symbolic form: a system which provides a means of expression, through the use of *symbols*. Language is the example most often used.

symbolic interactionism: the approach to meaning-creation in social life which stresses the activity of individuals and groups, and the availability of shared meanings through the use of common symbols. The theory emerged in the University of Chicago in the 1920s. The best known of its adherents in the first generation were G.H. Mead and William James, The second generation included Herbert Blumer and Everett Hughes, while the later groups can be represented by Erving Goffman, Howard Becker and others. (See also *interactionism.*)

synchronic: an approach to the study of language which interprets the structural relationship between elements, rather than their development over time. Synchronic studies attempt to understand the internal structures of text and speech.

synchronisation: the process of putting sound on an audio or film track so that it appears natural and unforced. Lip synch is where actors re-record lines so that they be synchronised with the visible evidence on-screen. (See also *synchronous sound.*)

synchronous sound: sound that provides a simultaneous accompaniment to the image; synchronous sound is essential where an audience watches a character speaking, or when the source of an on-screen noise is clearly identified. If the sound track does not follow the action, especially lip synchronisation, the film is said to be 'out of synch'.

syndication is the practice of selling a single story, comic strip, or feature to a number of outlets; also the distribution of programmes to individual television stations and the sale of newspaper material to overseas publications.

synopsis: a general overview or summary of an article, essay, book, or film, radio or television narrative. Usually written out or printed, in the case of film, television and radio, it may be spoken, heard in voiceover, or presented with accompanying excerpts from the production concerned.

syntagm: a syntagm is a combination of units which forms a signifying message. The units are taken from paradigms and are selected according to a governing principle of logical choice. So, for example, a musical score is made up of choices from the entire *paradigm* of notes.

syntax is the rules of sentence formation, or the component of mental grammar that represents speakers' knowledge of the structure of phrases and sentences.

T

tableau: a scene from television or film, which features actors who remain silent and motionless. It is taken from theatrical practices in the ancient world, and is intended to create an emblematic or symbolic effect on audiences. Some directors have used the tableau successfully, though rarely as an unselfconscious device; it is usually justified or given some context by other references, sometimes in films which deal with historical events. Peter Greenaway's films, for example, contain such references.

tabloid: a newspaper printed on sheets half the normal size; the term tabloid is often used as a reference to popular journalism.

tabulation is the arrangement of data (obtained from questionnaires or other sources) in the form of tables.

Talbotype: an alternative, though now largely unused term for the photographic images produced by William Henry Fox *Talbot*. The images are usually known as *calotypes*.

talent: a slang term used, especially in America, to describe performers who appear in front of the camera, including actors, newscasters, reporters, announcers and so on.

target audience: that group of individuals identified through age, ethnicity, class, or other demographic or psychographic means, which forms the core market for a particular product.

teaser campaign: an advertising campaign which attempts to arouse the curiosity of its audience. It does this by producing an incomplete message, a single image, or some other puzzle. As the campaign continues, the advertiser gradually releases further information which, retrospectively, makes sense of the material which has already been seen.

technological determinism is the doctrine that technological development is an autonomous force, leading to (or determining) social change, rather than emerging from specific social trends or the demands of an economy. This kind of approach has been called the 'technology-push theory', where the adoption of new technologies may secure future economic advantage; this means that innovations are taken up by nation-states before the market actually demands their use. The weakness in the argument is the implication that technology lies outside the social and economic sphere, when it is ultimately a product or manifestation of social and economic forces. Some may see it as 'separate' because of the way that technological innovation takes place in specialist environments controlled by powerful corporations, and is eventually 'revealed' to the public.

telegram: a communication made by telegraph, which was superseded in the UK in 1982 by the 'telemessage' (though retained for international communication).

telegraphy: a method for communicating messages across distances, first patented in 1837 by Cooke and Wheatstone. The telegraph used a series of compass needles which were deflected by a magnetic field produced when an electric circuit was closed. Also in 1837, the American inventor Samuel Morse made a telegraph system which was eventually supported (in 1843) by the United States Congress. Telegraph cables spread rapidly throughout Europe and America. In 1850, a telegraph cable was laid across the English Channel. Telegraphy is still used in a variety of public message systems, such as the Stock Exchange telex service.

telephone: an instrument that converts sound waves into electrical impulses, and these impulses back into sound. The first telephone system was established in Connecticut, in 1878, by Alexander Graham Bell.

teletext: a data service, which appears on a television screen as graphic or textual information.

television: television is a technological enterprise, driven by market forces, which has achieved immense importance as a cultural form. Although television is only one of a number of commodities which make up the economy of individual households, its status as a medium for cultural reproduction means that it will always remain at the centre of attention. It is assimilated into domestic life through the familiarisation of content.

Television content is organised into established genres, such as news, documentary, situation comedy, and so on. Each genre is recognised by audiences and produces a set of general expectations which must be fulfilled if audience loyalty and interest is to be maintained. In Britain, the diversity of genres is one reason for the appearance of choice and cultural diversity. While the mutation of genre is entirely possible, dramatic ruptures in established programme types can sometimes cause considerable agitation (witness the criticism directed at the satirical programme 'Brass Eye', based on its 'dishonest' appropriation of the documentary form).

The earliest practical demonstration of television took place in January 1926, when a Scottish engineer called John Logie Baird used a camera and photo-electric cells to convert light into electric current, scanning the object he wished to transmit and producing a picture composed of thirty lines. A research team from the company EMI soon developed a rival system to Baird's, based on electronic scanning. The two systems, electronic and mechanical, were tested against each another. Baird's method was troubled by mechanical failure, so the British government selected EMI to set up the world's first high-definition television service. Transmission began in 1936 and continued until the outbreak of the Second World War in 1939.

In its early years, television depended on finding suitable material to broadcast, and did not significantly alter the forms it reproduced; on the whole, it attempted to find a suitable mode of address which would allow television to be accepted as a legitimate cultural form by the small middle class audiences it could reach. The birth of commercial television in 1954 was an important factor in the creation of new ways of addressing mass audiences. Accusations of triviality and the unthinking reproduction of limited subject-matter, was one of the major criticisms voiced by the 1962 *Pilkington* committee.

Debates around television turn on issues of quality, its supposed role as an agent of dominant interests, and in recent years the effect of *deregulation* (thought to accelerate the fragmentation of public culture). The future of television will be determined by the fact that it has become, in the words of David Morley and Roger Silverstone ('Television Audiences', p. 203) 'a key technology for the selling of other technologies'. However, it not only displays advertisements which introduce a range of goods, it lies at the centre of proposed developments in computer technology and home entertainment. Opinion is divided as to whether television will assimilate other forms or will remain an essentially separate technology.

Telstar: a communications satellite launched on 10 July 1962. It transmitted the first live television pictures between the United States and Europe. These transmissions could not be continuous because Telstar was not *geostationary,* and orbited the earth every 157.8 minutes.

terrestrial broadcasting: broadcast systems which transmit programme signals from ground-based stations to audiences, as opposed to *satellite* transmission. In Britain, this means the BBC and the independent companies as opposed to B Sky B and other satellite companies.

text: any product of authorship (single or multiple) embodied in a recognisable structure (e.g. narrative or non-narrative), which assumes one of many guises (including the novel, film, or other coherent form) and which is the site of cultural interpretation. Breda Luthar (in 'Identity Management and Popular Representational Forms') explains that 'a popular text is ... a piece of objectified culture and at the same time a producer of specific identities'. In other words, 'the content and aesthetic form of a text convey its meaning only through the reception and interpretation which is defined by the common experience of recipients, and objectified in social memory'.

textual analysis: the process of identifying and evaluating the meaning of a text, through a study of content, form (internal structure) and the social context in which it was produced (including relationships with other texts and the way it is received by audiences). A text is an 'objectified' cultural artefact, whether a newspaper article, film, radio programme or other format.

In textual interpretation the following areas must be considered, where appropriate; image, colour, sound, and language. These elements, their relationship to one another and to their wider cultural context, will immediately suggest a wealth of *cultural references,* expressed through design, visual and aural connotation, discourse and address, narrative reference and so on. Recognised methods of textual analysis include basic linguistic studies of phonology, syntax and semantics, more advanced analysis of style and address, content analysis (where the occurrence of certain types of content is recorded), semiological approaches (which search for the concepts suggested by signs), structural analysis (which asks how the internal elements of the text are arranged), studies of narrative (which examine patterns of cause and effect), empirical comparison (where the world of the text is compared with other sources), discourse analysis (the attempt to identify 'social narratives') and ideological analysis (concerned to establish what types of belief are being propagated in what contexts). Contextual analysis is an important procedure, related to empirical approaches, while an enquiry into the effect of mediation on textual form could be applied where an original text has been re-presented by the media.

theory: a set of ideas formulated from observation, intended to provide a coherent explanation for the existence and behaviour of phenomena (things which occur or change in the world). In media and communication studies, a great variety of theoretical perspectives have been advanced. What follows is a brief overview.

Film theory, especially that associated with the journal 'Screen', has used psychoanalytical approaches, together with a strong feminist perspective; Althusserian Marxism has also been employed to explain subjectivity and address in the cinema.

The study of interpersonal communication was dominated for years by the variant imported from the United States, which looked for hidden psychological states behind utterance. Myers and Myers' 'The Dynamics of Human Communication' (1985) and Patton and Giffin's 'Interpersonal Communication in Action' (1981) read like manuals for good citizenship but do not study real exchanges.

Mass communication research has been strong in the United States, with a number of studies of effects in evidence (see *effects* and *two-step flow*). Within the North American tradition, *functionalism* is one significant sociological approach to communication.

Symbolic interactionism, associated with the work of George Herbert Mead (1863–1931), places language at the centre of human communication. Symbolic interactionism studies the human perspective on events, and the social outcomes of communication.

Usually applied to mass communication, Marxism has provided a powerfully radical critique of the media, from quite simple positions which perceive the media as reproducing dominant ideology, to the more complex and less critical cultural perspective associated with the Centre for Contemporary Cultural Studies in Birmingham (see *hegemony*). Political economy theory, revived in recent work like Vincent Mosco's 1996 study, concentrates on analysing structures of media ownership and control.

Feminist theorists have pointed to the physical, intellectual and symbolic exclusion of women, in the media industry, in the academy, in representation and in language; even more significantly, feminist theory has extensively radicalised the perspectives it has studied. A number of male-centred psychoanalytical approaches (associated with the first wave of *spectatorship theory*) and many post-structuralist studies of power and identity, have been transformed into radical critiques by feminist intervention. The domestic consumption of mass media forms has provided a particular focus for feminist researchers.

Structuralism, particularly the form associated with de *Saussure*, remains a great influence on textual interpretation. Post-structuralism and deconstruction emerged in response to the fixed and seemingly sterile rationalism of Enlightenment thought. Deleuze, Guattari, Lyotard, Foucault and *Derrida* are all associated with this development, while postmodernism represents a late riposte to all 'totalising' and repressive discourses. *Postmodernist* thinkers see the 'information society' as a significant departure from past forms of social organisation. In recent years, interest in *discourse analysis* and new theories of power has gathered pace, to the extent that it has become a major force in media and communication studies. Discursive theorists are usually split between 'social constructionists' (the world created and maintained through discourse) and *realists* who believe it is still possible to perceive a world which lies outside human invention.

Therborn: Goran Therborn is a Marxist sociologist whose contribution to communication theory lies in his work on subjectivity, ideology and discourse. Therborn does not see the modern worker as entirely oppressed by the state, but as a subject who is given opportunities which may eventually lead to an oppositional stance. The process he identified is known as *subjection/qualification.*

third cinema is a term invented in 1969 to distinguish cinema made in less developed nations from Hollywood productions (first cinema) and European art films (second cinema). Third cinema is characterised by its political orientation, dealing with the effects of colonialism, class conflict and sex inequality. Other themes include the armed struggles which many exploited nations experienced, and the difficulties of implementing progressive policies in underdeveloped countries. Cuba is an example of one country whose cinema displays a strong oppositional perspective. Latin American and many African film-makers are also notable for their analysis of political power. Established third cinema directors include Ousmane Sembene (Senegal), Octavio Getino (Argentina), Tomas Guttierez Alea and Humberto Solas (Cuba).

thought may be defined in a number of ways; as the process of cognition, the power of reason, a reflective state, or an individual idea. It may also describe a *world-view* (as in 'modern thought'). Harré and Gillett ('The Discursive Mind', p. 47) call thoughts 'composite' conceptions, made up of particular ideas about specific objects and general concepts about the world.

These conceptions include images, linguistic features, and more abstract elements (which are used, for example, when a mathematical property is considered). Arguments about the nature of thought include debates about its relationship to language and to action (see *thought/language* and *pragmatism*). J.M. Moravcsik ('Thought and Language', 1990) believes (p. 71) 'one can think of humans as basically curious ... calling for explanations. According to this conception thought is not fundamentally action-oriented, but has as its primary function the articulation of reality into a series of explanatory patterns'.

tight shot: a camera shot which frames its subject matter very closely, used when attention to detail is important and little movement is required.

Todorov: Tzvetzan Todorov, a Bulgarian who came to France in 1963 and collaborated with Roland Barthes, is known for a number of works on structuralism and the literary text. He also produced a study of Columbus' encounter with the inhabitants of America, called 'The Conquest of America: the Question of the Other' (1982). He is known within media studies for his contribution to narrative theory, which has been applied to film and other forms. Todorov argues that narrative in its most basic form, works through a series of five 'transformations', which are:

1 a state of equilibrium
2 a disruption of the state of equilibrium through an action
3 a recognition of the disruption
4 an attempt to repair the disruption
5 a return to the initial state of equilibrium.

These changes are not made on a random basis, but are generated by the operation of cause and effect. The principles which produce the cause/effect relationship are possibility, probability, impossibility and necessity, all relating to the actions that occur during the narrative. It is sometimes difficult to relate this to actual narratives.

For example, it sometimes appears that a story actually starts with a disruption. Todorov's answer to this problem is to argue that the real beginning of a narrative is found, not necessarily at the start of the sequence, but at the point which provides a point of explanation for the whole tale.

traffic lights: the three-part traffic light system was used by Leach in 1974 to demonstrate how semiological meaning is created through the relationship between signs. On the face of it, the use of individual colours (red, green and amber) provide a straightforward demonstration of how structures of meaning operate. The signifier red has the signified stop, green stands for go, while the amber light means get ready to stop/go. Hodge and Kress ('Social Semiotics', 1988) argue that semiology neglects the contextual features of culture, which include setting and participants. In the case of a large Australian city, motorists produce a quite different reading of the lights. According to Hodge and Kress, the amber light in particular is often read as a signal to speed up and get through the lights before they turn to red.

transaction: the performance of a communicative exchange between two or more participants.

transactional analysis: a little-used psychological approach to interpersonal communication, which argues that specific 'ego states' lie behind utterances. The idea, advanced by Eric Berne in 1964, was that everyone is able to operate from one of three basic types of ego state. These are parent, adult and child. There are also certain sub-divisions, but the principle of the system remains the same. Each condition is the repository of certain behavioural traits: the parent is responsible, caring, but critical; the adult is rational; the child spontaneous, creative, but rebellious. The theory is that utterances can be studied in order to determine which ego state is being used during the exchange, and thus which strategic position an individual should best use to respond. Transactional analysis has largely disappeared from communication studies, owing to its inability to analyse actual utterances, except as evidence of hidden psychological conditions. Its virtue lies in its view of interpersonal communication as a series of strategic moves.

transformation: in grammar, a rule of sentence construction which moves one element into a new position, transforming the structure of the sentence but not necessarily its meaning. The first point to note is that, within a sentence, it is possible to identify a number of different elements, including determiners (the, this, a, etc.), verbs, nouns, and so on. In addition, two sorts of 'phrase' are present; noun phrase and verb phrase. The movement of one of these phrases is responsible for the 'transformation'.

'Introducing Transformational Grammar' (1994), by Jamal Ouhalla, presents this example: 'I can solve this problem'. Here, the noun phrase is 'this problem' and the verb phrase is 'I can solve ' ('can' is known as a modal auxiliary). When the noun phrase is moved to the beginning of the sentence, it reads 'This problem, I can solve'. The theory of transformation works on the idea of *Chomsky's* 'deep structure'. This states that, underlying all sentences, a basic level of organisation exists which can generate different 'formulas' which share the same basic meaning. So, for example, the sentence 'the train driver ate the sandwich' and 'the sandwich was eaten by the train driver' mean the same thing, even though their surface structure is different.

transmission: in communication theory, a form of communication which is linear and usually proceeds in one direction. Many studies of media communication describe it as the transmission of information from a source to a receiver. Transmission also refers to the sending of electronic information between two terminals.

transmission speed is the speed at which various types of data are transmitted through a communication circuit, expressed as words per minute, characters per second, bits per second, etc.

transparency is the degree to which social relations in a class/patriarchal society can be seen for what they are; some theorists think that the media obscures the true relations of power.

travelling matte: a *matte* shot in which foreground and background details are filmed separately, and the matte itself is changed in each frame. A travelling matte is used when movement needs to be represented.

treatment: any adaptation of a play, book, or (usually) literary production which is intended for cinematic or television use. A treatment sometimes forms an intermediate stage between the initial idea for the project, and the *shooting script.*

triangulation: in research, the use of a variety of methods in order to check findings and supplement results. Triangulation does not mean that there will be an absolute guarantee of accuracy, but rather that the researcher will be able to answer any challenges to his or her research in a more assured manner, using a variety of findings.

two-step flow is a theory of effects which emphasises the role of opinion leaders and other human influences during elections. The American researchers Lazarsfeld, Berelson and Gaudet conducted a study of the 1940 presidential election campaign. They examined a number of issues, including the voting predispositions of social categories (socio-economic status, religion, residence, occupation and age were all taken into account). The level of interest in the election was also assessed, and how this related to the final decisions of voters. The media campaign was, obviously, high on the researchers' list of variables.

One aspect of influence on voting was, however, undervalued until later on in the election campaign. This was the the fact that individuals were strongly influenced by what their acquaintances thought about the candidates. Discussions with friends, relatives and other individuals was reported more often than exposure to political messages on radio or in print. This possibility had not been built into the research hypothesis. As a result, Lazarsfeld and his co-workers formulated the 'two-step flow' theory of communication and influence. They believed that some people among those they had studied acted as opinion leaders, and were characterised by their high level of exposure to political messages and their high level of interest in the election. Other individuals, the theory stated, used these opinion leaders as vital conduits of information. Lazarsfeld et al. noted that 'ideas often flow from radio and print to the opinion leaders and from them to the less active sections of the population' (see 'The People's Choice', 1948).

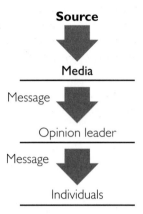

Two-step flow

typage: in film and television, the use of certain physical or social 'types' to represent particular qualities, social forces, or behavioural patterns. Studies of heroes and heroines, and of villains and their female accomplices, have been carried out on a number of occasions. Emanuel Levy, for example ('Social Attributes of American Movie Stars', 1990) examined the social attributes of American movie stars, discovering a great deal about the values espoused within US society through the choice of social type used in a variety of films.

typeface: the various types of printed character available to typographers. Typefaces include Palatino, Courier, Helvetica, Baskerville, and many others.

typescript: a typewritten document, now more likely to be word-processed. The usual term in publishing is 'hard copy'.

typesetting: the process of arranging type into a coherent form, based on a faithful reproduction of the original manuscript.

typo: an abbreviation of 'typographical error'.

typography is the art of composing print and page layout; originally it included the printing process itself, but is seldom used in this way now. It includes the production of text and graphic design. Although computer software programs allow greater access to the elements of design, it cannot teach individuals how to set out a page.

ultra high frequency (UHF): the band of frequencies from 300 to 3000 MHz.

ultraviolet: light which lies outside the range of human vision.

underexposure: incorrect shutter speed, insufficient light, or the use of too small a shutter aperture can lead to underexposure, where a photograph lacks detail and appears too dark.

underground cinema: generally, any small-scale 'artisanal' production with social or political aims which conflict with those of the state or the cultural establishment, but particularly associated with the rise of the New American Cinema Group, formed in 1960 to oppose what it believed to be the moral corruption underlying dominant cinematic forms. The movement was 'underground' because many of its products would have been proscribed under the United States' censorship laws. Practitioners of underground cinema included Stan VanDerBeek, Kenneth Anger, Jack Smith, Stan Brakhage, and Andy Warhol.

uniaccentual sign: Volosinov's term for a sign which has been given an 'eternal character' by the ruling class. The ruling faction in society is supposedly hostile to the *multiaccentual* character of *language*. This is because the wide range of meaning in language reveals the existence of a struggle between opposing social groups. Language must therefore be 'disciplined', in order to force each sign to produce one dominant meaning. In practice, it is probably impossible to restrict language in this way, and perhaps doubtful that any ruling group would try to channel *signification* when social control is perhaps more easily attained through the *fragmentation* of meaning.

unit production: a type of film production prevalent during the classical period of the *Hollywood studio system*. Unit production consisted of groups of camera operators, lighting technicians, and directors, who were assigned a producer for a number of projects. Different production units would work on specific genres; biopics or Westerns, for example.

United Artists: one of the smaller *Hollywood* studios, formed in 1919 by a group which included D.W. Griffith, Douglas Fairbanks, Mary Pickford and Charlie Chaplin. It began as a distribution company for its own independent productions, but was restricted by the fact that the major studios controlled most of the cinemas required for exhibition. Among the company's well-known productions were Chaplin's 'Modern Times' (1936) and 'High Noon' (1952). United Artists was bought by a Las Vegas businessman in 1981, and was amalgamated with MGM. The combined group was briefly part of the Turner Broadcasting System, was then sold to an Italian entrepreneur, and finally taken over by the French bank Crédit Lyonnais.

unity: in the work of the ancient Greek philosopher Aristotle, theatrical presentation is supposed to obey the three 'unities'; of time, place, and action. This meant that dramas would ideally have to take place in real time, and would not represent more than the action which could take place in the space of one day.

Universal Pictures: a studio founded in 1912, part of the smaller grouping which included United Artists and Columbia. Universal's early stars included Lon Chaney and Rudolf Valentino. In the 1930s, the studio specialised in making horror films. After overcoming a financial crisis in the early 1930s, Universal was re-launched and attracted well-known stars to its 'stable' by offering them a percentage of profits from films in which they appeared. It acquired International Pictures in 1946 but was taken over by Decca records in 1952. Ten years later, Decca was incorporated into Music Corporation of America (MCA). Universal continued to produce films for television, as well as some major features like 'Jurassic Park' in 1993.

universal structures: this term refers to the idea that all languages share certain structural features. Noam *Chomsky's* observation that all infants throughout the world acquire language in a similar way suggests, in turn, the existence of structures in the brain which are common to all humans.

unmatched shots: the practice of cutting from one shot to another, apparently unrelated shot, thus disturbing the *continuity* of action. It is used in some types of avant-garde film.

unpredictability: in film, encounters with situations which are not part of the intended narrative or structure. Sometimes, unexpected incidents recorded on film are retained as part of the *mise en scene*. The *Lumières* encountered the unpredictable when filming 'Barque sortant d'un port', recording a boat slewed off course by waves. Rossellini, in 'Rome Open City', made in 1945, showed an 'ambush' on German soldiers which included a dog which ran across the field of vision. The moment is kept in the film, because the realist aesthetic is not disturbed by such accidents.

user friendly: used most often of computer software, 'user friendly' means systems and applications which are easy to learn and straightforward to use.

user interface: the point at which a computer system and the person using it 'interact', including the use of instructions from system to user which appear on-screen, the use of the mouse, keyboard, printer, etc.

uses and gratifications: a theory of textual consumption which emphasises audience use of what they see, hear and read. Media texts are thought to provide information, reinforcement of identity and values, integration into the social environment, and entertainment. In 1970, James Halloran noted that 'we must get away from the habit of thinking in terms of what the media do to people and substitute for it the idea of what people do with the media'.

Uses and gratifications theory emphasises the freedom of choice exercised by viewers, despite some evidence (Goodhart, 1975 and Barwise, 1982) to suggest that a great deal of media consumption is unselective and based on force of habit. As an idea, uses and gratifications has occasionally been used to oppose those studies which stress the power of the media to shape public perceptions. Shaun Moores ('Interpreting Audiences', 1993) argues that it is (p. 7) 'a psychological conception of human personality which focusses narrowly on the media's functions for the individual'. He also thinks there is a tendency in uses and gratifications research to 'overplay audience freedom and ignore issues of ideology completely'.

V

values are ideas about the relative worth of things and the nature of good and evil. Values are applied to things, events, people and so on, rather than being an inherent part of such phenomena. The operation of values may be found in group interaction, public *discourses,* and language, where the naming and *categorisation* of things often reveals the values which are thought to reside within them.

verbatim: from the Latin for 'verb' and 'literatim' comes verbatim, a literal or word-for-word report. When someone is quoted verbatim, the result is supposed to be an exact reproduction of what he/she has said, though journalistic practice does not extend to recording breathings and pauses, as would be given in records of speech used for conversational analysis.

verisimilitude: the impression of truth or a close resemblance to actual life. In film, the quality of appearing close to the real.

vernacular: the speech of a region or sub-culture. The concept of the vernacular is a type of speech that is unforced, and not deliberately learned. (See also *received pronounciation.*)

vertical integration is the ownership of more than one level in the corporate structure of supply and distribution. In the case of the film industry, this might be the ownership of the supplier, the distribution network and the exhibitors (a network of cinemas).

video: from the Latin 'videre', to see, video is the technology used for recording and playing television programmes, films, exercise cassettes, training films, 'home movies' and so on. Video cameras have revolutionised production practices, while the use of video recorders has made viewers less dependent upon the primary output of broadcast television.

video box: a Channel Four innovation which encouraged public response to its programmes. A number of booths fitted with recording equipment, were placed in strategic locations. Individuals could use the facility to make statements, some of which were selected and broadcast.

video nasties: a type of video narrative which shows acts of cruelty or extreme violence. The term came into prominence in the early 1980s as video recorders became increasingly widespread and children appeared to gain access to violent films.

The argument used by groups like the National Viewers and Listeners Association, was that children would watch such material and then carry out violent acts themselves. The British Parliamentary Group Video Enquiry took the view that video nasties gradually lose their power to shock, leading young viewers to seek yet greater levels of visual barbarity. Arguing against this view, the media researcher Martin Barker attacked the 'desensitisation' argument, claiming that it made 'a stupid equation between judgment and emotion'. Barker believed that the loss of the 'shock response' did not lead to the loss of an individual's critical abilities. Court action in 1982 led to the withdrawal from circulation of several video nasties. The issue was again brought to public attention during the trial of the boys who killed two-year-old Jamie Bulger. They were alleged to have watched a violent video called 'Child's Play III'. Margaret Ford, of the British Board of Film Censors, writing in 'Sight and Sound' in 1994, noted that 'Child's Play III' 'has now achieved notoriety far beyond its power to frighten or distress. Its symbolic power is immense'.

Video Recording Act: a 1984 Act designed to restrict the access of young people to '*video nasties*'. It focused on the classification of video tapes and the censorship of material thought to be unsuitable for home viewing.

videotext/teletext: a service which provides information in the form of text and graphics, via telephone cables, to individual television sets. In Britain, the BBC's service is known as Ceefax, while the commercial equivalent is known as Teleview.

viewpoint: the relationship between a subject and the angle and distance of the camera which records the scene.

violence: the study of violence is usually concerned with *representations* of violence in narrative fiction. Footage of state violence in wars, or any other form of actuality showing conflict, does not appear to cause controversy.

One of the earliest enquiries into the harmful *effects* of on-screen violence was carried out by the National Council for Public Morals, which was composed of representatives of all Britain's moral reform groups. In 1917, the Council took evidence from nearly fifty witnesses, including social workers, policemen, doctors, probation officers and members of the film community. The Council reported that the problem of juvenile crime was too complex to lay at the door of the cinema, and that the cinema did not cause violence but 'suggests the form of activity rather than [providing] the impulse to it'.

One of the most influential theories of violence and its treatment by the media is found in Stan Cohen's 'Folk Devils and Moral Panics' (latest edition, 1987). Cohen observed the response to those youth sub-cultures regarded as deviant; he used the term '*amplification of deviance*' to describe a cycle of public agitation, negative reporting, increased police interest in the group concerned and renewed publicity through the media.

Popular targets for campaigns against 'media violence' have included video nasties, comics, films and cartoon shows. Despite research carried out by Gunter and Harrison which showed that the amount of violence on television had declined from 1.1 per cent of output in 1986 to 0.61 per cent in 1994/5, the debate over the significance of violence in the media continues to generate new controversies. In 1996, Warner Home Video delayed the release on video of Oliver Stone's 'Natural Born Killers', after a British MP had lobbied against the film.

virtual exchange: Bernard Beckerman's description of theatrical presentation, in which there is no actual interaction between actors and audience, but an exchange of sorts based on the performance and address of the play.

virtual reality (VR): the technological simulation of an environment which makes an impact on the human senses, to such a degree that they respond almost as they would to stimuli in the real world. The creation of virtual reality is achieved at present through three major simulations; vision, sound, and the sensation of touch.

The computer-generated image is achieved by calculating the location of three-dimensional images in space. This calculation is based upon a perspective which assumes that a camera is placed in the position of the viewer's head. It is easier to 'map' artificial shapes than natural objects. One frame of a high-quality animation can take half an hour of programming. As Sally Prior writes in 'Virtual Reality: Beyond Cartesian Space' (see 'New Technologies of the Screen', 1993) 'current state-of-the-art VR worlds are not convincing enough to be seriously confused with the 'real thing' '.

The ultimate aim of many virtual reality programmes is to create a world that at least provides a complete immersion of the human subject. In order to achieve this, the following elements would need to be reproduced: visual, auditory, haptic (touch, temperature and pressure), proprioceptive (concerning the body's configuration), vestibular (orientation, movement and acceleration), olfactory (smell) and taste. The current uses of interactive VR systems are games, training in engineering and medicine, the reconstruction of 'heritage' sites and military combat simulation.

voice-activated: a microphone or other device which is activated by the human voice. When transcripts are required for *discourse* or conversational analysis, voice-activated tape recorders are sometimes used.

voiceover: in film and television, the use of a commentary which accompanies the narrative; the narrator remains unseen. Voiceovers are sometimes called 'commentative sound', and are positioned outside the world of the film itself. Some writers believe that the voiceover 'closes down a text', leaving the viewer 'little room for interpretation' (Watson and Hill, p. 244). However, the exact relationship between commentary and the text may vary depending on the way the *narration* is used.

vox pop: an abbreviation of '*vox populi*', a Latin term meaning 'voice of the people'. It is used in television and radio to describe street interviews with members of the public, when opinions are being canvassed on various issues. It sometimes appears as a technique in *party political broadcasts*, though actors are often used to 'mimic unscripted' responses.

voyeur: an individual who views others from a hidden or secret location. The concept of voyeurism is used in *cinema* studies to describe a number of positions which allow the viewing of others without their knowledge (though these others are representations on film). The first is that of the spectator, who observes from a darkened auditorium. The second is that of the camera, which also observes from a privileged location. In addition, characters within the film often watch other characters. In most cases, the voyeur obtains an insight into to a secret world. Critics of film point to the regularity with which voyeurism is focused on female characters, though there have been some limited changes in cinematic *representation* which display men as the objects of the female gaze.

VR: see *virtual reality*.

warm-up: the practice of entertaining a television or radio audience before a show is recorded, in the misplaced belief that they will be more enthusiastic about the proceedings and will show this in their applause, etc.

Web: see *World Wide Web*.

white balance: a control on a video camera which is used to achieve the correct colour balance. If the white balance is not used, white areas on the recording will appear with a green tinge.

wide-angle lens: a lens which has a *focal* length shorter than the diagonal of the film plane. The standard wide-angle lenses for 35 mm film are 35 mm, 28 mm, 24 mm and 20 mm. The chief effect of using such a lens is the apparent distortion in spatial relationships. A wider lens will allow more to appear in the frame but objects will appear to be further away.

widescreen: any process which is used to produce a cinematic aspect ratio greater than 1.33:1. Alternatively, a form of television set which is able to transmit the PalPlus format (used by BBC 2 and Channel 4 since 1994). The types of film widescreen best known to audiences are CinemaScope, Super Panavision, Technirama and Techniscope. CinemaScope was first introduced in 1953 by Twentieth Century Fox, in an attempt to attract audiences back to the cinema. Fox held the rights to the anamorphic lens, invented by Chretien in 1927. This lens squeezed the image during filming and then, through the use of a reverse anamorphic lens during projection, threw the image on the screen at a ratio of 2.66:1. Two rivals to CinemaScope were Cinerama, a system introduced in 1952 but which proved uneconomic to run, and VistaVision, introduced by Paramount but unable to compete with the commercial strength and acumen of the Fox group. The successor to CinemaScope was Panavision.

Widescreen projection

will to power: found in the philosophy of Nietzsche, the will to power is the idea that the human unconscious includes a drive to obtain knowledge and to secure control. Discourses, therefore, are supposed also to contain a will to power, in the sense that they are used to secure material benefit for the groups which use them.

wipe: an effect in film and television, where one scene is gradually replaced with another.

wire: a term used for a 'wire service', a news agency which provides its subscribers in the broadcast media with information. The information is sometimes coded with one of a series of letters, designed to indicate the relative importance of the news.

wireless: the use of telegraphy to send messages via electromagnetic waves. A number of scientists, working at the end of the nineteenth century, pursued experiments in which signals were sent between two separate locations, without the use of intervening wires. The pioneers of wireless telegraphy included William Preece, Heinrich Rudolf Hertz and Guglielmo Marconi. Marconi received £20,000 a year from the British Admiralty for the use of his his wireless system, which used Morse code to send signals between ship and shore. (See also *radio.*)

world-view: any coherent perspective held by a group about the nature of social reality; the term 'world-view' should not imply that the outlook described is either generous in its philosophical embrace, or particularly accurate. It suggests instead a perspective which provides answers, however limited, to all questions about the nature of lived experience. World-view is usually associated with a particular class or other social faction. It is sometimes also used to describe the attitudes, values and beliefs of a particular culture or era, as in 'the Athenian world-view' or 'the mediaeval world-view'.

World Wide Web: an international network of computer sites which offers, in the main, commercialised information. The Web contains multimedia data, including graphics, audio and video material.

wrap: in film or television production, to 'get a wrap' is to finish a scene.

written communication: any printed or handwritten material (including comics, magazines, newspapers, letters and essays) which initiates or sustains an act of communication.The functions of written communication include story-telling, *socialisation,* social affiliation and the simple provision of information.

WYSIWYG: stands for 'What You See Is What You Get', referring to the type of computer software program where the on-screen display closely resembles the hard copy print-out, identical in size and closely reproducing other features like font and design.

XCU: a script direction which stands for 'extreme close-up'.

xenon lamp: a high efficiency discharge lamp used in xenon projectors, producing a bright light; such lamps have largely replaced carbon arc lighting.

Xerox: a company that makes photocopiers, taken from 'xerography', an electrostatic process which reproduces printed matter. Ink in a powder form is fused to the paper through the application of heat.

youth culture: a concept which applies to the postwar recognition of new sub-cultures. Increased affluence and independence meant that the *norms* and values of young people could no longer be assumed to match those of their parents. Academic studies of youth cultures examined gangs (mods and rockers in the 60s, for example) and other 'counter cultures'. Functionalists looked for an explanation of the phenomenon in the functions that youth culture performed for its adherents and for the wider society. Eisenstadt (1956) believed that an extended period of youth was necessary for socialisation into what had become a very complex society. A well-known contribution to the debate came from the Centre for Contemporary Cultural Studies in 1975, with their volume 'Resistance through Ritual', which saw youth culture as a form of resistance to subordination. Cohen (1972) argued that skinhead culture was a desperate attempt to reclaim a lost form of working class community. Since the 1980s, the problems faced by young people have included low income, unemployment, homelessness and so on. This, some believe, has led to a decline in collective forms of expression. However, the rave/dance culture is one example of a (now commodified) youth culture which has managed to thrive in a depressed social landscape.

Z

zip code: a zip code is a group of five digits used by the US Postal Service to designate any large company or organisation.

zoetrope: an early animation device consisting of a drum which held a long strip of drawings. Each individual drawing would show a different phase in a simple sequence of movement. Vertical slots in the drum allowed the viewer to look inside; when the drum revolved on its pivot, the drawings would appear to form a continuous movement. It was invented in 1834 by W.G. Horner.

zoom: the practice of changing the focal length of a zoom lens, in order to make the subject of a film appear to move either closer to, or further away from the camera.

zoopraxiscope: a device invented by photographer Eadweard Muybridge (1830–1904) which he used to project images of human and animal movement. The photographs consisted of a series of pictures which showed the individual stages in a series of events. These images were mounted on a transparent disc which was attached to a central shaft. The shaft revolved in front of a lens, behind which a lantern provided illumination for the show.

Zoopraxiscope

MEDIA AND COMMUNICATION REVISION LISTS

At Advanced level, Media and Communication appear as two distinct subjects. Communication Studies (run by the AEB) covers more ground because it considers all aspects of human communication. Media Studies, on the other hand, gives more detailed attention to 'mass communication'. At the time of writing, it was offered by four separate boards (WJEC, NEAB, AEB and Cambridge).

The great diversity of Media and Communication work at undergraduate level, including Media Arts, Media Studies, Communication and Cultural Studies courses, also suggests that some common themes and perspectives need to be identified. What follows, therefore, is an amalgamation of sources, set out in alphabetical order under nine headings, each containing between 12 and 20 essential terms each.

Audiences and Reception

Aberrant decoding
Active audience
Audience
Counter-culture
Decoding
Ethnography
Foreknowledge and expectation
Identification
Lifestyle
Mass audience

Moral panic
Negotiation
Norms
Opinion leader
Phatic communication
Phonetics
Readership
Spectatorship
Sub-culture
Voyeurism

Human Communication

Address
Categories
Cognition
Convention
Expression
Exchange
Gender
Group communication
Identity
Imagined communities

Innateness
Interaction
Interpersonal communication
Language
Perception
Norms
Role
Self
Sensory perception
Speech

Industries and Production

Advertising
Broadcasting
Cinema
Cybernetics
Journalism
Institution

News Corporation
News International
News values
Photojournalism
Public service broadcasting
Radio

Issues and Controversies

Access
Artificial intelligence
Bias
Deregulation
Disinformation
Effects

Globalisation
Impartiality
Information society
Piracy
Quality
Violence

Media Technologies

Analogue
Cable
Camera
Compact disc/CD
Cyberspace
Digital technology
Information technology
Multimedia

New media
News
Photography
Printing
Satellite
Studio system
Television
Virtual reality

Perspectives and Approaches

Critical pluralism
Empiricism
Exchange
Feminism
Functionalism
Hypodermic model
Interactionism
Marxism

Phenomenologism
Pluralism
Postmodernism
Realism
Post-structuralism
Structuralism
Transmission/linear
Two-step flow

Power, Ownership and Control

Address
Agenda-setting
Bureaucracy
Censorship
Conspiracy theory
D-notice
Domination
Hegemony
Hierarchy

Ideology
Incorporation
Interpellation
Manipulation
Manufacture of consent
Monopoly
Market share
Organisations
Propaganda

Social Processes

Categorisation
Consent
Culture
Determination
Enlightenment
Interaction
Legitimation
Mediation
Narcotisation

Reinforcement
Representation
Signification
Social identification
Socialisation
Society
Stereotypes
Subjection/qualification
Surveillance

Texts and Analysis

Connotation
Content analysis
Context
Conversational analysis
Deconstruction
Denotation
Dialogics
Discourse analysis
Genre

Intertextuality
Linguistics
Narrative
Polysemy
Signifier/signified
Signs
Texts
Textual analysis
Semantics

EXAMINERS' TERMS

INTRODUCTION

The terms used in examination questions demand careful attention. Each term has a particular meaning which requires a certain kind of answer. The list below gives a definition of terms used in Media and Communication papers. Notice that there is a difference between a question which instructs you to do something (as in 'describe', 'analyse', and so on), and a 'true' question (which asks 'how might' or 'in what circumstances would' something occur).

Analyse: pick out the individual features of a topic, argument or theory, and determine their essential nature and value.

Assess: estimate the relative value or usefulness of a theory or theories, by examining the strength of argument and quality of evidence used in its/their support.

Consider: weigh up the merits of an argument, or the worth of empirical evidence, by measuring their quality against established criteria.

Compare: identify the differences between two or more sources, in order to estimate their relative value or completeness.

Contrast: set two issues, arguments, collections of data, etc., in opposition in order to establish their differences.

Critically discuss: carry out a thorough, in-depth examination of an issue, by presenting or summarising the various ideas/arguments it advances, before making a judgment on its overall worth.

Define: state the precise range of meaning suggested by a word or other linguistic unit.

Describe: draw out the characteristics of an event, argument, topic, issue, etc., by giving a detailed account of its essential features.

Discuss: examine an issue by going through the process of argument or debate, giving reasons for and against the various positions encountered, and examining their implications.

Evaluate: judge the worth of something, with reference to its accuracy, usefulness, or truth.

Examine: look in detail at an argument, topic or evidence, in order to find out how convincing, useful or trustworthy it is.

Explain: clarify an issue or event by interpreting its meaning and providing reasons for its character or form.

Give examples of: provide relevant, distinct examples (usually for the purposes of backing up an argument or illustrating a point).

How might: a preamble to a question which asks the candidate to speculate on the possible effect (of one thing on another) or outcome (a choice between two alternatives), using his/her knowledge and understanding to reach a defensible conclusion.

How successful: estimate to what degree a theory provides a convincing explanation for a particular phenomenon.

Identify: set out the main features or elements of an approach, issue or perspective, either within the main body of the essay or as individual points. Where strengths and weaknesses are mentioned, this will require an evaluation of arguments as well as the simple description of points.

Illustrate: provide some form of textual reference in support of an argument.

Interpret: translate the meaning of something into a clear and readily understandable form.

Justify: demonstrate the validity of a position (usually that held by the candidate) by providing adequate argument and evidence for the view taken. Likely objections to the viewpoint must be answered within the essay.

List: reproduce a number of points to demonstrate recall of a topic's main features.

Outline: set out the most important points, general principles, or main characteristics of a subject, placing emphasis on structure and relationship, but omitting less important details.

Relate: give a narrative account of something (as in 're-tell') or demonstrate the relationship between things (as in compare x to y).

Review: provide an overview or survey of an area of study.

State: present arguments, facts, or details in a clear manner, free from elaborate forms of presentation or flowery language.

Summarise: cut material down to its essential content, giving a concise account in which details are sacrificed for the sake of clarity.

Suggest reasons for: put forward possible explanations for the occurrence of specific events.

To what extent: decide to what degree a theory or viewpoint gives a valid or adequate account of events or developments.

Trace: follow the development of a theory or circumstance from its original appearance, through to the present.

With reference to: argue a case or consider evidence, mentioning the particular issue which is set out in the exam question.

What do you understand by: the candidate must explain his/her interpretation of an idea, issue, theory, model, or term.

What is meant by: give a definition of a term or concept, describing its use and meaning within the subject as a whole.

With reference to other sources: cite knowledge other than that which is already suggested by the title itself.

WRITING ESSAYS

INTRODUCTION

The requirement to produce essays forms an important part of all Media and Communication courses. It is a useful exercise because it helps to organise students' ideas in a structured form. It also teaches the skills of argument. Information is, therefore, learned for a purpose and not simply for its own sake.

Essays form an important link between tutor and student; they enable each to check what has been learned, and to identify positive strengths as well as weaknesses. What follows is a 12 point guide to writing essays.

12 point guide

1 An essay is a formal exercise; do not use informal terms, slang expressions, or asides to the examiner/tutor.
2 Essays require careful planning; make a plan before beginning the work, showing the different stages to be followed.
3 Essay titles must be studied carefully; the first task is to identify the key words in the title so there is no confusion about what is really being asked.
4 Wherever possible, a first draft should be produced.
5 All essays require the use of evidence: every time a major point is made, it should be reinforced with a reference (from an event, theory, or textual example).
6 Following the principle set out above, assertions (where an idea is simply stated without evidence) must be avoided.
7 Essays should be structured with care, beginning with an Introduction; this should define the terms used in the title, provide a brief account of which aspects of the topic will be covered, and give some indication of the student's attitude to the topic under discussion.
8 Student essays require clarity and the use of straightforward language; the issues may be complex, but the language and arguments used must be as clear as possible.
9 Anything which marks time or falls under the heading 'waffle' must be cut out; 'padding out' work does not gain marks.
10 All writing must be presented in paragraphs; each paragraph should deal with one topic, or should develop the argument used in a previous paragraph.
11 The conclusion to the work must be based on, and sum up, the arguments made in the main body of the essay.
12 The essay title must always be kept in mind; it is advisable to write it out on a separate piece of card and to place this to one side of the essay, so that it can be referred to throughout the course of the exercise.

Analysis: three levels of response in essay-writing

High grade

Clear understanding of title – initial definition of terms – clear agenda set at beginning – ability to deploy relevant theory – accurate recall of factual references, theory, or events in support of argument – high standard of basic skills – good organisation throughout – sophisticated understanding of factors influencing media and communication events – strong conclusion

Medium grade

Adequate understanding of title – definition of terms – generally clear agenda with some minor deviation – basic knowledge of theory – supporting reference accurate but perhaps somewhat mundane or sketchy in places – adequate basic skills – sound organisation with perhaps minor deviation from the task – some evidence of understanding of factors influencing media and communication events

Low grade

Misunderstanding of aspects of the title – inability to offer full definition of terms – consequent tendency to rely on speculation or assertion – references often vague or inaccurate in some respect – basic skills shaky, forming a barrier to appreciating the argument – poor organisation – confusion about the factors which influence media and communication events

A BRIEF GUIDE TO IN-DEPTH ASSIGNMENTS

In many 'A'-level (and some undergraduate) programmes, coursework is divided into two areas: a written study and a practical task. The written work is variously described, as an extended assignment, a study in depth, a research report and so on. Typically, it requires a clear sense of purpose, an active commitment to investigation, and the ability to record and present results in a coherent fashion. Primary and secondary research will inform the early stages of the work.

Students begin by choosing one part of the syllabus or course. They then identify a particular area of interest, negotiating a topic (and a suitable approach to that topic) with their tutor. The following guidance material is based on the WJEC's A3 extended assignment.

Writing an A3 Introduction

All investigations must be clearly focussed if a successful investigation is to be made. The Board warns that 'the more general the title, the more general the approach ... thereby resulting in less successful grades'. The project must be 'manageable in terms of time, resources, word limit and method'.

The purpose of the A3 project is to give candidates 'the opportunity to demonstrate their analytical and research competences on a topic of their own choice'.

The A3 assignment must focus on media **texts –** these make up the leading element of the whole exercise. The following question must be answered: *how does the text in question 'work' – what key devices are used to construct what kinds of representations?*

Answer the following questions:

1 What texts are you using?
2 What is meant by 'devices' and what particular devices are used to create meaning in the texts under investigation?
3 What representations do these devices produce?

The next question to consider is *what does study of the texts in question reveal about the context and relations of their production?*

This asks you to focus your attention on what can be learned about the context (the elements which surround the text) and the ways in which the text is produced – this task must be achieved through studying the text or texts concerned.

4 Identify the context (events, discourses, issues) surrounding the text/s you are using
5 What types of production, and particular features of production, are revealed through a study of text?

Once this is understood, you must provide some material which demonstrates how the texts in question are selected, interpreted and used by audiences. This means a) finding out what theories of audience use are relevant to your study and b) testing real audiences to see if the kinds of response match the theories examined.

The introduction should contain:

1 the title
2 the purpose of the project
3 a description of the scope of the project, referring to theories to be used and the types of research to be conducted.

Examples of titles

A

'An examination of Marilyn Monroe's rise to fame and her effect on a particular audience, plus her representation by Hollywood and genre applied. Particular emphasis on the films 'Some Like it Hot' and 'Gentlemen Prefer Blondes'.

B

'Monroe: an Analysis of her Image'.

Comment on these titles in the light of the Board's requirements.

Extracts from introductions

A

'Marilyn Monroe died over thirty years ago. Her death was surrounded by intense mystery. How could, people have asked, someone as wonderful as her have died in such circumstances? Born as plain 'Norma Jean' in 1926, Marilyn was denied the usual happy childhood most take for granted'.

B

'Marilyn Monroe's image is everywhere, thirty years after her death. She is featured on billboards, posters and commercials. Her image has launched a thousand merchandising crazes. Monroe was built on an image constructed by Hollywood ... I shall analyse the created Monroe image – its cinematic/social construction; why her original look had to be altered and what it meant to the public and publicists'.

Comment on these passages in the light of the Board's requirements.

Examples of titles

C

'Representations of violence in the Media; the key devices in their construction; their importance to the film industry and their effect on audience'.

D

'Violence on the Television – is there too much Broadcast?'

Comment on these titles in the light of the Board's requirements.

QUESTIONS TO USE FOR TEXTUAL ANALYSIS

Apply the following questions to each media text studied:

a) **Content**

What different types of material can be identified?

Is the content of the text 'mainstream' or 'alternative'?

b) **Form**

How is content arranged?

Is the form of the text 'mainstream' or 'alternative'?

c) **Context**

Where is this material likely to be found?

What does the text reveal about the social context in which it circulates?

What kind of discourses are mobilised in the text?

d) **Audience/Address**

To whom is the text addressed?

What kinds of address are used?

e) **Industry/Institution**

Which industry (radio, television, etc.) produces this type of text?

To which institution (e.g. BBC) does the text belong ?

textual analysis

MEDIA AND COMMUNICATION
BIBLIOGRAPHY

Alasuutari, P in (1992) *Media, Culture and Society*, Vol. **14**, No. 4, Sage

Alasuutari, P (1995) *Researching Culture*, Sage

Allen, R (1994) *Broadcasting enters the Marketplace*, John Libbey

Allport (1954) *The Nature of Prejudice*, Addison Wesley

Althusser, L (1965) *For Marx*, Penguin (1969)

Alvarado, M (1987) *Learning the Media*, Macmillan

Ang, I (1991) *Desperately Seeking the Audience*, Routledge

Arens, WF and Bovée, CL (1994) *Contemporary Advertising*, (5th ed), Irwin

Argyle, M (1988) *Bodily Communication*, Methuen

ASA *Advertising Under Control*, Advertising Standards Authority

Atkinson, M (1984) *Our Masters' Voices*, Methuen

Barker, M (1989) *Comics: Ideology, Power and the Critics*, Manchester University Press

Barker, M and Petley, J (1997) *Ill Effects*, Routledge

Barnuld in Patton, BR and Griffin, K (1981) *Interpersonal Communication in Action*, Harper and Row

Baudrillard, J (1981) *Simulacra and Simulations*, Galilée

Baudrillard, J (1979) *Seduction*, Macmillan

Beetham, D (1996) *Bureaucracy*, Open University Press

Bell, A (1991) *The Language of News Media*, Basil Blackwell

Bennis, W in Myers and Myers (1965) *Managing by Communication* (1982), McGraw-Hill

Billig, M (1991) *Ideology and Opinions*, Sage

Binkley in Hayward, P and Wollen, T (1993) *Future Visions: New technologies of the screen*, British Film Institute

Bolter, JD in Crawley, D and Heyer, P (1995) *Communication in History*, Longman

Bordwell, D (1985) *Narration in Fiction Film*, Methuen

Bourdieu (1991) *Language and Symbolic Power*, Polity

Branigan, E (1992) *Narrative Comprehension and Film*, Routledge

Branston, G and Stafford, R (1996) *The Media Student's Book*, Routledge

Bremjer and Roodenberg, H (1991) *A Cultural History of Gesture*, Polity

Bruck, PA in Wosro, J and Mosco, V (1992) *Democratic Communications*, Garamond Press/Ablex Publishing

Burgoon, M, Hunsaker, FG and Dawson, EJ (1994) *Human Communication*, Sage

Carey, J (1987) *The Faber Book of Reportage*, Faber

Centre for Contemporary Cultural Studies (1975) *Resistance through Ritual*, Hutchinson

Chaffee, S in Korenzy, F and Ting-Toomey, S (1992) *Mass Media Effects across Cultures*, Sage

Chen, KH (1991) *Postmodernism* in Media, Culture and Society

Chomsky, N (1965) *Aspects of the Theory of Syntax*, MIT Press

Chomsky, N (1972) *Language and Mind*, Harcourt, Brace Jovanavich

bibliography

Coates, J (1993) *Women, Men and Language* (2nd ed), Longman

Cobley, P (ed) (1996) *The Communication Theory Reader*, Routledge

Corner, J, Harvey, S and Lury, K in Hand, S (1994) *Behind the Screens*, Lawrence and Wishart

Corner, J (1996) *The Art of Record*, Manchester University Press

Corner, J (1991) in *Media, Culture and Society – Postmodernism*

Coulthard, M (1985) *An Introduction to Discourse Analysis*, Longman

Coulthard, M (1992) *Advances in Spoken Discourse Analysis*, Routledge

Crissell, A (1986) *Understanding Radio*, Methuen

Crowley, T (1989) *The Politics of Discourse*, Macmillan

Cruz, J and Lewis, J (1994) *Viewing, Reading, Listening*, Westview Press

Culler, J (1985) *On Deconstruction*, Routledge

Curtis, E (1984) *Ireland: the Propaganda War*, Pluto Press

Davies, K, Dickey, J and Stratford, T (eds) (1987) *Out of Focus*, Women's Press

Derrida, J (1967) *Of Grammatology* (trans) Johns Hopkins University Press (1976)

Dines, G and Humez, J (1995) *Gender, Race and Class in the Media*, Sage

Eldridge, J, Kitzinger, J and Williams, K (1997) *The Mass Media and Power in Modern Britain*, Oxford University Press

Ellmore (1990) *NTC's Mass Media Directory*, NTC

Elsaesser, T (ed) (1990) *Early Cinema: space, frame and narrative*

Evans, H (1983) *Good Times, Bad Times*, Hodder and Stoughton

Feldman, A (1997) *An Introduction to Digital Media*, Routledge

Fiske (1987) *Television Culture*, Routledge

Foucault, M (1977) *Discipline and Punish*, Allen Lane

Fowler, R (1991) *Language in the News*, Routledge

Fromkin, V and Rodman, R (1993) *An Introduction to Language*, Harcourt, Brace Jovanavich

Galtong, JT and Ruge, M (1965) 'The Structure of Foreign News' in *Journal of Peace Research*

Game, A (1991) *Undoing the Social*, Open University Press

Genette, G (1976) *Mimologiques*, Poetique

Gerbner, G and Gross, N (1976) 'Living with television' in *Journal of Communication*

Gibson, W (1984) *Neuromancers*

Giddens, A (1991) *Modernity and Self-identity*, Polity

Giddens, A (1993) *Sociology* (2E), Polity

Gill, D and Adams, B (1992) *ABC of Communication Studies*

Glasgow University Media Group (1976) *Bad News*, Routledge

Glasgow University Media Group (1980) *More Bad News*, Routledge

Glasgow University Media Group (1982) *Really Bad News*, Readers and Writers

Glasgow University Media Group (1985) *War and Peace News*, Oxford University Press

Glass, AC and Holyoak, KJ (1986) *Cognition*, McGraw-Hill

Goffman, E (1959) *The Presentation of Self in Everyday Life*, Anchor Books

Goffman, E (1976) *Gender Advertisements*, Macmillan

Goldsmith, A (1979) *The Camera and its Images*, Ridge Press/Newsweek Books

Gorbman, C (1987) *Unheard Melodies*, Indiana University Press/British Film Institute

bibliography

Gramsci, A (1971) *Selections from Prison Notebooks*, Lawrence and Wishart

Greenwood, JD (1994) *Realism, Identity and Emotion*, Sage

Grice, P (1975) *Studies in the Ways of Words*, Harvard (1989)

Gross, R (1992) *Psychology*, Hodder and Stoughton

Habermas, J (1986) *Theory and Practice*, Polity

Hall, J (1994) *Coercion and Consent*, Polity

Hall, S (1980) *Culture, Media and Language*, CCS/Hutchinson

Halloran, J (1970) *Television and Delinquency*, Leicester University Press

Harre, R and Gillet, G (1994) *The Discursive Mind*

Harris, D (1992) *From Class Struggle to the Politics of Pleasure*, Routledge

Harvey, D (1990) *The Condition of Postmodernity*, Blackwell

Hayward, S (1996) *Key Concepts in Cinema Studies*, Routledge

Herman, ES and Chomsky, N (1988) *Manufacturing Consent: the political economy of the mass media*

Hodge, J in Benjamin, A (1991) *The Problems of Modernity*, Routledge

Hodgson, FW (1987) *Modern Newspaper Editing and Production*, Heinemann

Hogg, M and Abrams, D (1988) *Social Identifications*, Routledge

Hoggart, R (1957) *The Uses of Literacy*, Chatto and Windus

Hood, S (1983) *On Television*, Pluto Press

Hume, D (1977) *An Enquiry Concerning Human Understanding*, Hackett Publishing

Hunston, S in Coulthard, M (1992) *Advances in Spoken Discourse Analysis*, Routledge

James, G in Barrett, E (1988) *Text, Context, Hypertext*, MIT Press

Jensen, KB (1995) *The Social Semiotics of Mass Communication*, Sage

Johnson-Laird in Mellor, DH (1990) *Ways of Communicating*, Cambridge University Press

Jowett, GS and O'Donnell, L (1986) *Propaganda and Persuasion*, Sage

Kaplan, EA in Allen, RC (1992) *Channels of Discourse, Reassembled*, Methuen

Keeble, R (1994) *The Newspapers Handbook*, Routledge

Klapper, JT (1960) *The Effects of Mass Communication*, Free Press

Labov, W in Atlatis, JE (1970) *The Logic of Non-Standard English in Linguistics*, Georgetown University Press

Langley, P (1993) *Managing Sociology Coursework*, Causeway Press

Larrain, J (1989) *The Concept of Ideology*, Hutchinson

Lawson, A and Garrod, J (1996) *The Complete A–Z Sociology Handbook*, Hodder and Stoughton

Lazarsfeld, PF, Berelson, B and Gaudet, H (1948) *The People's Choice*, Duell, Sloen and Pearce

Leiss, W, Kline, F and Thally, S (1990) *Social Communication in Advertising*, (2nd ed), Routledge

Levy, E (1990) 'Social attributes of American movie stars' in *Media, Culture and Society*, April 1990

Lewis, W in Masterman, L (ed) (1984) *Television Mythologies*, Comedia/MK Media Press

Liebes, T and Katz E (1993) *The Export of Meaning*, Polity

Lowery, SA and deFleur, ML (1995) *Milestones in Mass Communications Research* (3rd ed) Longman

Luthar, B (1993) Identity management and popular representational forms in Drummond, P, Paterson, R and Wiliss, J *National Identity and Europe*, British Film Institute

Lyon, D (1994) *Postmodernity*, Open University Press

Macdonell, D (1986) *Theories of Discourse*, Blackwell

Malvern, L (1986) *The End of the Street*, Methuen

Manchester, W (1989) *In Our Time: the world as seen by Magnum photographers*

Marchand, R (1986) *Advertising the American Dream*, University of California Press

Maslow, A (1954) *Motivation and Human Personality*, Harper and Row (1970)

Mattelart, A (1991) *Advertising International*, Routledge

McLuhan, M (1964) *Understanding Media*, Routledge and Kegan Paul

McQuail (1987) *Mass Communication Theory* (2nd ed), Sage

McQuail (1992) *Media Performance*, Sage

McQuail and Windahl (1993) *Communication Models*, Longman

Meehan, D (1983) *Ladies of the Evening*, Scarecrow Press

Monaco, J (1981) *How to Read a Film*, Oxford University Press

Moores, S (1993) *Interpreting Audiences*, Sage

Moores, S (1996) *Satellite Television and Everyday Life*, John Libbey

Moravcsik, JM (1992) *Thought and Language*, Routledge

Morley and Robbins, K (1995) *Spaces of Identity*, Routledge

Morley, D (1992) *Television Audiences and Cultural Studies*, Routledge

Morley, D (1980) *The Nationwide Audience*, British Film Institute

Mosco, V (1996) *The Political Economy of Communication*, Sage

Mulgan, G (1990) *The Question of Quality*, British Film Institute

Mulvey, L (1975) *Visual Pleasure and Narrative Cinema in Popular Television and Film*, Oxford University Press (1981)

Murdoch, G and Golding, P in Curran, J *et al.* (1977) *Mass Communication and Society*, Edward Arnold

Myers and Myers (1985) *The Dynamics of Human Communication*, McGraw-Hill

Neale, S (1980) *Genre*, British Film Institute

Nofsinger, RE (1991) *Everyday Conversation*, Sage

Norton-Taylor, R (1991) *Index on Censorship*, Index on censorship

O'Keefe (1990) *Persuasion*, Sage

O'Sullivan, T, Hartley, J, Montgomery, M, Saunders, D and Fiske, J (1994) *Key Concepts in Communication and Cultural Studies* (2nd ed), Routledge

Oakes, PJ, Haslam, SA and Turner, JC (1994) *Stereotyping and Social Reality*, Blackwell

Ouhalla, J (1994) *Introducing Transformational Grammar*, Edward Arnold

Outhwaite, W (1994) *Habermas: a critical introduction*, Polity

Patton, BR and Giffin, K (1981) *Interpersonal Communication in Action*, Harper and Row

Pinker, S (1994) *The Language Instinct*, Penguin

Poulantzas, (1980) *State, Power, Socialism*, Verso

Price, S (1993) *Media Studies*, Longman

Price, S (1996) *Communication Studies*, Longman

Propp V.(1929) *Morphology of the Folk Tale*, University of Texas (1969)

Raymond, J (1993) *Making the News*, Windrush Press

Rimmer, S (1995) *Planet Internet*, McGraw-Hill

bibliography

Robins, K and Webster, F (1987) *Information Technology: Social Issues*, Open University Press

Ryle, G (1973) *The Concept of Mind*, Penguin

Sarap, M (1988) *Introductory Guide to Post-structuralism and Postmodernism*, Harvester/Wheatsheaf

Saussure, Fde (1915) *Course in General Linguistics*, Fontana (1974)

Schlesinger, P (1978) *Putting Reality Together*, BBC News/Constable

Semin and Fiedler (1992) *Language, Interaction and Social Cognition*, Sage

Shaw, M (1994) *Global Society and International Relations*, Polity

Shipman, M (1988) *The Limitations of Social Research*, Longman

Shotter, J (1993) *Conversational Realities*, Sage

Silverman, D (1993) *Interpreting Qualitative Data*, Sage

Sim, S (1992) *Beyond Aesthetics*, Harvester Wheatsheaf

Spybey, A (1996) *Globalisation and World Society*, Polity

Stallabrass, J (1996) *Gargantua: Manufactured Mass Culture*, Verso

Stewart, R (1993) *The Reality of Organisations*, Macmillan

Strauss, AL (1987) *Qualitative Analysis for Social Scientists*, Cambridge University Press

Sturmer, C (1993) *Channels of Resistance*, British Film Institute/Channel 4

Taylor, PM (1992) *War and the Media*, Manchester University Press

Tetzlaff, D (1991) 'Divide and rule' in Media, Culture and Society, Vol **13**, No 1

Therborn, G (1980) *The Ideology of Power and the Power of Ideology*, Verso

Thompson, EP (1968) *The Making of the English Working Class*, Penguin

Todorov, T (1982) *The Conquest of America: the Question of the Other*, Harper and Row (1984)

Trowler, P (1996) *Investigating Mass Media* (2nd ed), Harper Collins

van Zoonen, L (1994) *Feminist Media Studies*, Sage

Watson, J and Hill (1997) *A Dictionary of Communication and Media Studies* (4th ed), Edward Arnold

Wernick, A (1991) *Promotional Culture*, Sage

Williams, R (1983) *Keywords*, Fontana

Wittgenstein, L (1953) *Philosophical Investigations*, Oxford University Press

Young, J *The Drugtakers*

Zizek, S (1994) *Mapping Ideology*, Verso